THE ARABS AND THE WORLD
Nasser's Arab Nationalist Policy

THE ARABS
AND THE WORLD

Nasser's Arab Nationalist Policy

By CHARLES D. CREMEANS

Published for the
COUNCIL ON FOREIGN RELATIONS
By FREDERICK A. PRAEGER, *Publisher*
New York • London

Published in the United States of America in 1963 by
Frederick A. Praeger, Inc., Publisher
64 University Place, New York 3, N.Y.

Published in the United Kingdom in 1963 by
Frederick A. Praeger, Inc., Publisher
49 Great Ormond Street, London W.C. 1

THE ARABS AND THE WORLD: NASSER'S ARAB NATIONALIST POLICY

For information, address Council on Foreign Relations,
58 East 68th Street, New York 21

FIRST EDITION

Library of Congress catalog card number: 63–10459

Printed in the United States of America
by American Book–Stratford Press, Inc.

For a list of Council publications see pages 337 and 338.

For my father
Walter R. Cremeans

PREFACE

I attended a Middle Western liberal arts college and went directly after graduation in 1936 to teach in the American College in Assiut, Egypt. The college itself was familiar ground, a part of a long-standing effort by Americans of good will to bring education, medicine, and religion—their religion—to people less fortunate than they. But around it lay Egypt, like another world, a world for which my education had left me completely unprepared.

The history, philosophy, and literature which I had studied was, of course, all Western. I had studied the history of the ancient world, but I had learned—or assumed—that the point of ancient history was that it led onward and upward, as it were, to the twentieth-century West. The Arabs I had come across in world history were cast in the role of unsuccessful opponents of the West, their place in history redeemed by the fact that they had passed on to the West certain Greek books which otherwise might have been lost.

Quite clearly my education needed rounding out, and Egypt became both classroom and teacher for my postgraduate studies. It taught me the importance of perspective, and how differently the world looks from the Middle East than from the Middle West. It taught me the basic importance of poverty and oppression to the political outlook of much of the world's population. From Egypt and the Egyptians I also learned to look at my own country and its attitudes and policies with an objectivity I might never have learned at home.

At the time I first went to Egypt there were rumblings of the greatest revolution of our time, the revolution of the submerged peoples of Africa and Asia. My students at Assiut College were caught up in the excitement of Arab nationalism. I watched them make the first steps toward the comprehension of their nationality, of the Arab community, and of that community's place in the world. Since that time I have watched the Arabs move step by halting step to legal independence and then to the independence that comes to those who take charge of their own destiny.

I have also watched my own country respond to the Arab revolution and to the wider movement of liberation of dependent peoples. I came to the conclusion that much of America's difficulty in meeting the international situations created by these revolutions lay in the tendency to assume that people whose international behavior is based on different motives, and is organized, directed, and explained differently from that of the established nations, have no foreign policy at all. Communist foreign policy, though it challenges European tradition, is far enough within that tradition to be understandable as foreign policy. Nehru's neutralism has been much more difficult, but still, his comprehension of the Western mind and of Western methods has made it possible for him to convince the West that he has a policy that deserves consideration. As far as the Arabs and the African nationalists were concerned, however, it has often been thought much the easiest thing to dismiss their activities in the international arena as sheer opportunism, erratic and unsystematic. The natural consequence of such a judgment has been an inability to foresee policy moves by Afro-Asian leaders and a tendency to treat each incident and crisis as though it were separate and accidental, a thing in itself.

Long observation of Arab behavior in international affairs, plus some familiarity with Arab psychology and the ideas of Arab nationalism, convinced me that there was a foreign policy of Arab nationalism as consistent and as firmly based on doctrine and interest as Western foreign policies. It seemed to me important that an effort be made to look at Arab foreign policy from the inside out, to understand the wellsprings of Arab international behavior, and to see Arab objectives as they appear to Arab eyes.

It was my good fortune to find Philip E. Mosely, Principal Research Fellow at the Council on Foreign Relations, interested in these ideas. The Council, having appointed me a Research Fellow in 1960–61, called together a study group of members and a few guests with special interest, knowledge, and experience in Middle Eastern affairs. With Mr. Russell H. Dorr as chairman, the group included: John S. Badeau, John C. Campbell, John Dorman, Goldthwaite H. Dorr, Parker T. Hart, J. C. Hurewitz, Charles P. Issawi, Harry F. Kern, Francis A. Kettaneh, Hal Lehrman, Derwood W. Lockard, Harold B. Minor, Fred M. Nelson, Richard H. Nolte, Johnston F. Northrop, Don Peretz, William R. Polk, George W. Ray, Jr., Kermit Roosevelt, Walter R. Sharp, John Slawson, and S. D. Turner. These men brought a wealth of varied experience and an array of unusual talents to bear on the questions I posed and the problems I set before them. The academic world, business, journalism, and government were all ably represented. While we were holding our meetings President Kennedy appointed two members of the group to key ambassadorial posts in the Arab world: John S. Badeau to Cairo and Parker T. Hart to Jidda.

During the winter of 1960–61 the group met six times. The discussions, comments, arguments, recollections, and disputes on problems with which I was dealing in my book were invaluable. The book, however, is in no sense a group product. It was not intended to be so and, in looking back, it is hard to conceive how a collective work might have been written on the subject or what it would have said, for in its discussions the group clearly demonstrated the lack of consensus in America on the broad range of questions involved in Arab-American relations.

Members of the group had their moments of disillusionment and discouragement about trends in the Middle East and especially about relations between America and the Arab world. Much of the excitement that had suffused the study of Arab problems in the 1950s had passed away as increasing familiarity with those problems dampened hopes of finding solutions. Throughout the discussions, however, a deep sense of the significance of the questions at issue and their far-reaching implications was evident. The members of the study group agreed that however difficult the problems of American relations with the Arabs may be, there is no turning away from them.

Despite the absence of consensus, the study group was immensely helpful in providing, with many wise suggestions, a wide range of reactions to the author's ideas. The chairman and several members kindly read and criticized portions of the manuscript. Richard Nolte, William R. Polk, and Don Peretz have been particularly helpful. I have benefited also from the encouragement of the Council's Committee on Studies, from the advice and assistance of John C. Campbell, Senior Research Fellow at the Council, and from the editorial assistance of Percy W. Bidwell. Harold F. Linder gave me useful assistance in making important contacts. I also wish to thank Miss Lorna Brennan and the secretarial staff of the Council for their careful work on my manuscript. Full responsibility for the end product is mine.

My work is based in part on books and journals written in European languages, but the burden of the book rests on long reading of the Arab press and radio broadcast transcriptions and —most important—on many conversations with Arabs ranging from chiefs of state and cabinet ministers to that much quoted source in the Middle East, my own cook. Government officials and private citizens all over the Arab world and on both sides of the Armistice lines talked with me at length and assisted me in many different ways. A number of Asians and Africans—diplomats, journalists, and businessmen—with knowledge of the Arab situation also were helpful. Although records of conversations were kept and often drawn upon, I have decided that direct quotations could not be used without embarrassing people who in good faith had engaged with me in private conversation.

Many of my friends—Arabs, Americans, and others—who contributed to my opinions may disagree with the way they are stated in this book. But I shall be satisfied if the book leads more Americans to think about the world as it looks to the Arabs and if it demonstrates to some Arabs that an American can be sympathetic and honest in his evaluation of their situation and their efforts to improve it.

The book reflects the complexity of its subject. Neither Gamal Abdel Nasser and others who make Arab foreign policy nor Arab scholars or journalists have produced a complete statement of the doctrine on which that policy is based. None has tried to make the kind of analysis of the policy and its background which I have attempted. As a consequence it has been necessary for me to rely much on the evidence of events and on pronouncements made in response to immediate situations. Yet I have sought to make mine an analytical rather than an historical approach. Events illustrate and explain the ideas which are my main subject. My endeavor has been to make the ideas dominate in setting the theme and to use events to document them, at the risk of chronological confusion.

The first chapter introduces the theme by setting forth the new dimensions of international politics and the Arab response to them, and points out the implications for the United States. The second chapter presents the man who has been the most important symbol and leader of Arab foreign policy and describes his personal style and techniques in foreign affairs. The next three chapters are concerned with the basic influences and limitations upon Arab foreign policy and international behavior. Chapter III presents Arab nationalism in the context of the psychological circumstances which shaped and stimulated it; IV and V describe the physical and institutional situation in which the Arabs live. Another group of three chapters are historical, though not an account of the succession of events. Chapter VI discusses the Arab reaction to their own history and the effect of their recent historical experience upon their view of the world; VII and VIII describe Arab behavior in the international arena in the period since the Palestine War. Chapter IX presents the Arab-Israeli conflict as it affects Arab thinking on foreign policy and as an aspect of Arab relations with the outside world. Chapters X–XII are concerned with Nasser's Arab nationalist policies in the Arab area, in Afro-Asia, and toward the great powers; they also touch on prospects for the future. In the final chapter I have examined alternative courses of action open to the United States.

CHARLES D. CREMEANS

October 1962

CONTENTS

THE ARABS AND THE WORLD
Nasser's Arab Nationalist Policy

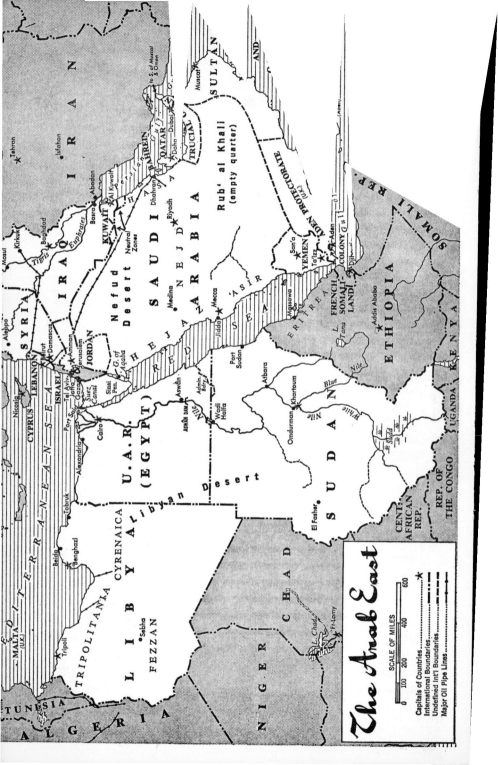

The Arab East

INTRODUCTION

The great upheaval which, starting in the American and the French Revolutions, changed the shape of the Western world has now spread to Africa and Asia. Improved communications and technology have awakened in underprivileged peoples the desire for independence, self-determination, and material progress. The resulting outburst of human energy is both a tribute and a challenge to the West. Coming at a moment when nuclear weapons and the ubiquitous struggle between the Western and the Communist powers have changed the dimensions of international policy, it modifies and complicates the pattern of international politics.

Americans, who of all people have benefited most from the great democratic-scientific revolution that began in the eighteenth century, find that the desire to protect their gains makes it difficult to be understanding of the new revolution. In Western eyes the constructive potentialities of the Afro-Asian struggle for independence and self-determination are too easily blurred by the violence, extremism, and frequent irresponsibility of its protagonists. Americans, also, find it hard to appreciate the intense resentment of underprivileged peoples toward the predominant position of the Western powers in the world, and toward the control they exercise directly or indirectly over their lives and opportunities.

The United States and what it stands for remain a powerful influence throughout Africa and Asia. But the tides have been running against the American and Western role in the great revolutionary transformation of our time, the transition of the underprivileged peoples from the morass of the past into the modern world. The Western powers have failed to assume the leadership of which they are capable and to convince the Afro-Asian peoples that they believe in this transition. Moreover, the Communists have shown great ingenuity in turning the underprivileged peoples against the West.

In this situation it is of vital importance that the United States understand the nature of the revolution and what its leaders believe and want, so that by adjusting its position and its approach this country can assume the role for which its traditions and its interests qualify it—a role which otherwise falls to the Communists. But the role of the United States cannot be one of domination like that of the Western powers in the East in the nineteenth century. A new approach and new techniques are required.

The Arabs of Northeast Africa and Southwest Asia—the Arab East—occupy a very special position in the Afro-Asian revolution and in the West's relations with it. Always geographically strategic, the region they occupy lies now between the centers of international communism and Africa, a critical frontier of the Afro-Asian revolution. Politically also, the Arabs occupy a strategic position; since 1955, the Arab nationalists, particularly Abdel Nasser in Egypt, have developed an approach to international affairs which has had, and is likely to have, increasing influence among emerging nations throughout the Afro-Asian world and in Latin America as well.

For the United States, neutralism or nonalignment, as practiced by President Nasser of the United Arab Republic and increasingly throughout the Arab world, presents significant and difficult problems. In the Department of State there are many embittered men who at one time or another committed themselves to the proposition that the United States could "do business" with Nasser. Americans without a chance to gain firsthand knowledge are apt to have a narrow, often prejudiced, view. Some have appeared to be prepared to turn the whole business of the Afro-Asian revolution over to the Communists. Others explain everything as the work of the Russians or the consequence of their influence, and accuse those who point out that the revolution has a validity of its own of being naïve about communism. Many Americans, moreover, are so emotionally committed to Israel that they can see the area's problem only in terms of the security of Israel. Any attempt to understand or explain the Arab position becomes anti-Israel in their eyes and is likely to evoke the charge of anti-Semitism.

Thus Arab attitudes and policies in international affairs—the Arabs' view of their rightful place in the world and their idea of how they ought to go about getting there—are not only of significance for American leadership in the most explosive revolution of our time; they challenge, also, the ability of Americans to think objectively under the cross fire of pressures and fears, and to adapt their traditional policies and institutions to the realities of a changing world.

I

ARAB FOREIGN POLICY:

Implications for the United States

In 1953 an American Arabist, who was driving across the desert near the borders of Kuwait and Saudi Arabia, saw in the distance a cluster of Bedouin tents. He drove there and found a group of men sitting around the coffee fire. When he sat down to accept the traditional hospitality of the desert Arab, his eye lighted on a battery radio, so he asked his hosts to what stations they listened. "All the great nations," they said, "Radio Moscow, the Voice of the Arabs from Cairo, BBC, and the Voice of America." The American, impelled by interest and the force of long professional habit, asked what differences they detected in the outlook and purposes of the various states as shown by their broadcasts. The younger men deferred to the elder sheikh, who turned the matter over in his mind for a long time and then answered: "The Russians live to the north; the English to the northwest; the Egyptians to the west; and the Americans far across the sea. The ruler of Russia is a very strong man named Stalin. The English have a queen. Gamal Abdel Nasser, who rules the Egyptians, is a soldier. The American ruler, Eisenhower, is also a soldier. All these powerful rulers distrust and dislike each other, so one day they will have a big *razza* [the traditional warlike raid of one desert tribe on another]. What we fear," he said, "is that they will decide that our desert, which is in the center of the world, is a good place for their *razza*."

The desert sheikh's estimate of the situation was very like that of the Arab governments. The fact that in 1953 Bedouins of the desert, as well as the Arab governments, were aware of the rivalry of powers and of its implications for their welfare reflects a great change. In the world of the more sophisticated urban Arabs, an even more important change had taken place to which their leaders and their governments responded with new ideas and new policies. After centuries in the backwaters, the Arabs have entered again the main stream of international affairs as a force to be reckoned with by the great powers, a factor in the international equation. In place of inward-turning traditionalism there has emerged a dynamic conception of Arab goals and the means for attaining them.

Forty years ago the foreign relations of Arab states were devised in London, Paris, and Rome, with the outlook and interests of the metropolitan countries predominating. Local situations and interests were usually calculated in terms of the relations of the individual state or other political entity (whether colony, protectorate, League of Nations mandate, or nominally independent state) to its European ruler or partner, seldom with respect to the area as a whole. Local governments were dominated by ruling families and an elite of pashas, beys, sheikhs, and princes, whose many privileges were dependent upon their relationship with the representatives of the particular European power which by occupation, treaty, or League of Nations mandate, and with the consent of the other European powers, had assumed a position of predominance in their country. A certain amount of political life and activity had begun to develop on the European pattern and nationalism was a growing political force to which even the pashas occasionally deferred, but the ultimate sanction on Arab political activity was still to be found in the presence of European troops. They never were too far away to be brought into any picture that threatened to get out of focus; that is, from the perspective of the interested European government or the "native" privileged monarchy and upper class linked with it. The European powers attributed great importance to the Arab states' foreign relations. While they granted step-by-step modifications of their authority in other areas of government, this function was always reserved, along with control over defense and security matters and over finance. In due course this outside control of foreign policy came to have symbolic significance to Arab nationalists as a denial of an essential attribute of sovereignty and the most important mark of independence. At this early stage, however, the Arabs in general showed little awareness of international affairs or concern about them. Street demonstrations and other expressions of public indignation became more common, but public opinion was the concern of the security forces rather than of the foreign-policy makers.

In the period between the two world wars, as European control was slowly reduced, the responsibilities and powers of local governments increased. Furthermore, in the essential but not always objectively determinable matter of readiness for self-government, all the Arab countries made important advances. The really big changes, however, began during the Second World War, reaching their culmination in the postwar years. They have provided opportunities for the Arabs to move forward to complete independence, and to take their place on the world stage under their own colors and with policies devised to achieve their own purposes.

One can now speak, without too much inaccuracy, of an "Arab foreign policy," meaning thereby a body of principles which the governments of the various Arab states will support, more or less consistently, and a set of goals which they and their peoples cherish. The common policy has been made possible and has been shaped by a series of changes both in world politics and in the internal affairs of the Arab states, principally the change in the number and the position of the great powers and the new role of the small states; the political and social revolution within Arab society; and the crystallization of Arab causes and the growth of the idea of Arab unity.

The inability of Great Britain and France to play their former role, the unwillingness (and probably the inability) of the United States to take it up, except in a limited way, and the rise of the Soviet bloc to the position of chief rival of the Western powers—all these things changed the Arab situation fundamentally. The obvious value of a policy of playing off rivals for favors against each other had long been well understood in the Arab part of the world. But for years the dominant Western European powers, though rivals, had generally agreed among themselves which was

to have free run in each of the Arab territories. Now there was
not only the United States to play off against the British and
French, but also the Soviet Union to play off against them all. It is
not necessary to attribute malice or deviousness to the Arabs to
explain their seizure of new opportunities for political maneuver.
Previously they had had only the Western powers to deal with.
Now they had the West and a formidable rival of the West. Previously they had had the choice of various kinds of alliances with
one Western state; now they had the choice of alliance with the
West, or with the Soviet bloc, or independence of both.

A NEW ROLE FOR SMALL NATIONS

States and peoples without military or economic power, requirements for action in the past, now can play an active and significant
role on the world stage. Disparities in strength may be greater
than ever, but outside powers are no longer in a position easily to
translate military superiority into political influence. The precarious world balance is partly responsible. In addition, the world-
wide revolution in communications and awareness has created a
new environment for international affairs. The Western public has
new power and will to influence its governments to take action
favoring the self-determination and economic development of the
underprivileged peoples. In a quite different way and for different
reasons, but with similar consequences, Communist countries have
supported the aspirations of developing countries and colonial
peoples.

The United Nations provides a forum where new nations can
bring their problems and attitudes to the attention of the whole
world. Even peoples without national status—like the Algerian
nationalists before winning independence—can send their representatives, sponsored by some friendly nation, to lobby in the halls
of the UN, where they often obtain treatment very close to recognition as representatives of legitimate states. The frequent deadlocks
in the Security Council, and the consequent rise in the importance
of the General Assembly, have given small states opportunities to
participate in negotiations on major world issues. When the United
States and the Soviet Union were facing each other from irrecon-

cilable positions on disarmament and UN reorganization at the General Assembly in October 1960, Nasser, with the leaders of four other states—Sukarno of Indonesia, Nkrumah of Ghana, Nehru of India, and Tito of Yugoslavia—came forward with recommendations made from the neutralist point of view. Regardless of the value of the effect of this initiative, it had great significance for Nasser and for many Arabs. For them it symbolized a new world situation in which an Arab leader at a critical moment in world affairs could stand with other world leaders, playing a major role in the world forum.

The admission of new African states into the United Nations and the emergence of the Afro-Asian group as the potential arbiter of General Assembly decisions opened a new vista for the Arabs and the nations with whom they share so many interests and attitudes. Because of their common feeling of resentment for past exploitation and discrimination, the prospect of vindication by participating in shaping their own and the world's destiny is deeply satisfying.

THE REVOLUTION OF SUBMERGED PEOPLES

The Arab world has experienced the feeling of participation in a world-wide revolution of submerged peoples, a movement with deep historical roots and growing power, a new force in world affairs. Even to uneducated radio listeners in the remoter parts of Arab lands, the world has appeared to be increasingly dominated by the struggle between two groups of great powers. Hence the idea that the newly awakened peoples, the underprivileged and the downtrodden, by pooling their numbers and uniting their voices could exercise some control over their own destinies, won ready acceptance.

Growing anti-European feeling and sometimes consciousness of race was added to the sense of kinship and community of interest. There was increasing awareness among the Arabs of the struggles for liberation and self-determination being waged and won by non-white peoples of Asia and Africa against the same overlords who dominated the Arab countries. All these peoples, it became evident, cherished common goals—independence, economic development, and modernization—goals which seemed attainable on acceptable terms only through freedom from European and American domination. So from the Philippines to Latin America since World War II a wave of national assertiveness with racial overtones has been rising, a fierce demand for modernization and for the place in the world that modernization brings. This has affected the Arab peoples, buoying their hopes for achieving nationalist goals.

Ferment within the Arab states themselves has not been the least of the influences upon the incipient Arab foreign policy. In several states since World War II the classic pattern of monarchy surrounded with its privileged agents and supporters has given way. Revolutions have put into power men of middle-class origin, most of them from the military officer corps or elite groups of Western-educated technicians. These men believe in change, an attitude which has influenced their approach to foreign as well as to domestic policy.

ARAB UNITY AND ARAB CAUSES

Arab unity is an ideal with a long history. It still remains an ideal rather than a program, although in the past few years it has taken on more and more practical political meaning and has exercised increasing influence on the foreign relations of Arab states. Today, there is a real sense of identification with, and involvement in, the future of the area as a whole. Arab nationalism is an attitude of mind which almost all Arabs claim to share; "Arab causes" and "Arab questions" are those international issues on which Arabs believe they should present a common front. Actually, sometimes they do and sometimes they don't. Often agreement is reached on goals while the means to their achievement are bitterly disputed. Nevertheless, agreement on common goals, and the intensity with which many Arabs believe in them, is a new and significant advance.

Certain great issues automatically bind the Arabs together: their mutual interest in freedom from great-power interference; their common experience in winning independence, and shared fears of attempts to abrogate it; the sacred cause of Arab lands not yet free of foreign rule.

In 1956 the British-French-Israeli invasion of Egypt evoked resentment throughout the Arab world. It was commonly believed that the attack was directed not against Egypt alone but against all Arabs, or, more specifically, against Arab nationalism. Fear of the great powers and hostility to them, expressed in anti-Western or anticolonial attitudes, are not unambiguous or unalloyed. Many Lebanese are torn between their attachments and their hostility to the West; the Jordanian, the Saudi, and the Libyan monarchies, and the rulers of the Persian Gulf sheikhdoms all have reasons for maintaining ties with Western powers; the King of Jordan is even willing to associate himself with the West against the Communist powers. But most Arabs agree on the dangers of involvement with the great powers, and on the necessity of maintaining Arab solidarity against their interference.

Israel is the issue which has done more to unite the Arab world than any other. The Arab states were unable to coordinate their efforts to prevent the establishment of the state of Israel. They could not agree on an armistice or on the status of the Palestinian lands, or on the future of the Palestinian refugees. But they have been united in their consistent refusal to recognize Israel or to make any gesture that would help it establish itself in the community of nations.

Algeria, although farther removed than Israel from the eastern Arab states, has presented a more theoretical issue but one similar in its power to evoke Arab solidarity. Agreement on the righteousness of the rebel struggle for independent Algeria, and recognition of the Front of National Liberation and its provisional government as representative of the Algerian people, have tended to unify the Arab states in their dealings with the West and in their conduct in the United Nations.

In recent years, as their horizon has broadened, Arabs have also treated the Israeli and Algerian issues as part of the problem of colonialism going beyond the confines of their own region. Solidarity on the larger questions of the relations between the great powers and the submerged peoples of the world has provided a common ground for the international activities of the Arab states. Experience in formulating common positions and taking joint action on these matters in the United Nations and elsewhere has tended to strengthen the sense of community of interest among the Arab states and to create a common outlook on world affairs. Thus they have moved forward into a role based on fairly consistent views covering developments both in their own Arab world and in the larger world beyond.

THE NEW ARAB APPROACH TO INTERNATIONAL POLITICS

Often, but not always, led by Gamal Abdel Nasser of Egypt, and frequently, but not always, with the cooperation of all the Arab states, there has emerged since the Second World War something which may be described as an Arab position in international politics. This position is based on the idea of eventual Arab unity and on the maximum utilization of the resources of the community as a whole for the common interest. It emphasizes independence of outside control as its primary objective and the economic development of the several states and of the area as a whole. In carrying out the theme of independence it opposes alignment with great powers on the ground that this derogates from the sovereignty of small nations. It supports an independent policy commonly called "positive neutralism." It utilizes the techniques of maintaining relations with the two great-power groupings and seeking to balance them against each other, as well as encouraging rivalry between them in the support of Arab development. It also seeks to strengthen the Arab position in world affairs by associating it with the Afro-Asian and the nonaligned states.

The forces which the Arabs utilize or take advantage of are not the classic supports for foreign policy. They have little military or economic power of their own. That they have been able to make their voice heard in international politics reflects both their own skill and the new dimensions of the world of the second half of the twentieth century. They have taken advantage of the strategic significance of their territory and of the importance of its oil deposits to the world economy to manipulate the great powers, and they have taken full advantage of the opportunities offered in the United Nations and other forums. Without significant wealth or power they have made much progress toward the achievement of their goals.

The foregoing observations need qualification. Arab foreign policy is conducted on two levels: the level at which the interests of the national states are dominant, and the level at which Pan Arab interests are controlling. Even within the principal levels there are differences of approach, owing to the contrast in basic orientation between the states which have gone through social and political revolutions and those in which traditional regimes continue to rule. And, of course, there are frequent occasions for dispute among states within each group. Each state has special interests and problems which influence its outlook, even on the most generally accepted goals of Arab nationalism.

A division of great importance is that between Egypt and the other Arab states. Egypt's size, wealth, and economic development, as well as its position as the greatest Arab cultural center, enable it to play a preponderant role and to command a following throughout the area. At the same time Egypt's advantages tend to push the other states into opposition to it. Even so, because of Nasser's emergence as the recognized spokesman for Arab nationalism and Arab unity, and with the Egyptian revolution being accepted by many as a prototype for change, Egypt's foreign policy is often identified with Arab foreign policy. Occasionally, it has been in fact very close to being a policy for the area rather than of a single state. Governments which have attempted to deal with Nasser as the chief of the Egyptian state have sometimes found that they were dealing with Arab nationalism itself.

Nasser, the outstanding spokesman and protagonist of Arab nationalism, has done more than any other leader to apply it in foreign policy. Yet he did not create Arab nationalism; it was a force in the area before he appeared on the scene and will certainly survive him. His policy of "positive neutralism" is echoed by leaders in other Arab states, even by those who have little reason to love him, because of his great prestige and influence, and because he speaks for a movement which has its roots deep in the area. Nasser is both an Egyptian leader and a Pan Arabist, a spokesman for Egyptian and Arab nationalism. Others on the political stage sometimes take their cues from him and often react to his initiatives, but he on occasion must respond to them and take account of their wishes when he formulates his policy and calculates his actions.

In effect, Nasser alone, although he is the most compelling and effective spokesman for Arab nationalism and rules the most important Arab country, does not make Arab foreign policy; his policies and his position in international affairs cannot be understood except in the context of the policies and positions of the other Arab states. Although complex and diverse, the Arab area is more understandable as a whole than in its parts. On many issues it plays a role in foreign affairs as a region rather than as a collection of individual states.

THE ARABS AND THE GREAT POWERS

The revolutionary changes in Arab attitudes and behavior in international relations have made obsolete the traditional assumptions and policies of the Western powers. European nations, which until World War II with a relatively small expenditure of resources and effort dominated the Arab area and guided its development, have seen their ability to affect the course of events dwindle. The United States, although it plays a greater role in the area than before, has not replaced them. The Soviets have moved in with a rush, expending impressive amounts of energy, money, and other resources without, however, openly adopting the parental attitude which characterized the prewar relationship of the British and French to those Arab states with which they had special ties. Only in the sheikhdoms of the Arabian littoral and in Aden does the old system prevail, hardly an anachronism where people and their rulers are still living in the nineteenth century, or earlier.

None of the powers—not Britain or France, the United States or Russia—has found a means of dominating the Arab world as the European powers did in the nineteenth century, nor have they discovered a new policy which would protect their interests, as they defined those interests in an earlier period. For a new attitude pervades the Middle East, a self-assertive nationalism which suspects the motives and interests of the great powers. New tactics also are employed, taking advantage of new features in the world situation which make the nineteenth-century diplomacy of pro-consuls, gunboats, and paternalism either impossible or, if tried, ineffective.

The Soviets in the past few years appear to have done extremely well in evolving and applying new policies directed toward the Arab states. Although they gave initial support to Israel, they soon discontinued it and, without committing themselves to hostile action, upheld the Arab position in their propaganda and diplomacy. The U.S.S.R. became the chief supplier of arms to the Arabs while Israeli arms came from the West.

The principal Communist advantages in dealing with the Arabs have been psychological and political. Like the United States they were free of any record of Middle Eastern colonialism. However, as the open and avowed opponents of the Western powers and having no stake in the *status quo,* the Communists were in a position to support every revolutionary tendency of the Arab nationalists, encouraging the impression that they have a common interest in breaking the grip of the Western "imperialists" on the emerging peoples. Beginning with the 1955 arms deal with Egypt, the states of the Communist bloc have skillfully provided military and economic assistance in impressive quantities. Their terms, though perhaps less advantageous economically than those offered by the West, appealed to the Arabs because they stipulated no commitment to political orientation or alliance. Nasser and other Arab leaders on their part, in order to reduce their dependence on the West, consciously sought to increase their association with the Sino-Soviet bloc.

Given their advantages and the suspicion of the West which was so widespread in the Arab world after World War II, it seemed possible that the Soviets would soon draw the Arabs into their orbit. In fact they have not. In some ways they have had as much difficulty as the West in their relations with the new states. The Soviet Union, too, suffers from the disadvantage of being a great power; to the newly emergent states all strong nations are suspect. To many Arabs, and certainly to the politically sophisticated ones, the Soviet Union is identified with local Communist parties, which have been caught often enough in subversive activities to be regarded as dangerous enemies of national independence. This is particularly true in countries where all political parties, and secret ones especially, are suspect. Finally there is the basic incompatibility between nationalism and communism.

Arab experience in dealing with the Soviets since 1955 has considerably dimmed many of the latter's initial advantages. Soviet contracts have often proved to be as difficult to implement as Western contracts. More important, however, to Arabs in official positions and to many of the politically alert were the lapses in the Soviet pretense of disinterested support. The Arabs are going through a revolution which shapes their attitudes and dominates their actions; it also limits the approaches which outside nations can make to them because it eliminates the possibility of using policies not compatible with the revolution or which appear to seek to oppose or turn it back. For the United States the important thing to remember is that the revolution is more of our making, by far, than of the Communists' making. It is part of the social and economic revolution, the revolution of modernization which began in Europe, reached its most vigorous peak in the United States, and is now stirring the submerged peoples of all the world to assert themselves, searching for a place, an independent role in the modern world.

The United States should be in a better position than the Soviets to support and take advantage of this revolution. Its success is compatible with American interests and with the American conception of what the world ought to be like, whereas it is antipathetic to the Communist goal of a regimented world dependent upon Moscow's lead. Taking advantage of this opportunity, however, may be the most difficult task that the United States has ever faced. The necessary adjustments may be beyond any nation's capacity, but failure may mean the rapid slide of the uncommitted third of the world into the Communist orbit.

PROBLEMS FOR THE UNITED STATES

The United States has demonstrated its acceptance of the principle of self-determination and its readiness to support the weak against the strong in granting Philippine independence, in its support of Indonesian independence in the late 1940s, in the Suez crisis of 1956, and in its dealing with the newly emerging African nations. To the Arabs, however, the United States appears always to be excusing itself from supporting some measure of great importance to them, or to some other emergent group. While claiming to believe in self-determination, this country seems to them to prefer stability to change and to be unwilling to jeopardize its ties with Great Britain, France, or another ally.

No satisfactory defense of U.S. policy is possible while the Arabs remain unable to understand the importance of our commitments to the defense of the non-Communist world. The question arises, however, whether America's definition of its responsibilities does not often give excessive weight to the support of those allies who are deemed important in the anti-Communist coalition, even when they are fighting hopeless battles against forces which in the long run they cannot overcome. The case of France in Algeria was the most extreme example. The American position may also have often been influenced by unwillingness to accept rapid change, lag in understanding, or fear of the consequences of recognizing and acknowledging the claims of the emerging Asian and African states.

The revolution within the Arab states is far from complete; no one can be sure where it is going or even who are its true representatives. Its leaders, although they may speak with great positiveness about general goals, are not certain how they should go about achieving them. There are often wide differences in opinion between responsible officials in Arab states and great sections of the articulate public. We also have the spectacle of several Arab leaders who, while professing attachment to the goal of Arab unity, engage in violent personal attacks on each other and become involved in intrigues and subversive movements in each other's states.

The traditional American practice is to accept existing chiefs of state as the rightful spokesmen and proper representatives of their peoples and to deal with disputes between the United States and individual state governments as they arise. Naturally the State Department has been inclined to support and work with foreign leaders who behave in a friendly manner, who are willing to accept the basic assumptions of American foreign policy, and who are willing to cooperate in attaining its objectives. Such a course has not always proven successful, however. Accepting Nuri el Said as the legitimate representative of Iraq and following his advice and counsel on Arab affairs seemed justified and normal; he headed the government in power, was friendly and cooperative with the West, and associated his country with the anti-Communist Baghdad Pact. The revolution of 1958, however, demonstrated how unrepresentative he was and how weak a reed for the United States to lean on. It has seemed to some that the proper way to deal with Nasser was to treat him merely as the president of Egypt and later of the United Arab Republic[1] but not to acknowledge that any greater significance attached to his position. This, too, proved difficult, because politically, though not legally, he did stand for something more. For example, the picketing of the Egyptian ship "Cleopatra" in New York, in the spring of 1960, produced a boycott of American ships by dock workers throughout the Arab world. But neither of these examples could be described as easily avoidable mistakes in U.S. policy, for in neither case is it certain that we would have done better by choosing an opposite course. The U.S. government could not have ignored Nuri and established some kind of relationship with revolutionary forces in Iraq, nor could it have at any stage announced that it proposed to deal with Nasser as the representative of all the Arab states. Both courses would have been impractical; they would have created as many difficulties as they solved.

It is essential that awareness of the reality and the force of revolutionary movements show through acts of American policy, giving the impression that the United States is fully conscious of the shape of the modern world and is not pigheadedly devoted to conservation of the *status quo*. A major difficulty is that Arab nationalists, like most revolutionaries, are inclined to ignore the dangers involved in getting what they want before they are ready for it.

DIFFERING ARAB AND AMERICAN VIEWPOINTS

In addition to obvious differences in culture, religion, language, customs, and manners between Arabs and Americans, there are

[1] The United Arab Republic (U.A.R.) was formed in 1958 by the union of Syria with Egypt. In 1961 Syria withdrew from the union, but Egypt is still known officially as the United Arab Republic.

important conflicts in points of view deriving from the very different stage in development of the two peoples and their place in the world. America is wealthy, relatively secure, accustomed to being looked up to and imitated. It has stable political and economic institutions and the oldest written constitution in use in the world. Democratic procedures, freedom of speech and publication, freedom of enterprise in the economic sphere, and national independence have become articles of faith for Americans and canons by which they judge the worth of other countries. Though dedicated to progress and change from its inception as a state, events have thrust upon the United States the role of protector of half the world and also, at least by inference, that of guardian of the *status quo* in all non-Communist countries.

The Arabs are desperately poor and recently have become aware of their poverty and lack of distinction. Now they are terribly anxious to regain the esteem and influence they once enjoyed. They have inherited a system that prescribes traditional formulas for religious, political, and economic conduct, but Arab nationalists have been won over to the religion of progress and modernization. Their traditional culture had no place for democracy (at least not on the Western pattern), or for freedom of speech, or free economic enterprise, except in certain places and times. Their sense of urgent need for accomplishment leads them to adopt more efficient, less complicated means of government than democracy; the resultant centralism and authoritarianism does not clash with traditional forms. The Arab nationalist has no patience with American cautiousness about change. The *status quo* is what he hates and fears; the prospect of chaos has few terrors for him.

Islam is probably closer to Christianity and to Western philosophies than are the other great Asian religions, although its complete, closed, self-sufficient system contrasts sharply with Western emphasis upon the interplay of ideas, tolerance of dissent, and fondness for self-criticism. Thus, there is room for much misunderstanding. The Muslim Arab who becomes westernized, some say, creates a second world for himself; he lives in two separate worlds with very little exchange between the two. Some Arab scholars trained in Western methods who can choose between working in Arabic or in Western languages say that the results of their research differ according to which language they use. Books written in English have to be rewritten, not just translated, to be put into meaningful Arabic. Conversely, Westerners who study Islam and Arab philosophy, it is sometimes said, either lose their contact with Western thought or remain Westerners observing an alien culture; they are never both Arab and Western at the same time.

In regard to foreign policy and diplomacy, it is often said that any attempt on the part of the makers of Western policy to understand and be understood by the Arabs is misguided. The assumption is rejected that it is possible and desirable to win the confidence of the Arabs. Foreign policy, it is held, must deal in realities, i.e., power and national interest, for only these can be understood both by the Arabs and the West.

But no culture or philosophy has ever been so self-sufficient as to be impermeable. If it is, it dies. Islam, in the days of its greatest vigor, showed itself capable of accepting and absorbing Greek science, and present-day Arabs show great interest and appetite for Western techniques and ideas. Moreover, in the present century, people all over the world have absorbed parts of Western culture until it has become accepted, in part at least, and adapted to local conditions in societies as different as Japan and India, in Africa and even in the Communist countries. Complete understanding across the board between Arabs and Americans may not be possible or likely, but it is wrong to assume that trying to expand the area of understanding is a waste of time.

The assumption that understanding of a foreign people and their culture is impossible or meaningless can only lead to the continuation of practices which often in the past have blunted and weakened American dealings with the Arabs. We formulate our goals in terms of our own interests, excluding the interests and desires of the people with whom we are dealing. We state our objectives in language meaningful to us but not necessarily to them. A broader formulation might reveal areas of agreement obscured by such a one-sided approach.

Despite the many differences, in two matters Arab and American points of view are very much the same: in emphasis upon independence and in interest in progress and modernization. The differences are likely to persist but their role in the Arab-American relationship might be diminished by greater exploitation of the areas of agreement.

For too many years the Western nations, including the United States, have been formulating policy toward the Arabs on the basis of Western assumptions, measuring it by Western values and standards. The time has come for a serious attempt to examine the Arab case from the inside out.

II

NASSER'S APPROACH TO
INTERNATIONAL POLITICS

President Gamal Abdel Nasser of Egypt is the leading practitioner of Arab foreign policy. He is not the creator or the arbiter of Arab nationalism's role in international affairs; his role has been more that of commander in chief, whose function has been to translate ideas into action.

Arab nationalist foreign policy cannot be understood unless due attention be paid to the wellsprings from which it flows. Nasser's role, however, has been of such critical importance in its recent development and he has become so much its pre-eminent symbol that it is well to consider his approach to international politics before looking to the wellsprings.

It is not yet clear whether Abdel Nasser will figure in history as a dictator who sought to extend his personal authority outward from Egypt and to mobilize the Arab, the African, and the Muslim worlds in an "anti-imperialist" bloc, or as a creative innovator in international politics who bent new forces to the purpose of restoring the Arabs to first-class citizenship in the world.

Today, Western opinion, as expressed in the press and in statements of political leaders, leans toward the dictator theory. Conrad Hilton, in a moment of enthusiasm and good will at the opening of the Nile Hilton Hotel in Cairo, referred to Nasser as the George Washington of his country. A much more common label in the West has been "Hitler of the Nile." Anthony Eden and Guy Mollet at the time of the Suez crisis warned the West that appeasing this dictator would lead to consequences as dire as those that followed the appeasement of Hitler and Mussolini.

Most popular, and many official, analyses of developments in the Arab world, ignoring Nasser's political and social ideology and the broad popular support for his struggle against foreign influence, concentrate on finding an easier and simpler formula in Nasser's personality. The whole situation in the Arab area, with its many international ramifications, has often been explained solely in terms of his ambitions. This explanation leads logically to the belief that remedies or changes can be brought about only through Nasser, or by influences acting upon him. Thus a great deal of time and effort has been devoted to figuring out what he is likely to do next. Middle East specialists, like the "Kremlinologists" among Soviet specialists, can be classified according to their theories of Nasser's motivation and intent.

In the Arab world the popular image of Nasser is well defined. It is not his military prowess or his position as chief of state, or his personal ambitions and his ability to realize them, that impress the Arab masses from Morocco to Iraq. His power and influence rest on his ability to symbolize Arab nationalism as an idea and as a practical force. As he walks on the world stage, millions of Arabs see him playing the role they would like to play and doing the things they would like to do. When Nasser denounces the "imperialists and their agents and stooges" and tells them that he will have no more of their interference in Arab affairs, he says things that are in the hearts of individual Arabs everywhere, and says them as they would like to say them if they could. When he challenges the great powers and takes daring risks in the name of Arab "rights and dignity," and gets away with it, the Arab masses feel an emotional lift and a satisfaction that no Arab leader has given them within memory. When Syria threw off Nasser's rule, many Arabs, including some who understood why the union had failed and others who disagreed with the policies pursued by its president, felt that an unhappy event had occurred and that Arab aspirations for unity had suffered a defeat.

There has been plentiful dissatisfaction with domestic policy in Egypt, and more in Syria when it was under Nasser's rule. The governing class in every other Arab country has shown much hostility toward Nasser but has approved his "Arab policy" and his role in world affairs, occasionally with some degree of hypocrisy. His foreign policy receives broad popular support. In spite of disagreements on specific policies, as a symbol of Arab nationalism he continues, even after the dissolution of the U.A.R., to enjoy an authority shared by no one. A well-to-do Egyptian Coptic Christian, who was in Great Britain at the time of the Suez crisis, gave expression to the meaning of Nasser's symbolic role as it affects even Arabs who have reasons to dislike his revolutionary regime. When asked if he had found it unpleasant to be in England at the time of the invasion of Egypt, this Egyptian of the old school said that he would not have missed it for anything. "For the first time," he said, "people took me seriously when they learned that I was an Egyptian and an Arab."

What is Nasser's real role? Is he a giant who molds historic forces to his own will, or is he simply the instrument through which these forces express themselves? As with most, if not all, historic figures, the answer is probably to be found in a combination of personal and historic factors. Nasser, a man of great abilities, has made these abilities felt by applying them to forces which were real and growing before he came on the scene. An examination of the interaction between Nasser the man and the forces with which he has become identified makes the popular Arab image of Nasser as the symbol and representative of Arab nationalism appear much more accurate than the common Western image of Nasser the dictator consumed by personal ambition.

INFLUENCES SHAPING NASSER

When Nasser was in school in Egypt, anti-British demonstrations were a part of every schoolboy's life. He frequently refers in his speeches to this period of political awakening. Like many of his contemporaries, he was influenced by the tradition of Egyptian nationalism going back to Saad Zaghlul, Orabi, and further. His nationalism was like theirs, short on doctrine and long on emotion, being mainly a fierce desire to make their country their own and to drive out the foreigner who ruled Egypt and disdained the Egyptians. Another favorite reference in his speeches is to the role of the British ambassadors in Arab countries: ". . . this region was in the zone of British influence," he has said, "our foreign policy was then planned by the British Foreign Office."[1]

Unlike the majority of his contemporaries, Nasser at an early age became a full-time nationalist, not just an occasional marcher and demonstrator. Thenceforward he made political planning and, ultimately, revolution his primary occupation and concern. He certainly read the writings and speeches of nationalists like Mustapha Kemal and Saad Zaghlul, although his public statements do not indicate that he has committed their words to memory or keeps their writings at hand. However, he frequently cites their example, along with that of many other nationalist heroes of the more distant past, including Saladin and Baybars, the Mameluke Sultan who stopped the Mongol invasion in Syria. He rarely cites nationalist doctrine or theory publicly or privately. His great interest in history probably indicates that the realities of practical politics have more meaning for him than theory.

Quite early in Nasser's career as a nationalist he began making contact with political organizations in order to study their operations. He and several of his friends were in close touch with the growing Muslim Brotherhood. Though they were concerned with discovering every source of Arab strength, they were too secular in outlook, too much influenced by their military training and too much interested in the fruits of science and progress on the Western model, to accept the conservative, traditionalist objectives of the Brotherhood. They were, however, attracted by the organization of this truly clandestine instrument for political action.

For the same reasons Nasser and his friends made contact with the Communist party in Egypt. He has said that when the Communists tried to recruit him, he refused because communism was a foreign ideology and he was interested only in Egypt's independence.[2] He kept contact with the Communists, however, through one member of his group, Khalid Muhieddin, who joined the

---

[1] Gamal Abdel Nasser, *President Gamal Abdel Nasser's Speeches and Press Interviews,* 1958 (Cairo: U.A.R. Information Department, 1961), p. 306. Hereafter volumes in this series will be referred to as *Nasser's Speeches.*

[2] *Nasser's Speeches,* 1959, p. 146.

Communist party. A friend, Ahmad Fuad, also acted as a kind of liaison officer. Nasser seems never to have absorbed much Communist doctrine, although he learned a lot about Communist organization and tactics.

The most important years of Nasser's life, before the successful revolution of 1952 saddled him with the burdens and responsibilities of power, were spent planning and creating a revolutionary organization. Nasser has been a revolutionary ever since, and his whole outlook and style have been influenced by this fact. He developed his ability as a leader within a small group of carefully selected companions upon whose loyalty he depended absolutely for his own safety and for the security of the enterprise on which they were embarked. In an atmosphere of plot and counterplot he learned the value of trusted lieutenants and the dangers of disloyalty and betrayal. This experience, rather than the fact that the revolutionary regime had the support of the army from the outset, probably accounts for the continued presence of numerous army and air force officers in high places in Nasser's circle of advisers and chief lieutenants. What appears to be a military regime—it was one for a time—is actually a revolutionary regime, run by the small group of old conspirators whose loyalty was tested in the days before the monarchy was overthrown. Specialists in a variety of fields, including foreign policy, have been added to the circle of advisers that surround the central core of power, but only two or three who did not share in the conspiracy against the monarchy have ever entered the inmost circle. Thus, Egyptian foreign policy is still made by revolutionaries with a military background. They have learned many lessons and are advised by able specialists, but their approach to foreign policy is still influenced by their experiences before the *coup d'état*.

These leaders came to power with hardly any goals in mind beyond achieving the revolution. Nasser, and other members of the revolutionary junta, believed that it would be enough to throw out the King and the corrupt elements around him and to turn the country over to honest men. Their quick disillusionment with politicians and parties they have made abundantly clear.[3] Insofar

[3] Gamal Abdel Nasser, *The Philosophy of the Revolution* (Buffalo: Smith, Keynes and Marshall, 1959), pp. 33–34.

as they had a foreign policy it was essentially one of Egyptian nationalism. They had only two objectives: to get the British out of the country and to unite the Sudan with Egypt. Abdel Rahman Azzam Pasha, Secretary-General of the Arab League and long an exponent of the Arab unity idea, quickly ascertained that the revolutionary junta was not interested in Pan Arab ideas and resigned his post. Having concentrated on political organization and action before the revolution, and approaching the responsibilities of power with practically no doctrine, it was inevitable that the revolutionary regime should adopt a pragmatic line in foreign policy.

The practical, operational approach is characteristic of Nasser and his colleagues. At first, with overwhelming domestic problems demanding their attention, they gave only a carefully rationed portion of their time and energy to the achievement of their two stated foreign-policy objectives, carrying on where the monarchy had left off in its negotiations with the British. Generally, their foreign policy tended to be reactive rather than creative. They adopted measures that seemed expedient and seized opportunities, but original initiatives were rare until Nasser, in the summer of 1954, emerged from his struggles with the opposition forces which had clustered around General Naguib. After that, Nasser turned his hand to international politics and developed the basic ideas which have provided a doctrinal framework for his initiatives in this field. Still, the old pragmatism and opportunism has remained as a continuing characteristic of his foreign policy and a reminder of his origins.

NASSER'S PERSONAL STYLE

All the thousand and one determinants of Egyptian foreign policy can be analyzed and evaluated, but final judgment cannot be made without due attention to the personal ingredient which Nasser brings to foreign policy.

Nasser's skill in handling people and in finding ready answers to difficult questions has been carefully and painfully acquired. He tells how ill at ease he was when he first went before the public after the July 1952 revolution. A particularly difficult moment came when he addressed the students at Alexandria University shortly after the signing of a technical assistance agreement with the United States had been announced. As he talked, a group of Communist students started heckling him by shouting "Point Four, Point Four." Completely bewildered about how to handle the situation, he began to fear that the meeting would get out of hand. Then, reacting instinctively, he called the loudest of the hecklers to the platform, got him in front of the microphone, and asked him to explain to the audience what Point Four was. When he proved completely unable to do so, Nasser finished his speech with the audience on his side. Since that time his skill in speaking has developed phenomenally.

Nasser takes his responsibilities seriously. People meeting him note how rarely he uses the personal pronoun, except to illustrate from his own experience some point which he is making. He is remarkably effective in conversation, even with unsympathetic interlocutors, because he considers every question and suggestion seriously, addressing himself to them as though they were new ideas deserving of fresh examination. He is not the type who lectures his visitors, although he enjoys plunging into an extended analysis of a question that interests him. Quite a number of persons who came unprepared to be impressed have been disarmed by Nasser's questions and by his skill in showing interest in what his visitor has to say.

Nasser in conversation gives the appearance of an eminently serious and reasonable man who has suffered many injuries and affronts which he cannot forget. He makes it clear that he is determined not to get into a position again, if he can help it, in which they can be repeated. But this sensitivity to injury and determination to stand up for his rights, and the rights of his people, do not detract from the impression that he is a man with whom other reasonable men ought to be able to do business.

Leaving a conference with some official or unofficial American, in which he has appeared as the epitome of responsible statesmanship, Nasser can go on a platform or before radio microphones and lash the United States up, down, and sideways for its "imperialist" and "neo-colonialist" maneuvers and its hostility to the Arab nationalist concept. His public speeches, and the propaganda which he directs and reviews, have a heavy emotional content. Obviously he feels that the Arab public must be kept stirred up if it is to play its role in achieving national goals. A good deal of Nasser's public speech-making, however, should be put in the educational rather than the rabble-rousing category. When delivering one of his long historical speeches, or one on economic development, or Arab socialism, he insists on attentive listeners and discourages applause and shouting.

When receiving visiting dignitaries at his home, Nasser is punctilious, dignified, and serious. The villa at the Abbassia barracks, where he lived as a lieutenant colonel before the revolution, now enlarged and redecorated, provides a touch of modesty to contrast with the triumphal arches, the anniversary parades, the honor guard, the banquets at Kubba Palace, and the elaborate ceremonies performed for Afro-Asian leaders and others who make Cairo a frequent rendezvous.

Nasser's insistence upon presenting a dignified public image was evident when he attended the United Nations General Assembly in the autumn of 1960. His was the figure of a man attending strictly to business. In his quiet, well-pressed and well-cut suit, he made a sharp contrast with flamboyant personalities like Castro and Sukarno. The contrast was strikingly exhibited in *The New York Times,* which one day carried a photograph of Premier Khrushchev gleefully hugging Fidel Castro and nestling his head in Castro's beard, and on the next day showed Nasser and Khrushchev standing solemnly side by side, for all the world like two executives meeting on a Long Island estate.

An important quality of Nasser's style is his habit of talking things over at length with his staff and advisers, with careful analysis and consideration of alternatives and of probable consequences. As time has passed, Nasser seems to have become less impulsive and more deliberate. A fear that many of his well-wishers share is that as he becomes more and more of an institution and as he takes more and more unpopular and difficult steps in his reform program, he is becoming isolated from his critics, finding it less convenient than formerly to exchange views with his advisers in midnight discussions.

TECHNIQUES

The techniques with which Nasser, as head of the revolutionary regime in Egypt, has pursued the interests of his country—and ultimately the wider interests and claims of Arab nationalism—evolved along with foreign policy itself.

Elimination of the influence of the "imperialists" from without and the "feudalists" from within, and the establishment of a middle class and secular but still Muslim regime in Egypt, were the original goals of the Egyptian revolution. Translating these objectives into action, particularly where relations with other countries were involved, made heavy demands on the inexperienced military junta known as the Revolutionary Command Council. The methods which they evolved in the early days of the regime for handling foreign relations have had an important influence ever since on the style as well as on the content of Nasser's foreign policy.

Policy Formulation and Decision-Making

In those days, all basic policy decisions, including formulation of aims and planning of tactics, were made within the Revolutionary Command Council which sat as a committee in almost continuous session. The favorite meeting place for these sessions, which often went on through the night, was Farouk's palatial boathouse on Gezira Island overlooking the Nile. There was lively interchange of ideas, with all members of the group presenting their opinions and insisting on being convinced of the wisdom of the majority decision. Often there were violent disagreements and emotional scenes. Nasser's personality was dominant, but so long as General Naguib remained the titular president, policy as well as tactics were the product of group decision. After General Naguib's removal from office in 1954 and the substitution of a cabinet system for the old Revolutionary Command Council in 1955, the importance of group decision diminished. The biggest change in the formulation of policy took place after the Suez crisis when the Presidency, as a separate office, became indisputably the source of authority, initiative, and decision. President Nasser's office was located in a gloomy old villa across from the Parliament building, while the staff of the Presidency, now the nerve center of the government for foreign policy as for all other affairs, was shifted to a new building behind it.

After Suez, a change took place in the method of making foreign policy partly owing to a change in Nasser himself. Most of his countrymen and many other Arabs believed that by his own *baraka* (the luck or magic of his personal star) he had won victories against impossible odds. He cannot have been entirely unaffected by this popular feeling about him. An even greater change took place in the attitude of the people around him. Men closely associated with him for years who had argued with him through interminable strategy sessions, giving as good as they got, began referring to him as *El rais* (the leader, or the president) and quoting his opinions as the final word on every subject.

After the union with Syria, and the establishment of the central government's headquarters in the grandiose old Heliopolis Palace Hotel, Nasser moved his offices to Kubba Palace nearby, where his staff rattled around in the echoing marble halls and spacious rooms whose dimensions and decor are constant reminders of the Muhammad Ali dynasty and the Egyptian feudalism which Nasser has sought to extinguish. (Some of his aides grumble about the anachronism of a revolutionary socialist regime occupying a palace.) Here and in other of Farouk's leftover palaces, Nasser can entertain royally—even the King of Saudi Arabia and his numerous entourage—without inconvenience. He is much better prepared for visitors of state than the President of the United States who has to send those whom he cannot fit into Blair House to Washington hotels.

Basically, however, the technique of decision-making in Kubba Palace has remained the same as it was in the Gezira boathouse; a small group of trusted, responsible men sits in consultation with the man at the center who has the final authority. These men who act as the closest advisers to the President have become more and more specialized in one or another field of government, but they are still essentially members of a revolutionary council whose credentials are loyalty to Nasser and his leadership and dedication to the ideas and objectives which he represents. A harder working group has seldom run a government. In a country and a region long noted for regarding public office as a door to private enrichment, where the people are ready to believe almost anything about their rulers, it is still widely believed that the members of Nasser's circle have not enriched themselves during their years in office. Their basic honesty and devotion to duty provide a constant contrast with vivid memories of the court circle and the behavior of King Farouk's officials and constitute one of the most important sources of popular support. That Nasser's top group has not yet succeeded in imposing its standards on the second and third echelons in government and the officer corps is clear enough. However, the tough reform decrees of July 1961 have reconfirmed their determination to reduce corruption in government and business.

Since the revolution the activities of the Ministry of Foreign Affairs have been limited to the routine of foreign representation and of the conduct of international relations. The Foreign Minister, Mahmoud Fawzi, a respected technician whose standing as a diplomat and official of the Foreign Ministry dates from the prerevolutionary period, has only a small role as a policy maker. Many other members of the foreign service who were identified in one way or another with the outlook and the attitudes of the prerevolutionary period were let go. At present some of the most important specialists in foreign affairs have come from the lower ranks of the original military group, or are military men who have had some experience in foreign matters. Saleh Gohar, for example, who was involved in armistice negotiations with the Israelis at the end of the Palestine War, for a long time headed the Palestine Affairs Department in the Ministry of Foreign Affairs. Mahmoud Riad, also a military man who was involved in early negotiations with the Israelis and served as ambassador to Syria in the critical period before the union, became presidential adviser on foreign affairs and later permanent representative to the United Nations.

The Premier and former Minister for Presidential Affairs, Ali Sabri, an air force officer who was in the original revolutionary group though not a member of the Revolutionary Command Council, has been, after the President, the senior official in the foreign-policy field. He has described his job as being like that of Governor Sherman Adams under President Eisenhower, but it actually encompasses a good deal more. He is an important point of contact between the President and representatives of foreign governments and plays a key role in the actual process of strategy formulation and policy-making not unlike that of the American President's Special Assistant for National Security Affairs. His brother, Hussein Sulficar Sabri, who has been involved in foreign affairs from the early days after the revolution, has served as Deputy Minister of Foreign Affairs. Dr. Murad Ghaleb, formerly an official in the Presidency, was for a time Under Secretary in the Ministry of Foreign Affairs.

The rapid response, particularly to challenges or affronts, which characterizes Nasser's conduct of foreign policy is made possible by the highly centralized system of policy and strategy formulation. Its explanation lies in the Egyptian—and Arab—sensitivity to insult, inherited from long years of discriminatory treatment by foreigners. The importance of restoring "dignity" to the Arabs is a favorite theme in Nasser's speeches and in Arab nationalist publicity. Nasser described his reaction to the withdrawal of the U.S. offer of assistance on the Aswan High Dam project in these words: ". . . we felt that this was an act which was directed against our dignity. This explains why we reacted by doing something to maintain our dignity."[4] He practically never lets an insult or slight, real or fancied, go unanswered. Discussing the picketing in 1960 by American unions of the Egyptian ship "Cleopatra" in New York, Nasser has said that his policy of standing up to the great powers "proved to be useful and helpful to us."[5] His willingness to take on all comers in the game of answering back has become famous. "Imperialism" and "Zionism," have been most often the targets of his wrath; their initiatives have frequently evoked a response in the next day's press. In the spring of 1959 when Premier Khrushchev, following Nasser's attacks on Communist activities in Syria and Iraq and denunciation of local Communists as agents of a foreign power, chided him for being a hot-headed young man, Nasser promptly answered: "Mr. Khrushchev's defence in favour of Communists in our country is a matter which cannot be accepted by the Arab people,"[6] and again, "Through our unity which

4 *Nasser's Speeches*, 1959, p. 420.
5 *Nasser's Speeches*, 1960 (April-June), p. 79.
6 *Nasser's Speeches*, 1959, p. 159.

enabled us to destroy imperialism and its stooges, we will, God willing, destroy Communism and dependence. There will be no new imperialism to replace the Western imperialism from which we have liberated ourselves."[7]

This readiness to talk back, and the speed with which his government has been able to make up its mind, have given Nasser a great reputation as a counterpuncher and master of agile footwork in foreign affairs. In large part, this reputation is based on the nationalization of the Suez Canal Company and on his handling of the crisis which followed. The effect and the ultimate outcome of this maneuver were magnified by a series of apparent triumphs in 1957 and 1958. Since July 26, 1956—the date on which Nasser announced the nationalization of the Suez Canal Company—many ears have been cocked to catch each anniversary speech. But those who awaited another historic surprise have usually been disappointed, even though Nasser's foreign policy continues to be marked by rapid responses. His style is less slashing than in the early days of the regime. His response to the Syrian coup in 1961, which many expected would loose a thunderbolt, was marked by judicious restraint.

The Use of Propaganda

Propaganda has always been an important tool of Nasser's foreign policy. He has a practical as well as a mystic belief in the power of public opinion in both national and international affairs. Discussing the Suez crisis he said: "The example Port Said set in 1956 was a turning point in world history because it proved that the treacherous powers cannot triumph over the will of a believing people . . . and that believing people can triumph over the strongest armies and the biggest states."[8] He was obviously impressed by the effect of world opinion, particularly African and Asian, on the course of events in the United Nations and on its role in the Suez crisis. Speaking at Alexandria in July 1957, on the first anniversary of nationalizing the Suez Canal Company, he said, "The world has now become interlinked, and it now feels every action that takes place in any of its parts. The world con-

[7] Same, p. 163.
[8] Speech at Port Said, December 23, 1960.

science no longer is confined to Europe and America. . . . There is the world opinion in Asia and Africa which supported us during the aggression and gave us assistance. This world opinion must be taken into consideration."[9]

Nasser follows the world press with great interest and personally participates in the formation of propaganda policy. When the independent newspapers and magazines in Egypt were nationalized in the spring of 1960, Nasser gave two reasons for the action. First, he said that the independent press was too frivolous, too much taken up with sensational news and scandalmongering. He said he needed the press to help educate the public to its responsibilities and to the need for self-discipline. A country in the midst of a revolution must, by popular dedication to duty and by sacrifice, pull itself up by its own bootstraps. Second, he charged that, because of pressure from advertisers and foreign interests, the press slanted its treatment of news in ways detrimental to the revolution.

He adduced a similar argument against restoring the multi-party system: namely that if party activity were uncontrolled, the Soviet Union would subsidize a Communist party in disguise, the Americans a "rightist" party, and the Arab nationalists would be left in the middle, less well financed than the other two.[10]

A salient characteristic of Nasser's propaganda and in fact of all Arab activities in this field is its defensive quality. Its resort to apologetics reflects Arab sensitivity to insult, the sense of being under attack.[11] Most Arab officials in the business of "information" or propaganda, when asked how they conceive their jobs, will answer, "to defend ourselves against attack." When asked by a representative of the British Broadcasting Corporation about charges of stirring up the people of Africa and the Persian Gulf against Great Britain Nasser replied: ". . . it is not a question of propaganda alone, but propaganda and counter-propaganda, and the question of independence and self-determination."[12] When questioned by a CBS representative about propaganda attacks on

[9] Speech at Alexandria, July 26, 1957.

[10] Interview with representatives of the Columbia Broadcasting System, April 7, 1958, *Nasser's Speeches*, 1958, p. 387.

[11] Wilfred Cantwell Smith, *Islam in Modern History* (New York: Mentor Books, 1959), p. 117 ff.

[12] *Nasser's Speeches*, 1959, p. 528.

other Arab governments he said: "We may be forced sometimes to resort to defensive measures. . . . We attack them only when they are used [by "imperialism"] in the battle against the aspirations of our people."[13]

Cairo radio's "Voice of the Arabs" and the Cairo press, both instruments of Nasser's foreign policy, exert a potent influence on public opinion in Egypt, and, to a less degree, in other Arab states. Westerners often attribute their violence and emotional extremism to Nasser, personally. But those who prefer their propaganda subtle and delivered in an apparently rational manner with a liberal admixture of "facts" will discover from an examination of the propaganda of Nasser's Arab enemies, Nuri el Said, King Hussein, and Abdel Karim Kassem, that Cairo has no monopoly on the kind of propaganda they find distasteful. The peculiar quality of Arab propaganda has been described as follows:

It is really a kind of poetry, the search for an adequate metaphor, the expression of political bitterness and frustration. In a sense it is a straining after accuracy. To express the idea of a nation that strengthens itself at the expense of another, what more exact and sober than to call it a vampire, what more economical of words, what more telling to an audience that is attached to poetry? Arabs are like Celts, who must say what they feel while they feel it; their language is not to be gauged as an Englishman's is, who prefers understatement to obtain the effects he wants, and who would rather the stresses of the mere moment were left unexpressed. Englishmen, with their distaste for language which says what one feels at one time, never perhaps to feel again, rather than what one feels at all times, often misunderstand Arabs, as they regularly misunderstand Celts.[14]

Nasser's use of public media of communication, however, is much more than indulgence in Arab fondness for poetic expression. Behind it lies a deeply held belief in the power of self-determination and its function in the field of political action and international policy. After his denunciation of the Baghdad Pact in January 1955, and to a much more pronounced degree after the Egyptian arms deal with the Soviet bloc, it became clear that he had struck responsive chords throughout the Middle East.

[13] *Nasser's Speeches,* 1958, pp. 379–380.
[14] Caractacus (pseud.), *Revolution in Iraq: An Essay in Comparative Public Opinion* (London: Gollancz, 1959), pp. 90–91.

As Nasser has become more and more clearly the symbol of Arab nationalism, the Arab masses everywhere have looked to him for guidance, responding to the stimulus of his voice and his example. At the same time the conservative Arab governments have become more and more apprehensive about his ability to influence their people. When, in 1957 and later after the Egyptian-Syrian union, conservative opposition began to build up, Nasser's propaganda stressed a theory which had become fundamental in his political strategy and tactics. The idea is that the social and political revolution which attracts the eager support of the Arab masses naturally arouses the hostility and opposition of those entrenched elements about to be displaced. It is these conservative elements—the kings, the pashas, and the great merchants grown wealthy on monopolies—that are leagued with the "imperialists," sometimes secretly, sometimes openly, and whose maneuvers to maintain the old order are supported by the Western powers. At times—after the arms deal, the Suez crisis, and the union between Egypt and Syria—the regime in Cairo may have believed that the conservative regimes would soon come tumbling down. When they proved less fragile than they had sometimes appeared, Nasser and his supporters were bolstered up by their confidence in the continuing support and allegiance of the masses throughout the Arab world who could be reached over the heads of kings and pashas. This belief fitted in with the idea of the self-determination of the "Arab nation," the assertion of the will of the entire Arab people to be part of a single community.

Cairo propaganda has been shaped by the concept of Arab self-determination as the ultimate arbiter of Middle East politics. In an address in Aleppo in 1958, Nasser said, characteristically, "I pledge myself to the Arab world, here from its northern frontier, to proceed with our struggle.[15] When asked by Dana Adams Schmidt of *The New York Times,* in 1959, whether the theory of the three circles of Egyptian influence described in his book, *The Philosophy of the Revolution,* indicated his wish to lead all the Arabs, his answer was:

Nobody can impose his leadership on the people. But everyone can express his opinion. If this opinion finds support, this does not mean

[15] *Nasser's Speeches,* 1958, p. 113.

that the author of the opinion seeks leadership or wishes to impose leadership on others. . . . But now we live in the second half of the 20th century—the age of ideologies and opinions. We announce our views and beliefs. If the countries surrounding us feel that what we say expresses their aspirations and that the slogans of our struggle are the same as those which spring from the depth of their conscience, this is a matter which totally differs from mere leadership.[16]

In effect, Nasser was saying that if the people decide that he is expressing their desires and choose to join with him, then something different from "leadership," in the sense of the assertion of his own will or authority, will take place. It is the will of the people which Nasser seeks to make the arbiter and the justification of the Arab nationalist revolution and his own role in it. In a speech in Damascus in 1958 he echoed the words of democrats and dictators alike: "The will of the people is the will of God." And he seeks constantly to arouse the Arab public to its power and responsibilities: ". . . we are a generation destined to shoulder great responsibilities," he has said, and again, "if we really want freedom and independence we must depend on ourselves alone."[17]

Representation Abroad

The revolutionary regime, at an early stage, planned to utilize all the various resources of the state in a coordinated effort to further its interests abroad. The centralized character of the strategy and policy-making organs of the government, the rapid growth of interest in Arab unity, and the quick realization that good representation abroad in a variety of fields strengthens the over-all position and resources of a country, were foundations on which the new plan was built.

The revolutionary regime encouraged and facilitated the placement of Egyptian teachers in other Arab states, where they had long been in demand. This export of educational skills was advantageous to Egypt because of its inability to furnish suitable jobs at home for its output of university graduates. It benefited, also, states like Kuwait and Libya with expanding educational programs and shortages of trained teachers. Egyptians employed as teachers in other Arab states, probably numbering more than three thousand

---

[16] *Nasser's Speeches,* 1959, p. 592.
[17] *Nasser's Speeches,* 1958, pp. 16, 75, 187; same, 1959, p. 361.

today, are indoctrinated before going to their foreign posts and are instructed to act as representatives of their country and its policies. From time to time questions have been raised in other Arab countries about the propaganda content of the instruction given by Egyptian teachers, with suggestions that they are participating in sinister subversive activities. Actually, Egyptian teachers are more effective, it seems, and more useful to Nasser's cause, acting within the normal bounds of their profession, behaving in other Arab countries much as they would in Cairo. Even so, they help to promote the long-range objectives of Nasser's foreign policy, thus revealing the advantages of the cultural and educational leadership in the Arab world which the city of Cairo has long exercised.

Another resource is the great Islamic university of Al Azhar, which trains theologians, teachers, and specialists in Islamic law for the entire Muslim world. The rector of Al Azhar and the Muslim leaders in Egypt are apparently willing collaborators with the revolutionary regime and subscribe to the main tenets of its foreign policy. Occasionally, statements made by the rector on public issues and events have indicated either consultation in advance with the government, or at least an interest in being helpful. In general, however, the revolutionary regime has avoided the appearance of using Al Azhar on behalf of its policies or invoking the support of Islam. Its backing is nevertheless real, and is perhaps more important because it appears to be voluntary.

A different kind of use of the power of Islam as a link between Egypt and the rest of the Islamic world is the Islamic Congress. Organized in the early days of the regime, the Congress was put under the direction of Anwar el Sadat, one of the original members of Nasser's revolutionary group and a member of the Revolutionary Command Council. Its object has been the encouragement of religious, cultural, and educational interchange among Muslim nations. Its effectiveness seems to have been modest.

In many other fields the representatives of Egypt have been active in building up relations with governments, groups, and individuals throughout the Arab and the Afro-Asian world, and in promoting cooperation and support for the nationalist-neutralist point of view. The Egyptian labor federation has aimed at international political goals.[18] Fuad Galal, a prominent Nasser lieutenant, played an important role in the Arab Graduates' Congress, an association of Arab university graduates which holds conferences where well-publicized discussion of political and foreign-policy matters has taken place in a strongly Arab nationalist atmosphere. Military missions in other Arab states at one time or another have provided further contacts. In short, the Egyptians have taken a leaf from the book of the great powers in organizing and coordinating various external activities, private and public, with foreign policy. The only thing new and surprising about all this is that it is part of the policy of an Arab state.

Clandestine Activities

In giving increasing attention to clandestine operations, also, the nationalist leaders have been following the example of other nations. In this field they started with considerable resources and advantages of their own. Intrigue and secret activity are as old as the Middle East. Their use as instruments of policy was stimulated by the widespread conviction that the "imperialists," particularly the British, were masters of clandestine techniques and constantly engaged in nefarious goings-on throughout the Arab world. The Egyptians' interest in counterespionage activities was aroused when they uncovered a number of what were publicized as Western operations directed against them. One of their discoveries was an Israeli operation, the exposure of which led to the bitter "Lavon affair" in Israel more than five years later. There were also plentiful intrigues among the Arab states themselves, the most spectacular of which involved payments, in amounts which only the Saudi King could have managed, to Abdel Hamid Serraj, Nasser's lieutenant in Syria, allegedly for the elimination of Nasser himself.

Of more importance, and of more concern to the outside world, were clandestine political operations designed to promote Arab unity and the triumph of the revolutionary Arab nationalist point of view. Answering charges that he was engaged in subversive activity, Nasser in a speech in Alexandria said, "Whatever event

[18] Cf. Keith Wheelock, *Nasser's New Egypt: A Critical Analysis* (New York: Praeger, for the University of Pennsylvania Foreign Policy Research Institute, 1960), pp. 266–267.

occurred any place in the world the headlines in the newspapers said that Abdel Nasser was plotting there. I called the British journalists and told them: 'This statement is not logical.' It is impossible for any person to have such organizing ability."[19] The Western press in 1957 and 1958 did give him credit for more clandestine operations than any one country could possibly have carried out. On the other hand, a series of revelations in neighboring countries made it clear that if Nasser was not responsible for everything, he was having a try at a few things here and there, and having his share of bad luck, too. In a fairly short period of time, Egyptian military attachés or other officials were caught distributing or stockpiling weapons, engaging in antigovernment propaganda, or making contact with dissident groups in Tunisia, Libya, Lebanon, Saudi Arabia, Iraq, and the Sudan.

Such revelations, however, did not point to the most important aspect of the situation behind these unorthodox political activities, namely, that the Egyptians, and later the United Arab Republic, had what no amount of money could buy and no amount of skilled personnel could create. They had genuine volunteers for service in the cause of Arab nationalism in every city and hamlet in the Arab world. These people looked to Nasser for guidance and were prepared to take action to bring about the spread of the Arab nationalist revolution. They practically lined up in front of every Egyptian embassy and consulate, asking for more specific orders than they got over Cairo radio—though those were sometimes specific enough to bring action.

The ubiquitous rioters in Amman, during the disturbances of 1957, were said to keep one ear cocked to the café radios blaring the Voice of the Arabs program from Cairo. When the Voice reported that the Arab patriots in Amman were attacking the British Bank of the Middle East, for example, the faithful listeners would rush to do just that, picking up stones from piles foresightedly placed in advance in strategic spots.

On the whole, actual planning and participation by Egyptians and Syrians, themselves, in clandestine activities throughout the area seem to have been overestimated. Not that the U.A.R. au-

[19] Speech at Alexandria, July 26, 1957.

thorities lacked interest in helping along revolutionary tendencies. But their ability to help has often been unequal to the enthusiasm of local nationalists, and also less than their enemies suspected.

Afro-Asian Solidarity

A wider dimension to Egyptian interest and involvement in the politics of the Afro-Asian revolution has been given by Cairo's role as a haven for political leaders in exile. This is probably what Nasser had in mind in answering the Indian journalist R. K. Karanjia who had asked if he (Nasser) was not in reality the "Commander in Chief of Arab Nationalism." The Egyptian leader replied: ". . . Cairo has become the base and capital of the Arab struggle from Oman to Algeria."[20] With no loss of accuracy he might have extended the territory to include a large part of Africa. The Egyptian capital, even in the days of British predominance, provided a refuge where political exiles from other colonial territories and representatives of aspiring political movements from all over the Middle East and farther afield waited and planned in safety. In Cairo during World War II Indonesian students did some of the planning which later led to the Indonesian independence movement and to the formation of the Arab-Asian bloc in the United Nations. Leaders of independence movements from French North Africa, including for a time the leaders of the Algerian independence movement and Ben Yusif, Bourguiba's rival for control of independent Tunisia, and many political exiles from sub-Saharan Africa also found hospitality and assistance in the Egyptian capital. The Afro-Asian Peoples' Solidarity Council, set up in Cairo as a kind of permanent center for implementing the resolutions of the Bandung Conference, enlarged that city's role as a center for Afro-Asian activity directed against "imperialism" and "colonialism" and in support of a third force of neutralist nations drawing strength from public opinion in Asian and African countries.

Still another technique of Nasser in the field of foreign affairs has been the linking of Arab nationalist forces with those of the Afro-Asian revolution through cooperation with like-minded leaders of other states. When Nasser met with Marshal Tito of

[20] *Nasser's Speeches,* 1959, p. 539.

Yugoslavia and Prime Minister Nehru of India in 1954, he was apparently struck by the advantages of association with them, as well as by what they taught him about international politics and policy. The Bandung Conference in the spring of 1955, a turning point in Nasser's thinking, confirmed him in the technique of taking positions on world issues in conjunction with other leaders of similar views. The Bandung Conference was followed by conferences at Brioni with Tito and Nehru, and by the exchange of visits with other chiefs of state whose foreign policies were keyed to the principle of nonalignment and neutralism. The Belgrade Conference of nonaligned nations in September 1961, sponsored by Yugoslavia and the U.A.R., was the culmination of years of talk and planning about how to make the nonaligned states a third force in world affairs.

Armed Force and Foreign Policy

One technique, which some might have expected to find listed here and which has not been, is the use of military force. Nasser has spent much of his country's resources on armaments since 1955, and the armed forces continue to be an important element in his regime. Arms constitute a threat of force which can advance his purposes. They can be used in nearby countries, as they have been used in Yemen, if the risks are judged to be acceptable. Military force as such, however, is not a major element in his foreign policy, except for defense.

There are several reasons for this. The Arabs in general, and the Egyptians more than most, are hardly now a militarily aggressive people. Despite the traditions of the Arab conquerors in the great days of the Muslim empire, the Arabs today, except for a dwindling group of desert tribesmen, are essentially political people. They are aggressive enough, but disinclined to seek to resolve issues by force.

Nasser is typical in this regard. Though trained as a military man and obviously much influenced by his experiences in the army and in the Palestine War, he has made himself the master of the new international politics in which advantage is made of weakness and in which world opinion and the vast machinery of international organization are brought into effective play. The Suez crisis, of course, provided the best example of the use of these tactics. Nasser has on many other occasions and in other circumstances shown himself more confident of his ability to find political and psychological solutions than military.

Nasser is a pragmatist in foreign policy. Style and technique, therefore, often seem to dominate his diplomacy—but this is an illusion. Behind the tools and the skilled hands is the workman himself, and the things he does with his tools are not simply the product of his skill—they are also a reflection of his purposes and of his philosophy. Even during the early days of the Egyptian revolution, when Nasser and his companions were forced to concentrate almost exclusively on the practical concerns of the moment, they were guided by the Arab nationalism which they had absorbed through the pores of their skin from the moment they were in any sense conscious of the world around them. With the passage of time and in the light of experience they began to elaborate and systematize the essential Arab nationalist principles into a doctrinal base for foreign policy. In this endeavor they looked beyond Egypt to find their resources and opportunities in the wider Arab community, in its physical attributes, in the history and psychology of the Arab people as a whole. It is to these fundamentals that we now turn.

III

NATIONALISM AND ANTI-WESTERNISM

Nationalism has been the key to Arab political thought and behavior for nearly a century. Like most nationalisms, Arab nationalism is both a creative effort to build a better world and a reaction against external forces and influences—in this case those coming from the West—which are believed to oppose and limit the Arab revival. Paradoxically, much of the stimulus to Arab nationalism itself has come from contact with the West and the result has been a strange balance between feelings of admiration and hostility for the West. This inner tension in the Arab psychology, particularly as it affects attitudes toward the outside world, is of basic importance to Arab behavior in international affairs.

The peculiar logic of Arab nationalism was illustrated in the report of a special committee "on the regularization of national dress" appointed in 1955 by the Egyptian Minister of Social Affairs. The committee, which included distinguished citizens and representatives of the academic and the religious world, recommended the gradual abolition of the traditional Egyptian national dress, viz., robes and turbans and also the long, nightshirt-like *gellabiya* which is the comfortable, inexpensive dress of the lower-class males. The committee proposed that the men of Cairo and Alexandria be given three years to change from their traditional costume to Western-type trousers and turtle-neck sweaters. European suits would also be acceptable. During the following three years the men of the larger towns would be required to make the change; subsequently the village dwellers would have to comply. Women's dress was not mentioned, being a matter which even this committee was unprepared to tackle.

To Western observers the committee's recommendations seemed inexplicable. In the midst of a revolution the Arab nationalists, they believed, would surely reject the proposed abolition of the national costume and the adoption of an absurd imitation of Western dress. But not so. The nationalists were most strongly behind the idea. One of them explained his attitude thus: "As it is now, tourists come to Egypt to be amused by the strange mixture of dress they see here. They think these old-fashioned costumes are quaint and take pictures of them so they can go home and laugh again. In London, Paris, New York, and Moscow, everyone dresses more or less alike in a kind of international, twentieth-century costume. We would like people in Cairo to look the same as in these other important cities; their dress ought not to be a curiosity and a reminder of our backwardness."

The committee's recommendations were forgotten, of course, but the reaction they evoked from the more extreme nationalists indicates how complex are the psychological factors in nationalism.

THE COLONIAL EXPERIENCE

Many of the attitudes which characterize Arab nationalists today and which have such an important bearing on Arab-Western relations have their origin in the colonial period. The evidence of that experience is by no means clear, but it does explain some of the internal tensions within Arab nationalism and in Arab relations with the West.

An examination of the "colonial" record in the Arab lands shows that the purposes of many Westerners were respectable, indeed admirable in the context of the times. They often included genuine interest, for the Arabs' sake as well as their own, in efficient public administration, public order and security, development of natural resources, of communications and transport, and in building up external trade. They put considerable effort into laying the foundation of modern—i.e., Western—legal and educational systems. Generations of British and French officials went home after a career in Arab countries convinced that the knowledge and the skills they had contributed outweighed whatever advantages and special privileges their governments and their fellow countrymen had enjoyed. Many hard-working administrators at the end of their careers believed they had surrendered their responsibilities more rapidly than was wise, even from the Arab point of view. Why did the Arabs judge them so differently? Could the European governments and their officials on the spot, in their exercise of authority, have avoided the tide of bitterness and suspicion that now runs between the Arab nationalists and the nations of the West?

A pervasive factor, of course, was the superiority-inferiority relationship between Westerners and Arabs, as individuals, and between Western and Arab cultures. The Arab revolt against this relationship was not entirely the result of contemptuous or overbearing behavior on the part of the representatives of the West. Arab resentment is in part due to "the sheer fact that the West is there. The Joneses by simply existing engender the distress of not being able to keep up with them."[1] It is true, however, that all British and French officials were not able and well-balanced persons; many second-raters took minor posts in the East where they could do better for themselves than at home, and with less effort. Many, doubtless, were drawn to the East where they could appease their own sense of inferiority by lording it over other people.[2]

The behavior of Europeans and Americans toward Arabs and other representatives of the less privileged cultures has changed a great deal in the last generation. The memory of the past, however, continues to have a profound effect upon Arab attitudes. In the personal experience of many Arabs are recollections of contemptuous and uncivil treatment by a Westerner who regarded himself as superior by virtue of being Western. A book called *Egypt and the English* sought to make a case for a firmer British policy in Egypt shortly after the harsh response of the British authorities

[1] Wilfred Cantwell Smith, *Islam in Modern History* (New York: Mentor Books, 1959), p. 103.
[2] See O. Mannoni, *Prospero and Caliban: The Psychology of Colonization* (New York: Praeger, 1956).

to the Denshawi incident of 1906 had indicated the fruitlessness of such an approach. It contains many passages typical of the attitude of mind which encouraged the growth of nationalism inspired by a feeling of rejection and injury. For example:

There is no question in Egypt more important than that of education, except the necessity of the English Occupation. To hear the Egyptian talk, you would imagine that his one desire was to improve his mind, to raise himself to the equal of highly-educated Europeans. As a matter of fact, the Egyptian has no mind. Certain superficial notions and effects of civilization he assimilates—no coloured man imitates the collars of Englishmen so accurately; but in intellectual capacity and moral adaptability he is not a white man.[3]

Again in a chapter entitled "The Guileless Egyptian" this author wrote:

There are gentlemen in Egypt as in other countries, and a high-minded Mohammedan gentleman of the old school is a very fine fellow. But it cannot be denied that the ordinary Egyptian has the ordinary faults of hybrids in an inordinate degree. He is a liar, a rogue, an assassin, as needs be and opportunities arise. As my informant in my chapter on Education wrote of the Egyptian boy, "He is in no sense of the word a sportsman, however proficient he may be at games; nor can he assume or appreciate the qualities of an English gentleman." As the boy cheats over his work, so the man cheats over his business. Taking a mean advantage is, to him, commendable strategy.[4]

Such open expressions of contempt were no less resented by sensitive Arabs than the many indications that the representatives of the West in their countries found the Arab people laughable. Egyptians and other Arabs have not failed to note that many British and American visitors, as well as newly arrived officials or persons associated with Western business enterprises, have come and continue to come with one or more of the works of Major C. R. Jarvis in their bags, books in which they can read endless stories of the experiences of this British official who made his long years in Egypt tolerable by seeing the amusing side of the antics of the natives with whom he came into contact.

The fact that amused contempt for the city Arab was often

[3] By Douglas Sladen (London: Hurst and Blackett, 1908), p. 73.
[4] Same, p. 89.

contrasted with romantic patronizing of the desert dweller has had little effect on the former and less and less effect on the latter. One of the first orders to be given the Jordanian army after the dismissal of General Glubb was for the replacement of the traditional red *kafia,* or flowing desert headdress, with British army-type berets. The reason for this order was that Glubb was believed to have fostered the *kafia* in order to keep the Jordanian soldiers simple, obedient Arabs of the old school, subservient and respectful of authority. The fact that the order was never carried out reflects the confusion of values involved.

The specific acts and expressions of opinion that produced the psychological response described above were not so much the expression of any policy as they were a natural, though discreditable and unfortunate, response of human beings to the situation in which they found themselves. Probably very little could have been done about the attitude of superiority which became more and more intolerable to the Arabs as their national self-consciousness developed.

WESTERNIZATION

Many perceptive Arabs will tell the Westerner that if he wishes to improve relations between his country and the Arab world he must try to understand Arab psychology. Thus he acknowledges his sensitivity to Western misunderstanding of the position of the Arabs and Western reluctance to take them seriously. Behind this feeling lies the Arab effort to respond to the challenges and the opportunities of westernization without sacrificing Arab cultural personality and identity. This struggle deeply involves every Arab with intellectual, technical, and professional interests; it lies at the heart of the psychological and cultural crisis that has engulfed the entire Arab people.

The spread of Western power, trade, and culture into Arab lands in the course of the nineteenth century aroused defensive reactions among the guardians of traditional culture and religion. The most prominent Islamic theorists, however, men like Jamal el Din el Afghani and his Egyptian disciple, Muhammad Abdu, took the modernist course. They called for a revival of Islam, a revival which would take into account the new world which the inflow of Western ideas and ways foreshadowed. This attitude influenced a few at the upper intellectual levels of Arab society while practical considerations opened other gates to westernization.

To men with a practical bent, the appeal of Western technology and its products was undeniable. Western firearms, machinery, and manufactured goods, and eventually Western agricultural techniques, methods of irrigation, communication and all the other products and methods of an industrialized society, they adopted eagerly without concern for political, psychological, or social consequences. Profit, performance, and improvement were powerful magnets drawing many of the most able Arabs into trading relations with the West. Some sought training in Western medicine, engineering, law, and military science. Learning Western languages, they learned how to think in Western terms, and to act and live more or less like Westerners. At first the adoption of Western techniques was easy and lacked political complications. Technology did not occupy a focal position in Islamic culture and hence the new techniques did not displace anything of great importance to its guardians.[5] Later the social and cultural dynamite with which these changes were laden began to explode.

In addition to influencing businessmen and technicians, whose interests were generally economic and practical, things Western appealed to certain elements of the Arab upper class for other reasons. Western luxuries were new and attractive, available only to the wealthy, and hence associated with the way of life of the Western traders and profiteers who swarmed into the cities of the Near East in the latter part of the nineteenth century. Many of these found a secure and favorable base of operation under the system of "capitulations" which afforded the protection of Western consuls backed up by Western military and naval force. The Arab businessmen who worked with the Western traders and the Arab political figures who cooperated with Western governments were rewarded with the means by which they could westernize their way of life. By the mid-nineteenth century in Egypt, later in Syria,

[5] Raphael Patai, "The Dynamics of Westernization in the Middle East," *Middle East Journal,* Winter 1955, p. 4. The article provides an interesting discussion of the whole subject.

and still later in Iraq, Western clothing, Western furniture, Western sports, and Western languages developed a snob appeal that cast reflections on everything Arab or "native."

The process of westernization was in many ways easiest, and had the best results, among the elite educated in Europe and America and in the European and American schools of the Middle East. The many members of this group on whom westernization sat easily became sympathetic and able interpreters of Western ideas and methods, contributing much to the constructive reorganization of their society. Many became representatives of the liberal spirit of the West. In Iraq, Jordan, and the Sudan, British education and traditions exerted a strong influence. In Syria and Lebanon, French culture and French thought were treasured. British, French, Italian, and American culture contributed to the lives of several generations of Egyptians. American schools and colleges, particularly the American University at Beirut, produced young men, and some young women, prepared for leadership and ready and able to understand the West. Girls' colleges run by Americans in Beirut, Cairo, and Assiut have influenced the lives of many Arab women and their families, giving new dignity to the place of women in modern Arab society.

The process of westernization, the transition from a traditional, closed and protected society to one that was modern, open, and exposed, aroused basic cultural conflicts. People were pulled out of their traditional pattern of life, but only a few really found complete and lasting satisfaction in the transplanted Western culture. For many it was only a collection of superficialities, changes in dress, manners, and habits. Furthermore, these changes often were accompanied by the disparagement and rejection of the religious and ethical standards of the traditional society they had left behind. A superficially westernized upper class which had cast aside the restrictions of traditional Islamic society became easily corruptible, more and more amoral, and lacking in self-discipline and interest in public service. New kinds and patterns of trade and industry stimulated by the West led to the development of a new urban middle class and a new urban proletariat throughout the Arab area which could find little in Arab traditions to guide them but which were unable to find or follow Western patterns in their stead.[6]

Along with the other changes brought by westernization came a most unhappy by-product: anti-Westernism. There was the tremendous contrast between Arab and Western civilization—the former still organized in the medieval pattern and only just emerging from centuries in the backwaters of the Ottoman Empire; the later bursting with self-confidence and energy, strong in the arts of power. Because Western superiority was so easily accepted, it was almost certain that the West would abuse its position and that the Arabs would resent theirs.

The West itself taught the ideas that inspired reaction against it. Freedom, independence, self-determination, nationalism, the sanctity of struggle against oppressors—all these the Westerners brought to the Arab world in books, instruction, conversation, and example. That the Arabs should soon turn them against their teachers was only natural. The West taught that no man or people should passively accept its fate, that it was wise and right to gather one's resources and overthrow any oppressor. The oppressor the Arabs found to be the West itself.

Conflict became inevitable when the Western powers moved in to provide stability and protection for trade and strategic interests. By making themselves the responsible authority, often aligned with forces of conservatism, the Western powers became the natural target of the nationalistic revolution.

Even the most enthusiastic Arab imitators of the West could not really become Westerners. Of this fact Westerners made them deeply conscious by refusing to accept any Arab, however much westernized, into full membership in their community. Many Arabs who became most deeply involved in and attached to Western culture suffered a sense of betrayal, the feeling that after giving their best efforts and gifts of mind and spirit to penetrate the secrets of Western culture they, as individuals, were rejected by Westerners. Bitterness was doubled when the westernized Arab lost contact with his own society in the process. Thus it was natural that many Arabs, satisfied that there was no place for them in

[6] See Daniel Lerner, *The Passing of Traditional Society: Modernizing the Middle East* (Glencoe, Ill.: Free Press, 1958).

Western society, should seek redemption in a return to Arabism.

Edward Atiyah, an Arab of Lebanese origin who after becoming deeply attached to British culture, particularly to English literature, went to live in the Sudan, has written in his autobiography of this sense of rejection among the educated class in the Sudan. They had revolted, he said, "not against oppression, injustice or economic exploitation—of which in the Sudan at least there was practically no trace—but against spiritual arrogance, racial haughtiness, social aloofness and paternal authoritarianism. . . ."[7]

Atiyah tells how he, long a devoted Anglophile educated in England, teaching English in the Sudan, became an Arab nationalist and eventually a sympathizer with the Soviet Union. The break came when the British Governor-General came to visit Gordon College.

> One day his excellency came to visit the College. The British staff lined up to receive him and were one by one introduced to him. The non-British staff were required to remain in their Common Room; there was no part in the ceremony for them. We sat in the Common Room like a poor relation banished to the kitchen during the presence in the house of the distinguished guest. . . .
>
> I walked home disgusted and enraged by this humiliation. . . .
>
> Thus I was liberated, not by an intellectual process, but by the force of an emotional reaction, originating in my own wounded feelings, from the shackles of a political outlook which had been implanted in me by all the influences of my early life. . . . I found myself understanding and sympathizing with that host of longings, half-defined as yet, passionate and largely confused but none the less real, which come under the designation of "the Arab awakening." My whole life went into reverse gear. I became myself an Arab nationalist. My sympathy went out to the Indians and the Egyptians, to the Egyptian revolution on which I had looked disapprovingly seven years before. . . .[8]

A like experience was undergone by many Arabs who had followed the ways of the West and found themselves in the no-man's land which A. H. Hourani describes as the fate of the Levantine:

> To be a Levantine is to live in two worlds or more at once, without belonging to either; to be able to go through the external forms which

---

[7] *An Arab Tells His Story: A Study in Loyalties* (London: John Murray, 1946), p. 165.

[8] Same, pp. 147–149.

indicate the possession of a certain nationality, religion or culture, without actually possessing it. It is no longer to have a standard of values of one's own, not to be able to create but only able to imitate; and so not even to imitate correctly, since that also needs a certain originality. It is to belong to no community and to possess nothing of one's own. It reveals itself in lostness, pretentiousness, cynicism and despair.[9]

When they turned back to their own culture, many of the elite of the generation of Arabs coming after World War I found it weakened, as they thought they had been, by contacts with a culture out of harmony with its traditions. However, some of the most prominent and successful students of the West and practitioners of the art of dealing with the Western powers remained relatively satisfied with the progress of events and with the prospects for the Arab independence. After the Anglo-Egyptian treaty of 1936, Taha Hussein, Egypt's most famous scholar, philosopher, and educator, argued in a book called *The Future of Culture in Egypt* that Egypt's progress toward the civilization, for the achievement of which independence was only a means, could best be made by sharing European civilization.[10] In Iraq, in Transjordan, in Syria-Lebanon, and in Egypt the rulers and chief political figures of the interwar period, although they had moments of bitterness, worked fairly consistently to push the representatives of the West steadily toward the acceptance of Arab independence. Nuri el Said in Iraq, Shukri el Kuwatly in Syria, Nahas Pasha in Egypt and their colleagues called themselves nationalists, demanding the eventual withdrawal of British and French power. But they were not anti-Western in the same sense as Nasser and Kassem and most of the school of Arab nationalists that has appeared since the Palestine War of 1948–49.

It was the generation which was in school in the interwar period, coming of age during the Palestine War, in whose lives and minds westernization went through a metamorphosis and came out as

[9] A. H. Hourani, *Syria and Lebanon: A Political Essay* (London: Oxford University Press, for the Royal Institute of International Affairs, 1954; 3d ed.), pp. 70–71.

[10] See C. E. von Grunebaum, *Islam: Essays in the Nature and Growth of a Cultural Tradition* (London: Routledge and Kegan Paul, 1955), pp. 208–216.

anti-Westernism. They became convinced that the struggle for independence and self-respect for the Arabs would never succeed if left to the "old guard" of upper-class politicians. For decades, they believed, those men had been playing along with the Western powers, pretending to work for national liberation, but motivated in reality only by the desire to hang on to their powers and pre-rogatives. So the younger nationalists became social revolutionaries as well as proponents of independence. For them Arab nationalism means revolution.

THE GOALS OF ARAB NATIONALISM

Nationalism is the driving force, the most important fact of life in the Arab world today. It is a frame of mind, an approach to the problems and challenges that confront the Arabs. Its significance lies in the wide, almost universal, agreement among Arabs that there is such a thing as an Arab nation. Flowing from their desire to be identified with each other in opposition to the rest of the world, it still leaves ample room for differences in expression and in application. The product of historical forces, of shared fears, hatreds and aspirations, it has never been expressed or defined in a single document. No man is its sole spokesman; it is the property of the whole Arab community.

All the streams of Arab thought and experience coming together in the mid-twentieth century have mixed their waters in the pool of Arab nationalism. Muddied by the winds of fear, ambition, and xenophobia, it nevertheless has a basic consistency, expressed in a few ultimate goals upon which there is general agreement: Arabism, independence, unity, reform, and progress.

Arabism

The goal here is the revival and assertion of the Arab character, and the achievement of a place of dignity, respect, and influence for Arabs in the world. Elements of traditionalism and of reaction against foreign influences are present but Arabism is more characteristically the feeling that the only way for the Arabs to be anything is for them to be themselves.

Independence

This, the most immediate and practical political goal of Arab nationalists, has deep psychological and spiritual significance. Over the years the meaning of "independence" has widened. The experience of the interwar years convinced nationalists that anything less than complete sovereignty was not sovereignty at all. Consequently, the search for complete independence has turned suspicion against foreign investments and economic interests, minorities with special connections outside the Arab world, and alliances and special relationships with great powers. For Arab nationalists independence is more than a legal or a practical matter; it involves a feeling of freedom and confidence in one's ability to act as one pleases—a condition of mind which in the Arab states, and other new nations, has occasionally inspired impulsive attempts to test the reality of freedom without thought for the consequences. Though there has been no dissent among the Arab nationalists on the validity of the goal of independence, there has been considerable difference of opinion on the question "When does an arrangement with a great power have 'strings' attached?"

Unity

On this goal there is virtually universal agreement among Arabs, although its practical meaning is not clear. As Fayez Sayegh explains, most Arab writers have devoted their attention to proving that unity already exists but have forgotten, or ignored, the obvious question of how to make it a meaningful reality.[11] Schemes such as the Sherif Hussein's Arab state (the object of the Arab Revolt of 1917), Nuri el Said's Fertile Crescent plan, the Arab League, and plans for expanding the United Arab Republic have always developed opposition and have been shelved or modified. Nevertheless, no Arab leader, public figure, or private citizen who wishes to retain his standing and influence with other Arabs would criticize the ideal of Arab unity or suggest that it will not eventually, in some form or other, come to pass.

[11] Fayez A. Sayegh, *Arab Unity: Hope and Fulfillment* (New York: Devin-Adair, 1958), p. 81.

Reform and Progress

Reforms designed to strengthen and develop the Arab world and to contribute to the welfare of its people are included in the roster of nationalist goals. Although the revolutionary regimes in Egypt, Syria, and Iraq and the conservative regimes in Saudi Arabia and the sheikhdoms differ considerably in their attitudes on specific reforms, both groups stand for economic progress and believe some reform of outmoded institutions is essential for a stronger and more prosperous Arab world.

THE ROLE OF ISLAM

The oldest and in some ways most effective contribution to Arab unity comes from Islam, including the ideal of Pan Islam, the association of all Muslim peoples. In the late nineteenth century Jamal el Din el Afghani and Muhammad Abdu were the most famous and effective proponents of Islamic reform and modernization, in order to achieve, in Abdu's words, "the regeneration and the strengthening of one of the Islamic States so that it may reach the level of the great powers and thereby restore Islam to its past glory."[12] Their activities stimulated succeeding generations of theorists and practical politicians to study and advocate modernism, reform, and the association of Islamic states.

In recent years powerful forces of secularism have reduced the apparent influence of Islam and Pan Islamic ideas, although the latter continue to play an important role. Nationalist leaders tend to be more secular and more westernized than their followers. They have won support from the masses probably in spite of, rather than because of, their secularism; their emphasis upon nationalist goals has evoked response from people whose frame of reference and pattern of values is Islamic rather than nationalist in the modern sense. Wilfred Cantwell Smith observes that "the Westernizing leaders have frequently been surprised to discover the degree to which they have let loose an Islamic upsurge."[13] But in recent crises leaders who apparently were willing to call upon every force of emotion which the political imagery of

[12] Quoted by Hazem Zaki Nuseibeh in *The Ideas of Arab Nationalism* (Ithaca: Cornell University Press, 1956), pp. 120–121.
[13] Cited, p. 81.

nationalism could evoke decided, nevertheless, not to set loose an Islamic *jihad* (holy war) for fear that, once started, they could not control it.

Professor Smith also makes the point that ". . . wherever nationalism has been adopted in the Muslim world, and in whatever form, the 'nation' concerned has been a Muslim group."[14] Despite the secularization and modernization of Arab society and despite the predominance of politics in the thinking of nationalist leaders, Islam is still more effective in defining the "nation" than race, political creed, or any other criterion except language. Nationalist leaders apparently believe that nationalism has a personal meaning for Arabic-speaking Muslims and that they can be counted on to identify themselves with the "Arab nation." Non-Muslims, whatever their reasons for calling themselves Arabs, are not trusted in the same way as those who bear the unforgeable credentials of hereditary membership in Islam. Small wonder that secular and politically minded Arab leaders are careful to attend Friday prayers and to observe the Ramadan fast more strictly than ever before, and that the externals of Muslim piety are being taken up everywhere by people who have no interest in Islam except that inspired by Arab nationalism.

Some contributors to the stream of Arab nationalism have combined Islamic revivalism with the ideas of Western liberalism and constitutionalism; others whose outlook is fundamentally xenophobic insist on the essential conflict between Islam and Christianity and the incompatibility of the cultures based on them.[15] One of the most important applications of Islam in political thought and action has been the Muslim Brotherhood, founded by an Egyptian teacher, Hassan el Banna, in the 1920s and later spread throughout the Arab world. The Brotherhood, a traditionalist and conservative group, advocated a theocratic state, a return to earlier Islamic social and ethical practices, and a boycott of non-Arab goods and dress. In certain social groups the Brotherhood had a strong appeal but it clashed inevitably with the secular modernists who came to dominate and control Arab nationalism.

14 Same, p. 83.
15 Cf. Nuseibeh, cited, particularly Chapters 7 and 8, and Von Grunebaum, cited, Chapter 11.

ASPECTS OF ARAB NATIONALISM

Arabism and Pan Arabism, ideas associated with racial, linguistic, and cultural unity, and with the proposed union of Arab states, have also contributed to the nationalist movement. Endless discussions of the meaning of Arabism, of the factors which determine who is and who is not an Arab, and the relation between Arabism and Islam have not produced authoritative definitions. Nuseibeh says, "In modern use, the term Arab stands for a political concept and has no ethnic or social significance."[16] History, language, and geography have made Arabs emphasize and wish to make something significant out of what they share in common. But it is not so much these elements in an individual's background as his decision to be an Arab that makes him one. Egypt, today the largest *Arab* nation, was *Egyptian* twenty years ago. It has become Arab by electing to join with other Arab states and by assuming an Arab viewpoint, one which professes to comprehend the interests of all Arabs.

The question whether Pan Arabism or Pan Islamism is a more useful political formula seems to have been decided pragmatically. The cooperation of all Islamic peoples for the realization of mutual interests is regarded by most politically conscious Arabs as an ideal, a hope for the future. At present the common interests of, say, Egypt, Iran, and Pakistan, are not easy to discern or strongly felt. Pan Arabism, on the other hand, has been given more practical political significance, if only temporarily in most cases, by the Arab League, the union of Egypt and Syria in the U.A.R., the association of Yemen with the U.A.R., and the union of Iraq and Jordan. Real political content has been given to Pan Arabism by the Syrian Baath party which has gained adherents and influenced political thinking in all other Arab countries. The Baath—the word means "resurrection" in Arabic—is determinedly secular and socialist in its ideology and its methods. It looks to the ultimate association of all Arab states in a Pan Arab state large and strong enough to defend its Arab character and follow an Arab policy. In Michel Aflaq the Baath has one of the few Arab political theoreticians. It boasts a consistent political

[16] Cited, p. 65.

philosophy and doctrine which sets it aside from most Arab political groups and movements. Rent by internal dissension and shaken by events, the Baath still has significance as a political party dedicated to the Pan Arab idea and not to the interests of a single state or regime.

Over the past years, hundreds of books and pamphlets have been published on Arab nationalism by a wide variety of Arab authors. Most newspaper stories with any relation to political matters have referred to it in some way or another. Public speeches and radio talks, of course, have added their contributions.[17] The discussion, however, has produced no systematic doctrine. Commenting on recent books and pamphlets on Arab nationalism Fahim Qubain says, "The large bulk of this material lacks . . . the intellectual content, the critical analysis, and the honest self-criticism necessary to make it of value to a serious study of the subject, except as a facet of it."[18] Amid this apologetic and unsystematic material suggestions are found that the Arabs must work out a systematic ideology before they can achieve their goals; others say that ideology can be developed in the course of an Arab revival, or after the fact.[19] Serious attempts to analyze Arab nationalism, like Nuseibeh's *Ideas of Arab Nationalism,* after stating its goals and describing its wide range of ideas, movements, and influences, end by defining it as a state of mind.

Precisely because of its fluidity, because it represents a pooling of attitudes and ideas rather than their distillation into a doctrine, Arab nationalism belongs more to the politicians than to the intellectuals. Abdel Nasser has taken Arab nationalism and made it his own, proving himself an incomparable virtuoso in countless renderings of the theme. He exercises leadership in the Arab world today because he understands and can play upon the hopes and the fears implicit in the Arab state of mind. He is "Mr. Arab," but, as there were other Republicans in the 1940s besides Mr.

---

[17] See Fahim I. Qubain, *Inside the Arab Mind: A Bibliographic Survey of Literature in Arabic on Arab Nationalism and Unity* (Arlington, Va.: Middle East Research Associates, 1960).

[18] Same, p. vi.

[19] Cf. Nissim Rejwan, "Arab Nationalism" in Walter Z. Laqueur, ed., *The Middle East in Transition: Studies in Contemporary History* (New York: Praeger, 1958), pp. 145–165.

Taft, there are other Arab leaders who can play the nationalist themes for other purposes. Packed full with emotion and disrespectful of order, Arab nationalism provides a tool with which demagogues can sway masses of people. But that does not mean it is a fraud. Arab nationalism certainly does not fit Western criteria for political doctrine—standards which, incidentally, are not always met by political movements in the West itself. Yet, when judged for what it is rather than for what it is not, the most remarkable thing about it seems to be the degree of unanimity of feeling and purpose in the Arab people which it reflects. There remains a profound impression of the forcefulness with which the background and inheritance of the Arab people have been focused on a few simple goals.

It is worth considering whether the unrelatedness of Arab nationalism as a political force to what the West believes to be politically realistic and effective may indicate not backwardness and disorder so much as a completely different approach by a society with experiences which are quite different from those of the West, but which are none the less authentic. It may also be asked whether such a political force, despite the fact that it fails to meet Western standards in all departments, may not have a raw power and a harmony with historical forces which gives it significant advantages in the world as it is today. In any event, Arab nationalism cannot be dismissed by the West solely on the grounds that it is unstructured and disorderly.

PERSPECTIVE

The great bulk of the material used to support Arab charges against "Western imperialism" is out of date. The methods used and objectives sought by the Western powers in the nineteenth and early twentieth centuries are generally recognized as unacceptable by modern standards and have been discarded. This fact few would deny, certainly not the majority of responsible officials in Western governments. Nineteenth-century Arabs, moreover, were not so keen for self-determination and independence as Arabs are today. In fact most of the arrangements at that time with Western powers were made with the collaboration of Arab leaders, and with the approval of that part of the public which had an opinion. The dynamics of military and economic power were very different one hundred or even fifty years ago. There can be little doubt that if the British and the French had not established themselves in the Arab area, other powers would have come in their place. Moreover, this area was not the only undeveloped region in which Europeans worked and traded. The degree of sovereignty which the Arabs retained, and the assistance they received in the gradual development of national institutions, reflected European recognition of their capabilities. To accuse the European powers of acting in their own interest, regarding themselves and their institutions more highly than those of the lands where they found scope for their trading and empire-building activities, is not a very serious charge, measured by the standards of the nineteenth century or indeed by those of any period in world history. It is simply the West's misfortune that the Arabs are now judging nineteenth-century conduct by mid-twentieth-century criteria.

A more serious charge is "neo-colonialism," the new devices and new techniques by which, according to Arab nationalists, the West is seeking to continue its hegemony. Military bases, alliances, and economic development programs "with strings attached," they claim, enable strong nations to exert influence over the weak. They cite as modern forms of imperialism the establishment of the state of Israel, the Anglo-French-Israeli invasion of Egypt in 1956, and the long French effort to maintain control of Algeria. The Portuguese colonies in Africa and white rule in South Africa and the Rhodesias they regard as survivals of old-fashioned imperialism.

It is a matter of serious concern to the United States and to the West in general that Arab nationalists seldom recognize the spectacular withdrawal, since World War II, of the British and the French from their empires in Asia and Africa and their efforts to facilitate the progress of so many of their former dependencies toward national sovereignty, independence, and economic well-being. Neither do they often take account of the American record on questions of self-determination.

It is one of the great ironies of our time that, while the West has been making unprecedented efforts to bring about in orderly fashion the independence of most of the territories over which it once exercised one kind of hegemony or another, the Arab nationalists, and many of their fellow champions of nationalism and nonalignment throughout Africa and Asia, have been devoting so much time and effort to accusations of "colonialism" and "imperialism." Even more ironic is the fact that they have so seldom turned their attention to the record of the Soviet Union, the one great imperialist power of our time whose acquisitions of territory and denial of self-determination to subject peoples have matched the progress of the West in the opposite direction.

It is probably not to be expected that Arab nationalists will soon become noticeably less emotional and prejudiced in blaming the Western powers for past injustice. But it is vitally important, for themselves as well as others, that they understand better the real nature of the threats which they face and the true character of the contest between the West and the Communist bloc. It is also important that Western policy makers who would encourage the development of that understanding should comprehend and take into account the Arab situation and the historical and psychological background of Arab suspicions of the West.

IV

THE ARAB SITUATION

Psychological factors influence the behavior of Arabs in the international arena to an extraordinary degree. Their sensitivity to wrongs done them, their determination to assert themselves, the fervor with which they follow and denounce the misdeeds of their enemies and opponents have probably had more to do with their role in recent international affairs than military or economic factors or strategic position.

Nevertheless, not even the Arabs can live and have their being in the realm of international affairs on feeling alone. Likewise, the United States and other powers cannot frame their policies toward the Arabs with the sole object of understanding them and soothing their feelings. There are certain hard realities which shape the position of Arabs in the world and which limit their ability to modify it. Although they change in significance with the onward movement of history, these realities remain in the background, irrespective of political leaders and political movements. They include the geographical and economic environment; the make-up and distribution of the population; social, political, and economic forces; the Arab states themselves as institutions and as repositories of interests and loyalties; the established relationships among those states and with their neighbors.

THE AREA

Language, culture, historical experience, and politics—above all politics—give the Arab East a special character and importance, make it a part of the world which must be considered as a whole by students and policy-makers. But in many respects diversity rather than uniformity is the keynote.

The geography of the Arab world contributes little to unity. The area has been compared to an archipelago;[1] a map of vegetation shows hundreds of islands, mostly quite small, of habitable area separated by seas or by barren deserts. These islands provide a wide variety of environment for their occupants. The valleys of the Nile and of the Tigris and Euphrates provide a secure and settled agricultural existence, which contrasts strongly with that of dwellers in the hills, mountains, and coastal plains of the east Mediterranean littoral and in the mountains of northern Iraq. In quite another world, the steppes and deserts nurture the tribal, nomadic societies scattered all across North Africa, the Arabian Peninsula, and into the deserts of Syria and Iraq. Through the religion of Islam, this desert culture has exercised great influence over the peoples of the entire area, producing a kind of unity that defies geography. Occasionally, the whole area has been ruled by a single authority, but conformity has never been characteristic of its peoples. Even under the long Ottoman rule, provincial diversity persisted within common Islamic and Arab institutions.

The strategic importance of the Arab world remains relatively constant. In this area the continents of Europe, Asia, and Africa come together, and the main routes by water and by air between two great centers of world population—the North Atlantic area and South and East Asia—pass through Arab territory. Its situation between Russian centers of population and power and the warm seas and territories to the south is another geographic fact of enduring significance. Turkey, Iran, and Pakistan are under more immediate pressures of Soviet expansion, but the Arab states are also affected by the proximity of Russia. Beyond them lies the vast territory of Africa. In today's international politics the fact that the Arab area is in both Asia and Africa has great significance and gives the Arabs a sense of importance as a link between the two continents.

[1] Charles Issawi, "The Bases of Arab Unity," *International Affairs,* January 1955, p. 42. This article is an enlightening discussion of factors contributing to unity and to disunity.

The passing of the caravan age, when the world's fate was decided by armies that marched on their own feet or rode on camelback or horseback, and now the decline of the railroad age as well, has in some sense reduced the significance of the Arab area as a land bridge. The changing role of sea power has inevitably affected the strategic importance of the Black Sea and the Mediterranean and the Suez Canal.

Except for the airlanes and the radio waves, the communications of the area are the heritage of the colonial regime. Roads and railroads were built to provide communication within each state and to seaports looking toward Europe. There is still no efficient overland communication between Egypt and the states of North Africa or between Egypt and Saudi Arabia or Jordan. Only an undeveloped desert road links Iraq and Syria.[2] The idea of Arab unity is strong, but the physical sinews are weak or entirely lacking. Furthermore, although in recent years the airplane and the radio have brought the Arab countries closer together than ever before, Israel, a hostile nation, is planted squarely across the bridge between the Arabs of Asia and of Africa.

Life in the Arab states today can be visualized and understood only if one keeps in mind the layer upon layer of civilization which lies below the surface, and not always very far below it. The traveler and the student of history need not be reminded that in the Arab East one can see evidence all around of past civilizations which have been absorbed into the amalgam that is the Arab world today. In Jericho, looking down into the archaeologist's trench, one can see the streets of an early Stone Age village. In Damascus, said to be the oldest inhabited site in the world, Roman columns stand on either side of the narrow street that passes through a market on the way to the great mosque which was once a Christian basilica. In Cairo one can drive across the river and a few miles south to Saqqara where some of the first of man's experiments in building with stone were conducted and quickly brought to brilliant fruition. On the east side of the river, nearer the modern town, are Roman columns and fortifications, and nearby a much rebuilt seventh-century mosque founded by the Muslim conqueror of Egypt when the Arabs themselves were just

[2] Same, pp. 42–43.

learning to build with stone. Many an Iraqi and Syrian face reminds the visitor of those on the Hittite and Assyrian monuments; in Lebanon one sees women wearing costumes like those of European ladies at the time of the Crusades.

How much or how little the different mixtures of past civilizations affect the outlook of the modern inhabitants of the Arab area is hard to tell, but it is easy to see the differences that mark the major regions today. One needs only to compare the capital cities.[3] The traveler who sees Cairo stretching from the Mokkatam hills, capped by the huge Muhammad Ali mosque with its needlelike minarets, across the river to the heights on which stand the three pyramids of Giza cannot miss the unique qualities of that city. It is Arab and Muslim, but also Mediterranean and Christian, at the same time traditional and modern. This great cosmopolitan center is part Arab, part African, and part European, and also, in an undefinable way, Pharaonic. It has been a melting pot, passive and receptive but culturally rich and creative for centuries.

No one could ever confuse Cairo with Beirut. The situation of this lively city announces its mission; its aggressive and individualistic people, so intent on their affairs, make clear that this is a city of traders. New apartment buildings, each more modern—or modernistic—in design and taste than the last, sprout overnight in the few remaining vacant lots and, almost before the paint is dry, someone opens a restaurant and nightclub on the ground floor. The Beirut urchin, who, when asked to add two and two, inquired whether he was buying or selling, is no myth. His counterpart is in every street of the city.

If without his knowing it our traveler could be transported over the mountain from Beirut to Damascus and be set down on the streets of that capital, he would not fail to detect the deception. Whereas Beirut looks to the sea, Damascus looks to the desert and to the holy cities of Arabia further south. A Muslim city, Damascus lacks both the cosmopolitanism of Cairo and the enterprising individualism of Beirut. It seems to contemplate itself, confident that the oasis in which it lies is the center of the Arab

---

[3] Robin Fedden, *Syria: An Historical Appreciation* (London: Robert Hale, 1955), Chapter 2, "Three Towns," dramatically sketches the character of Beirut, Damascus, and Aleppo, making clear the different personality of each city and of its inhabitants.

world and that all the other Arabs must look to it. Aleppo to
the north, again, could not be mistaken for Beirut or Damascus.
It is commercial enough and its life takes its rhythm from trade,
but Aleppo is an inland city—Syria, Iraq, and Turkey are its
trading area.

Baghdad, also, has its own personality. The great winding river,
the dusty brown plains, the yellow-brown brick of the houses and
walls which make the city blend with the landscape—all remind
one that it is on the edge of a vast continent; one feels Asia to
the north and east, with the Mediterranean far away. Riyadh,
with its crop of new buildings surrounding a mud-walled and fortified medieval city, tells the visitor more graphically than words
can of Saudi Arabia's wedding of traditional desert culture with
the modern world into which oil provides the admission fee.

The traveler experiencing this great physical diversity of the
Arab world cannot but be struck by the differences in perspective
which geography and situation create. In Baghdad the world is
different than it seemed in Cairo, and back in Cairo the perspective again is changed. Even the alien European or American sees
things differently in Damascus than he did in Beirut. Too much
can be made, possibly, of the striking differences in character and
outlook of the main Arab centers. Certainly it is no news that
New Yorkers and Chicagoans have different perspectives. The in-
dividuality of Arab regions is important, but Arab nationalism is
bringing them together. If they do come to share a common outlook to the degree that New York and Chicago do, a revolution
of vast importance to the Arab world will have been completed.

The Arabs and Their Neighbors

Geography separates the Arab states from the outside world as
well as from each other. Deserts separate Egypt from the countries to the south and west and limit Libya's contacts with other
countries. The Red Sea, the Indian Ocean, the Persian Gulf, and
desert to the north give the Arabian Peninsula an isolation of
its own. Iraq has mountains to the east and north, which hamper
communication for everyone but nomadic tribes. The only inhabited borders between Arab and non-Arab states, except for
the borders with Israel, are those with Turkey and Iran.

It is a commonplace of Arab nationalism that the Arab world stretches from the Arab (or Persian) Gulf to the Atlantic. This is true in the sense that in their cultural history the Arab East and the Arab West, the Maghreb, have much in common. But in political philosophy and in external policies there are marked contrasts.

The relative good feeling that accompanied the emergence of Morocco and Tunisia as independent states made them more cooperative with the West and less inclined to follow the neutralist line. On the other hand, Algeria's long struggle for independence, the spread of nationalism throughout Africa south of the Maghreb, and Moroccan and Tunisian differences with France have produced marked changes. Morocco and Tunisia have joined the Arab League. The Casablanca Conference of December 1960 brought Morocco and the U.A.R. together in support of policies like those Nasser had been preaching for years, and the Bizerte crisis of 1961 brought Tunisia closer, for a time at least, to the general U.A.R. position with respect to the Western powers. The provisional government of Algeria received the support of Egypt and the U.A.R. over a long period, though it rejected the more extreme aspects of Nasser's "positive neutralist" policy, showing great circumspection, for example, about turning to the Soviet bloc for assistance. As negotiations with France drew out, however, the provisional government showed increasing willingness to look for assistance to the Soviet Union and the Chinese Communists. In any case, there are clearly to be close ties between independent Algeria and Nasser's Egypt. One of Ahmad Ben Bella's first important political gestures after his release from imprisonment in France in 1962 was a visit to Cairo. On balance, however, it appears that the North African Arabs will be more likely to seek accommodation with the West than the countries of the Arab East, in part because of geography, but also because of stronger cultural ties with the West.

Israel, a neighbor only in terms of propinquity, lies in the very heart of the Arab world. Except for the movement of Arab infiltrators and Israeli military parties, the borders that separate Israel from its four Arab neighbors are as tight a barrier as exists anywhere in the world. The Arab boycott, Israeli security measures, and the atmosphere of hatred and the ever-present menace of violence draw a sharp line between the Arab East and the essentially Western state of Israel.

As far as the Arab states are concerned, Turkey is an alien country with few contacts in the Arab area and less influence. During the period between the world wars when Arab nationalism was developing, Turkey was completely absorbed in its own affairs. Then, as the Arabs emerged from the Second World War and entered the fires of the Palestine War and the struggle with Israel, they saw Turkey bloom as the favorite of the Western nations. Arabs believe they detect an attitude of superiority on the part of the Turks and resent it. Turkey's occupation of Alexandretta in 1939 in defiance of Syria's claim, its relations with the state of Israel, and its membership in the Baghdad Pact (later CENTO—Central Treaty Organization) have all contributed to the coolness of Arab-Turkish relations. Present prospects are not favorable to any improvement in those relations or to the development of common interests.

Arab relations with Iran have generally been as distant as with Turkey, although not marred by as many occasions for difference and distrust. Iran has a separate language and culture, and adheres to a sect of Islam not followed by the majority of Arabs. Since the nationalist revolutions in Egypt, Syria, and Iraq, the Shah's conservative regime has found it more and more difficult to find common ground with the Arab states. Iran's acceptance of the principle of a defensive alliance with the West against Soviet aggression, its membership in the Baghdad Pact and CENTO, and its refusal to join the Arab boycott against Israel have all contributed to the separation of Arab and Iranian interests. Nasser's angry severance of diplomatic relations with Teheran in 1960, on the pretext that the latter's well-known *de facto* relations with Israel were no longer acceptable, showed how deep was the gap between them. The year 1962 has seen a bitter propaganda battle by radio between Cairo and Teheran.

Arab ties with Africa are political rather than economic, and contemporary rather than traditional. It is true that Egypt and the North African Arabs share the same continent with the new states of Central Africa but they are separated by a great desert void over which for many years there has been little communication. The nineteenth-century Arab slave trader and the modern Syrian merchant have provided contacts, but not such as inspire African interest or confidence. Racial as well as cultural differences separate Africans from Arabs. To race-conscious Central Africans, Arabs are not black men, though they may not be treated as white men either.

Islam, though it means little in Arab relations with Turkey or Iran, may provide an important link between the Arabs and the Muslims in a wide belt south of the Sahara. One of the most striking phenomena of contemporary Africa is the speed with which Islam is winning converts among people who have lost their primitive tribal beliefs and who reject Christianity as the white man's religion. Egypt is making a considerable effort to turn this development to its political advantage.[4] The most effective bases for political connections between the Arabs and the new African states are the common problems of economic development, and of finding a place in the community of nations which will provide both independence and security, plus certain common psychological characteristics.

The Arab association with the world of Islam—the other Muslim states and Muslim communities that stretch from the Philippines to northern Nigeria—has little actual or potential political importance. The relationship appears to be very like that between Arabs and Africans. Their common religion and its cultural aura do very little to link Arabs with Turks, Pakistanis, or Indonesians. International politics are more effective determinants of action than religious and cultural ties, however real they may be. Muslim Pakistan, for instance, which many observers once expected would exercise an important influence upon the Arab states, has had much less influence than Hindu India, which has joined them on many international issues and whose rivalry with Pakistan coincides with the Arabs' distrust of that country's association with the Western powers.

[4] See William H. Lewis, "Islam and Nationalism in Africa," in Tibor Kerekes, ed., *The Arab Middle East and Muslim Africa* (New York: Praeger, 1961), pp. 63–83.

THE ARAB MAJORITY AND THE MINORITIES

Except for the Kurds of Iraq and Syria, the Armenians, the persons of European descent in Egypt and Lebanon, and a few scatterings of other minority groups, the sixty million inhabitants of the states of the Arab East today call themselves Arabs. The designation is political and linguistic, not racial. Twenty-five years ago the Christians would probably have called themselves Christians, or would have identified themselves with the national state in which they lived. Most others would have said they were Muslims. Only the people of the Arabian Peninsula and the desert dwellers in other parts of the area would have called themselves Arabs. Many town dwellers and settled farmers would have used the term contemptuously to distinguish the Bedouin of the desert from themselves. Today, it is used to designate one's language and to express one's identification with a common culture, and with Pan Arabism. A Christian Copt of Egypt, or a Lebanese Maronite, may call himself an Arab with mental reservations, noting under his breath that his people were on the land and civilized before the Arabs came out of the deserts of Arabia. But he will make the concession in order to identify himself with the majority, and to avoid being classed with the Europeans or other outsiders whose future in Arab lands does not look bright. Thus the politics of Pan Arabism provide the appearance, and some of the substance, of unity on the surface of a complex reality.

The minorities will continue to play an important role, but the outlook is for a steady deterioration of the privileges which have permitted them over the centuries to maintain a separate existence among the Muslim majority. From the time of Alexander the Great a community of European origin has lived and traded in Egypt and on the Levant coast, their security and prosperity guaranteed by the potential of interference by some outside military force. During the great days of the Muslim empires they lived on sufferance and frequently paid dearly for the right to live and trade. The Ottomans granted the European trading communities many of the privileges enjoyed by religious minorities under the *millet* system. Each community had its own religious leaders, its own courts, and dealt as a community with the imperial authority.

From the mid-nineteenth century the European communities, backed by the willing and vigorous support of their home governments, enjoyed extraordinary privileges, but they could not last. The Turkish nationalists abolished them in Ottoman territory. In Arab countries, with the rise of nationalism in its Western forms, the European communities have lost their favored position and have begun to dwindle in size and influence. Arab governments and the Arab community at large gradually insisted on a greater role for Arab personnel in business and other enterprises, and on the reduction or elimination of discrimination in favor of Europeans. This long process came to a point of culmination in Egypt at the time of the Suez crisis of 1956. Attacked by Israel, Britain, and France, the Egyptian government expelled a number of Jews and British and French citizens and warned all holders of British and French passports that it could not be responsible for their safety. This measure, together with a variety of veiled threats and pressures, and fears of mob violence like the Black Saturday disturbances in Cairo in January 1952, brought the realization that Suez marked the end of an era. It led to a flight from Egypt of tens of thousands of Jews, Greeks, Italians and other "Europeans." A similar flight from Syria, and from Iraq after the 1958 revolution, took place, though on a smaller scale as the European communities in both countries were much less numerous than that in Egypt.

The Egyptian government encouraged the emigration, especially of those persons who had the closest ties to European nations and who were least willing to accept Arab supremacy. The government thus aimed to get rid of foreign influence and interference, recognizing that the presence in a small country of a community of the nationals of a great power has in the past been a frequent excuse for intervention.

Although many have fled from the inhospitable atmosphere of rampant Arab nationalism, a community of partially assimilated Europeans and Levantines—mostly Greeks, Italians, Armenians, and Turks—remains in Egypt and will probably continue to live and work there. There are much smaller groups in other Arab countries. As Arab governments push more and more of their own people into top jobs in all kinds of enterprises, and as Muslim Arabs develop skills which for many years have been a near monopoly of Europeans and Levantines, these groups will probably become smaller and poorer. Businessmen and agents of foreign companies and institutions who carry European passports, as also the employees of Western oil companies in Saudi Arabia, Kuwait, and Iraq, will probably occupy different and less powerful positions than formerly.

Indigenous religious and ethnic minorities are likely to remain and to retain their separateness, giving the Arab area its traditional diversity.[5] About three million Muslims belong to heterodox sects like the Shi'ia of Iraq and the Alawites of Syria. The Druses of Syria and Lebanon, an heretical sect of Islam, are not aliens. These people do not hold themselves aloof from the main currents of political life, but they form culturally distinct groups which maintain their separate identity. Their separateness and fear of being dominated completely by the Sunni Muslim majority can produce important political divergences and conflicts, as, for example, the resistance of the Shi'ia leaders to General Kassem's leadership in Iraq in 1959–60.

There are also Sunni Muslim groups which do not speak Arabic and which are culturally separate. In Iraq and Syria there are about one million Kurds and about a quarter million Turcomans and Caucasians. The eight hundred thousand Kurds in Iraq are a particularly important, politically conscious minority occupying a strategic area contiguous with Kurdish communities of a million and a half in Turkey and six hundred thousand in Iran. Iraq's constitution of 1958 recognizes them as a separate group, but they present a serious minority problem. Wholesale clashes between them and government forces have taken place since the summer of 1961 and grown more intense in 1962. The Kurds of Syria are more widely distributed, but they also are conscious of their ties with Kurds outside. None of the Kurdish communities is likely to welcome the prospect of being swallowed up in a Pan Arab state.

[5] A. H. Hourani, *Minorities in the Arab World* (London: Oxford University Press, for the Royal Institute of International Affairs, 1947).

Since the establishment of Israel the Jewish population of Arab states, numbering about half a million, has been considerably reduced from former levels by the expulsion of most of the Jewish communities in Iraq and Yemen and by substantial emigration from other Arab countries. The Jews who remain are for the most part people whose roots are very deep in the ground. The wealthier Jews have adopted Western manners and a Western way of life. The poorer, however, live like the Arabs on their economic level. They have existed as a minority group in the Muslim world for centuries, accepting an inferior position and forgoing aspirations to political influence or special privilege. In situations of crisis between the Arab states and Israel, pressure on the Jewish communities increases, but normally they are accepted in their accustomed place.

The Christian minority of more than two and a half million, including a million or more Copts in Egypt and nearly another million Greek Orthodox and Uniate Christians in Lebanon and Syria, is firmly established. Religion provides a tie with the West, particularly for Lebanese Maronites, but politically most Christians in Arab lands consider themselves Arabs. Indeed, it was among the Christians that Arab nationalist ideas first took root in the nineteenth century. Having practiced for centuries the difficult art of surviving in the midst of an Islamic majority, the Christians are adept at reminding the Muslims that their religion enjoins toleration of other "religions of the book," of which Christianity is one. As much because they fear a Pan Islamic movement which would discriminate against non-Muslims as because they agree with the policies of Arab nationalism, many Christians have become staunch supporters of the movement, emphasizing its nonsectarian aspects.

Arab nationalist leaders, all Muslims now, have been ambivalent, adopting at one time Islamic and at another secular approaches to their political goals. The temptation to use Islamic chauvinism as a means of mass appeal has usually been checked. The Egyptian constitution of 1956 declared that Islam was the religion of the state. Then in a plebiscite many Copts voted for Nasser as president but against the constitution. The revised constitution, promulgated after union with Syria with its large Christian population, did not include the declaration on Islam. In Iraq the Kassem government, conscious of the large Shi'ia and Kurdish groups in the country and the small Christian community, has been careful to recognize these minorities and avoid full identification with Pan Arab or Pan Islamic movements. Lebanon, with its near balance between Christian and Muslim populations, is peculiarly dedicated to the preservation of minority rights and can be expected to maintain them, although the civil war of 1958 affirmed the relationship of its Muslims with the Muslim majority in surrounding Arab lands. But at that time it appeared that Western intervention could do very little to affect the course of politics in the Lebanon, despite the Western orientation of the Christian community.

What is the significance of the minorities for the international posture of the Arabs? The Kurds will remain a problem, possibly a channel for outside intervention in Iraq. Recent reductions in the size of the European communities, changes in their character, and the declining capacity of the European powers to influence the course of affairs in the Arab states have lessened the importance of minority questions in international politics. Religious and linguistic minorities are likely to participate increasingly in the political activities of secular nationalism, provided it remains secular, while striving to retain their own special personalities.

ECONOMIC FACTORS

As in the case of communications, the economies of the Arab states are organized on a national pattern and foreign trade is oriented toward European markets. This is in part the result of history and partly the consequence of the nature and distribution of the natural resources of the area. Apart from petroleum those resources are mainly agricultural, and the bulk of the agricultural product is consumed very near the point of production. Agricultural exports, the most important of which is cotton, have been traditionally directed toward the European market. Except for oil, mineral resources are few and contribute little to economic exchange within the area, or outside it. Only Lebanon and Jordan send more than half their exports to other Middle East countries, and they import considerably less than half their incoming goods from the Middle East. Egypt sends under 10 per cent of its exports to other countries in the area (7.2 per cent in 1959). It is the same with the oil-producing countries (Iraq, for example, sending only 4.3 per cent of its exports to the Middle East in that same year).[6]

Middle East oil, during the period of its spectacular development since the Second World War, has done more to separate than to unite the states of the area. The most striking aspect of the oil development picture is that more than half the world's proved oil resources have been discovered, and almost a quarter of the world's current production has been developed, in countries that are among the most backward and least heavily populated in the Arab area.[7] Oil now produces more than a billion dollars in revenue annually, the largest shares falling to Kuwait, Saudi Arabia, and Iraq. Now there are prospects of similar good fortune for another undeveloped and thinly populated Arab country, Libya.

Some of the blessings of the oil bonanza have spilled over into other Arab states, particularly Jordan, Syria, and Lebanon, over whose territory run the pipelines to the Mediterranean. For those countries, however, and for Egypt, poorly endowed with natural resources and bursting at the seams with population, the development of Middle East oil resources has brought little economic change. Characteristic of the rulers of the states which have oil is the view attributed to one oil-rich sheikh. To the suggestion that he use some of his wealth for the development of Arab states not so blessed, he is said to have replied, "If Allah had wished them to have oil he would have placed it under their lands as he did under mine." On the other hand, rulers who have looked for oil in vain, and who in some cases have greater need for development capital than their richer neighbors, and have better capabilities for utilizing it, feel that the spirit of Arab brotherhood and unity requires sharing the wealth. This view has stimulated political maneuvering and has put the brakes on the movement toward economic unity.

[6] UN Department of Economic and Social Affairs, *Economic Developments in the Middle East, 1958–1959: Supplement to World Economic Survey, 1959,* 60.II.C.2 (New York: Author, 1960), Table 30.

[7] George Lenczowski, *Oil and State in the Middle East* (Ithaca: Cornell University Press, 1960), p. 462.

Other economic facts and institutions, as well as foreign trade, draw the several Arab states into contact with and dependence on the outside world. Interest in development of inter-Arab economic relations and efforts to realize in a practical way the ideal of economic cooperation are increasing, but it will be a long time before such endeavors lessen the traditional dependence of the Arab economies upon European capital, markets, and technical assistance. The nationalization of economic enterprises has gone quite far in some countries, both by establishing state control and by injecting native personnel at all levels in foreign-owned enterprises and those directed by foreign or minority interests. In the more complex technical undertakings, such as steel mills, oil refineries, and many kinds of manufacturing, the Arabs will be dependent for some time on machinery, technicians, and managers brought from abroad. Also the intricate and important process of national economic planning and development in most Arab states will require extensive outside help. Even in Egypt, where local personnel have acquired considerable competence, the need for capital and special equipment will limit prospects for economic development. Thus, however determined the Arabs may be to attain political independence, they will be drawn into close relations with one or more great powers by necessities of economic development which cannot be denied.

There has been much discussion of the political consequences of economic relations between underdeveloped nations and great powers, particularly relations dominated by long-term development projects which involve substantial credits or the commitment over a long period of the exports of the underdeveloped nation. There has been, also, much criticism of Western, and particularly American, aid programs because of the alleged attachment of requirements of a political nature to loans and assistance projects, a state of mind of which the Soviet bloc has taken advantage by publicizing its willingness to offer assistance "with no strings attached." The fact remains that any substantial arrangement between nations, particularly between small and underdeveloped nations on the one side and great powers on the other, has ultimate political implications. Over the long run the ways in which the Arab states meet their needs for outside assistance in their economic development will have an effect on their international position.

An important factor in the Arab area's economic ties with the outside world is the extent of the dependence of Egypt, Syria, and the Sudan on the export of raw cotton. A steadily shrinking Western market for cotton threatens the very existence of Egypt and the Sudan and has necessitated a search for other markets. Since 1955 the Soviet bloc market has opened up until in 1961 it took about half of Egypt's cotton, the bulk of which had for years gone to Western European markets. The factors involved, of course, are extremely complex. Egypt's, and later Syria's, interest in arms and the Soviet interest in the political implications of becoming the arms supplier for these two countries have certainly been major considerations. There is, however, probably an additional factor in a long-term requirement of the Communist states for substantial imports of cotton. While their internal market for cotton goods is expanding, there seems to be little land in the bloc suitable for further development for cotton production. If this prospect proves to be correct, the dependence of Egypt, Syria, and the Sudan on cotton exports and the ability of the Communist bloc to absorb their production may be one of the most important determinants of the economic orientation of an important part of the Arab world.

The development of the oil resources of the Arab area has been carried out by the Western oil industry, and the great bulk of its product has gone into Western markets, particularly in Europe. This has had a profound effect on the internal economic development of the oil-producing countries where the companies have provided assistance in development going well beyond the oil industry itself. It has also had an important effect on the external policy and relations of the oil-producing countries. The fact that the governments of Iraq and Saudi Arabia, for example, have been dependent upon oil revenues provided by the activities of Western oil companies and the sale of oil in Western markets has not prevented the development of Arab nationalism in those countries or swayed their governments from an Arab nationalist foreign-policy line, although at times it has somewhat tempered that line. Events in Iraq since the revolution of July 1958 have been extremely interesting in that they have shown the unwillingness of a nationalist leader to abandon his country's relationship with the foreign-owned Iraq Petroleum Company, on which his oil revenues depended, even when that leader was closely involved with local Communists and pressed by nationalist forces to prove his revolutionary anti-Westernism.

The pressures in the oil-producing countries are increasingly strong for modification of present agreements on profit-sharing in favor of the host countries and for progressive steps to bring their governments and nationals into the operation of the industry, particularly at its higher levels. Recent price cuts have had the effect of inducing the producing countries to present a common front to the companies. However, the talk of expropriation and nationalization of the oil companies which was common a few years ago has diminished, and the evidence at the Arab Petroleum Congresses in Cairo in 1959 and in Beirut in 1960 was that, though the oil-producing countries will work steadily toward the day when they can run their own oil industries, they recognize that they will be dependent on the Western oil companies, though to a diminishing degree, for some time. The development of new oil fields in North Africa to the west of Suez and the expansion of oil production elsewhere make the dependence of Arab Persian Gulf producers on the Western markets even greater than in the past. There seems little likelihood that the Soviet bloc will become able to offer markets to these oil producers which might change their orientation, though it is distinctly possible that the development of China may open up vast new markets there which would have that result.

THE REVOLUTIONS OF AWARENESS AND EXPECTATION

All of the Arab area, as we have seen, is in a state of revolutionary transition from the traditional society of the past into an as yet unformulated adaptation to the modern world. The great urban centers are very much in advance of other areas, but the ferment is at work even in the deserts of Saudi Arabia and the mountains of Yemen. How this revolution, which involves every aspect of Arab life, works out will profoundly affect both the ability of the Arabs to conduct meaningful foreign policies and the nature and purpose of those policies as well.

One of the most important aspects of this internal revolution in Arab lands has been the result of changed opportunities for communication. In the past hundred and fifty years, and particularly in the past generation, a revolution of awareness has taken place which has brought a wider and wider circle of Arabs into contact with information and ideas about the problems of Arab statehood, and of Arab relations with the outside world. Education and the spread of literacy have been fundamental in this process. Islamic education contributed to the preservation of the traditional society, but it was the introduction of European methods, disciplines, and languages that opened new vistas affecting first the upper classes and those few chosen for technical or professional tasks and then spread its influence over a wider and wider segment of society. The example of the West and the desire to strengthen the capability of the Arab states to withstand the pressures of the West led to the encouragement of education and literacy by Ottoman and Arab rulers with a broad variety of points of view and policies.

In the course of the nineteenth century the printing press and popular newspapers opened new horizons for a widening group of Arabs and created a sense of identification with people and affairs outside the local community. These new contacts were not limited to those who could read; they extended to those who frequented coffee houses to hear newspapers read, as well as those who learned by word of mouth of what had appeared in the press. Books, produced by the new mechanical presses, made their contribution to the spread of ideas. To some extent the new newspapers and books propagated the traditional culture and defended traditional points of view, but the new media naturally attracted new and progressive ideas. More and more, even in parts of the Arab area where strict censorship was maintained, the new books dealt with foreign ideas and techniques and with the Arab objectives in new ways. The close identification of the Arabic language with the special and separate character of Arab culture lent a nationalistic quality to practically everything written in Arabic.

The radio further extended the opportunities of Arabs of all qualities and degrees, even in the most remote localities, to come into contact with the outside world. Neither schooling nor money was required to listen to the radio in the ubiquitous coffee house, and no measure of censorship or control could prevent the widespread radio audience from developing a greater degree of awareness of the neighboring Arab states, and of the world of great powers and international politics.

The cinema showed many people—all those possessing the small sum required for entrance into the cheapest seats and living within walking distance of a motion picture theater—the striking contrasts between the wealth of the West and their own poverty, and between Western conventions and institutions and their own. On top of all this, television has come to Baghdad, Beirut, Cairo, Alexandria, and Damascus.

Greatly increased ease of travel has also contributed to awareness of the outside world. In centers of population and sometimes even in remote regions, tourists and businessmen in steadily increasing numbers remind the Arab of the diversity of the world, of the differences between himself and outsiders and sometimes of the things he has, or would like to have, in common with them. In two world wars tens of thousands of soldiers and many civilians, living, working, and fighting in the sight of Arabs, showed them what Americans, Englishmen, Frenchmen, or Poles are like and how they behave. By their presence these foreigners gave lessons in world politics.

Judged by statistics, the Arab states are still underdeveloped in terms of literacy and communications facilities. Literacy ranges from 45 or 50 per cent in Lebanon, where it is highest, to less than 5 per cent in Yemen and Saudi Arabia. In between there is Iraq with 10 to 15 per cent literacy, Egypt with 20 to 25 per cent, and Syria with 35 to 40 per cent. Lebanon, with less than a million and a half people, has more than 45,000 licensed radio receivers. Iraq, with a population of more than six million, had in 1954 66,000. Egypt, with nearly twenty-five million, has at least half a million radio receivers. There are at least 137 cinemas in Iraq, 60 in Lebanon, 365 in Egypt, and 63 in Syria. Egypt produces in the neighborhood of 60 feature films each year. Iraq has some 30 newspapers with a combined daily circulation of 100,000. Little Lebanon has 40 daily papers with a total circulation of 100,000 and 150 weeklies with 150,000. Egypt has 46 dailies with a circulation of a half a million and 200 weeklies with a circulation of about 250,000.[8]

These figures—though out of date and certainly all considerably lower than a current survey would show—indicate that the Arab states do not have communications facilities like those of the more highly developed nations. But they show a development from practically nothing a few decades ago to a level where practically every interested person has access to a great deal of information about his own country and the outside world, even though much of it has been prepared for him by government specialists in "national guidance." The poorest and most ordinary people are exposed to a mass of serious material which, however biased, carries with it much information about other countries, the workings of the United Nations, international conferences, and the like. It should also be kept in mind that radio, television, and the cinema reach the illiterate, and that poor but politically conscious countries make much more intensive use of their communications facilities (e.g., the café radio set) than richer societies. Politics in the Arab states is not the same as in Western Europe or in the Soviet Union, but the Arabs nevertheless are a highly political people. One of the most striking developments in Arab lands since World War II has been the increased awareness of world affairs of people at all levels.[9]

[8] Cf. UN Department of Economic and Social Affairs, *Statistical Yearbook, 1959,* 59-XVII-1 (New York: Author, 1960), and UNESCO, *World Communications* (Paris: Author, 1956; 3d ed.).

[9] The author cannot write of this subject without recalling a personal experience. At the end of the second day of air attacks on Egypt that preceded the British and French invasion in 1956, the all-clear was sounded and I decided to try to get to my house in the suburb of Maadi, seven miles south of Cairo. On the way there, however, the sound of the Canberra bombers was heard overhead and the alert signal was sounded. A small band of policemen and hastily recruited national guardsmen stopped me at a roadblock in a lonely spot by the river. I got out of my car, quite uncertain what the attitude of such simple people would be toward Americans at a moment when their country was being attacked by the "West." To my astonishment, the question with which I was greeted was how the vote in the United Nations was coming on the Canadian resolution. The

The revolution of awareness has been accompanied by a revolution of expectation. Until very recently people in many parts of the Arab world, because they did not know how rich much of the rest of the world was, had no idea how poor they themselves were. Today they have not only seen and heard accounts of the wealth of the West but they have learned also that in much of the world it is considered the right of ordinary men to possess a certain minimum of material goods and to have opportunities to acquire much more. Furthermore, the doctrine of progress and the infectious optimism of those who believe in the magical power of science, industrialization, and economic development to transform poor societies have gotten through to the Arab masses. They believe there must be a way out, a formula, a system, a policy which, sweeping away the misery and the penury of the past, will bring them a brave new world, just as good as that enjoyed by the West and the Russians.

These two revolutions, of awareness and of expectation, have greatly changed the psychological conditions in which policy makers in the Arab East, and those dealing with the Arab East, must operate. No longer can relations between states be worked out between individuals in authority without reference to the demands and interests of the public. No longer do events of great importance take place without publicity and public discussion.

SOCIAL REVOLUTION

Accompanying the revolutions of awareness and expectation is a social revolution. There has always been a significant division between the urban and rural populations of the Arab world, and

---

men at the roadblock did not have a radio, but they had set up a messenger service, and in a minute or two a small boy came running up with an old envelope on which someone at the nearest coffee house had written down the votes as they were announced over the radio. How had Turkey voted? Iran? Pakistan? These policemen and guardsmen knew which were the critical states and were watching the progress of the vote with shrewd anticipation. They knew the role that President Eisenhower had played in the crisis and what Ambassador Lodge had said in the UN. I tried to imagine how similar people in 1882 had heard the news of the British invasion then and what they knew of the positions of other states around the world.

between the settled population and the nomads of the desert. The gaps that separate these groups have been considerably narrowed by the radio and by the growth of nationalist political activity with its appeals to the whole population, its public festivals, and its national crises in which everyone, regardless of class or occupation, is swept up in the excitement of danger and the flush of victory.

Westernization was once an effective barrier separating the small group at the top of the social structure from those immersed in the traditional society. A young man's choice—or his father's choice—of a school symbolizes an important dichotomy in Arab society. Choosing a religious school probably means wearing the long robes of the Muslim student, running a Muslim household in which the women are kept at home, and associating with those who maintain the traditional way of life. A Western-style school means Western clothes, a Western-type home with a certain amount of freedom for its women, use of Western languages, and a Western kind of job in business, government, or the professions, though all this may be tempered by a generous measure of nationalism and hostility to Western "imperialism and colonialism." But even so, the rise of nationalist sentiment has narrowed the gap between the man in the turban and robe and the man in the Western suit, by drawing the former into politics and the latter into more conscientious use of the Arabic language and more careful performance of Muslim rites, as at Ramadan.

The old upper class of the pashas is being leveled down and a new professional and business class is moving up. Thus a much larger, more homogeneous, and more articulate upper class is being formed. Land reform, nationalization, the breakup of monopolies once held by royal favorites, the end of the exclusive rights of a small class to acquire legal and professional skills—these and other changes have brought an end to the pasha and his world. At the same time the proliferation of jobs in government and in the increasing number of industrial and commercial enterprises, whether independent or under government sponsorship, is producing a new elite. Well over a hundred thousand students in Arab universities, and ten thousand in foreign universities, are the sources from which this new expanding upper class is being drawn.[10]

In all the Arab states the military officer corps has provided an important contribution to the new elite. The armies and air forces, even to a greater extent than government departments organized along European lines, have provided effective training and experience in organization and command, and have developed a sense of responsibility. The first generation of officers in the Egyptian and Iraqi armies to be drawn from all levels of society, rather than exclusively from the upper classes, produced the leaders of the revolutions of the 1950s. Many of them coming from the middle or lower middle classes brought with them political ideas opposed to those of the established order and to its dependence upon and association with Great Britain and the West. The military life gave them education, special technical skills, the habit of organization, and awareness of the political uses of military power. It was natural therefore, that these officers should take an important place among the new elite.

The new upper class is to be found principally in Egypt, Syria, Lebanon, and Iraq, nowhere numbering more than about 5 per cent of the population. In the other Arab countries it is very much smaller, but similar in general character and composition. Its members include both the sons of the old upper class, trained and adjusted to new political and professional forms, and members of the new group of educated professionals. Their credentials in every case include education, some technical or professional skill, and commitment to the idea of national development. In the Sudan the new elite, small as it is, is very much in charge; in countries like Saudi Arabia and Libya it is still in the wings waiting to come on the political stage.

Around this new elite in Egypt, Lebanon, Syria, and Iraq is gathered another 10 to 15 per cent of the population that looks to it for guidance and leadership. They include newspaper readers, frequenters of political meetings, active participants in public political activity, all of whom tend to be the avid Arab nationalists. They are the small shopkeepers, the skilled artisans, urban work-

[10] Francis Boardman, *Institutions of Higher Learning in the Middle East* (Washington: Middle East Institute, 1961).

ers, and petty civil servants who are just below the elite in education and economic position. Thus the politically articulate group—interested and actively involved in politics and in Arab nationalism—probably ranges from 20 to 25 per cent in Egypt, Lebanon, and Syria, some 10 to 15 per cent in Jordan and Iraq, and 3 or 4 per cent in the Sudan down to a tiny percentage in Saudi Arabia, Yemen, and the more remote sheikhdoms.

The political and social changes of the past twenty years have by no means eliminated the old upper class of royalty and friends and advisers of royalty, the holders of state monopolies, the great landlords and lords of commercial fiefs, tribal sheikhs, and village headmen. Only in Saudi Arabia, Libya, Kuwait, and the sheikhdoms of the Persian Gulf is this class still in control, but it has great strongholds still in the Syrian business community, in minority communities like the Kurds and Druses, and, at the top level, in rural areas. Religion, economic custom, and traditional habits of thought, which include deep mistrust of the central government and of change, tend to sustain its authority. This authority is waning, however. The centers of power are no longer in the hands of the remaining representatives of traditional ways; and the winds of change have fanned the cheeks of the rural peasantry as well as of the urban dwellers. Deep as the roots of their influence go, the inheritors of traditional authority find it more and more difficult to maintain themselves in the face of the unity and the propaganda of the new elite.

Arab society has always been characterized by the ease with which individuals could move from class to class. The changes that are taking place today have created a great deal of social movement, both by pushing the once wealthy upper class down and opening the way, via the schools, government, and the army, for poor boys to move upward. The fundamental element of Arab society remains, however, the great mass of the very poor at the bottom. Despite what both revolutionary and conservative regimes have done in recent years for the peasant masses, by building schools, hospitals, and community centers, by land reform and irrigation projects, their life in its essentials remains very much the same. But the revolutions of awareness and expectation have brought about one important change. In the tradition of centuries,

the Arab peasantry still meets its sufferings with patience and for-
bearance, but it cannot now be long until the masses respond to
the new stimuli by more than cheering the fireworks on independence day.

Both the revolutionary and the conservative regimes in the Arab
states are faced with the basic and desperately difficult problem of
bringing the people into the process of government in a meaningful
way. The times, and the activities of the governments themselves,
have created a rising popular demand for participation in politics.
The conservative regimes would like to satisfy the demand without destroying their traditional system. But the Iraqi revolt gave a
grim warning that even a serious economic development effort is
not enough.

In the revolutionary states the problem is different but equally
acute. Nasser and Kassem, who came to power as the champions
of the people against the corrupt regimes of the past, have retained
much popular support. They have found out, however, that carrying out revolutionary changes against the opposition of formidable
domestic and foreign antagonists, with the support of an enthusiastic but undisciplined public, required a strong centralized authority. Nasser has faced up to the fact, of which Kassem is certainly also aware, that corruption and the lack of a sense of public
responsibility are not characteristics manifested exclusively by officials of old-fashioned monarchical regimes. The consequence has
been that the state has evolved as the supreme authority, under
their charismatic leadership. But censorship, nationalization of the
press, and state direction of education have made it increasingly
difficult to present the other side, that is, the side opposed to that
taken by the government, on any issue of significance.

President Nasser has sought to make his recently created National Union into a vast pyramidal organization of debating societies in which all solutions—i.e., "the capitalist, the Communist,
and the 'socialist, democratic, cooperative' solutions"—can presumably be discussed. Recommendations then go to the president
of the Union, who is also president of the republic. Although the
recommendations usually, though not always, follow the official
line, the gesture is significant. In the U.A.R., Iraq, and other Arab
states the need to make plans, organize resources, and get on with

the job of development has generally overridden considerations of the value, or political necessity, of free public discussion.

For the time being the most pressing problem is not the masses, either rural or urban. Most of them who have an interest in political activity are satisfied by the opportunities provided by the state information program, public meetings and demonstrations, and, for the most avid, devices like the National Union. It is the intellectuals, including many members of the new elite, who tend to be unhappy and whose dissatisfactions are harder to meet. Most Arab intellectuals, even if they are the most defiant anti-Western nationalists, have imbibed some of the Western feeling for freedom of discussion and the value of the interplay of ideas on serious subjects. Many of them, even some who have positions of responsibility which command respect, continue to find it difficult to work effectively and creatively in a situation in which there is only one right answer to a question.[11] This situation, it should be noted, is found in revolutionary as well as in conservative states. Only Lebanon maintains, along with its free trade policies, a free market for ideas.

Americans and those Western Europeans who enjoy the free exchange of ideas should not forget how long it took to create the democratic institutions which make it possible. They should keep in mind the monumental problems facing governments which are trying in a few short years to make up for long centuries of stagnation while beset by dangers from within and without. These problems and these dangers form a part of the environment in which Arab foreign policy is made.

[11] Cf. the perspicacious article by Hisham Sharabi, "Political and Intellectual Attitudes of the Young Arab Generation," in Tibor Kerekes, ed., *The Arab Middle East and Muslim Africa* (New York: Praeger, 1961), pp. 47–61.

V

THE ARAB STATES

The several national states are basic elements in the Arab situation and are at present the principal instruments of action in the international arena. For the most part the states were the creations of the Western powers at the end of the First World War and so do not have deep historic roots. The fact that the Arab states are new while Islam and Arab culture are old does not, however, greatly reduce their significance. They contain most of the working institutions that control the life of the area and its relations with the outside world, and for some time these institutions are likely to be stronger and more effective than any new creations. The states are essential parts of the existing situation. In some way or other they will be part of any future reorganization of the area. It is therefore important to understand those aspects of their geographic and economic situations which influence their outlook and external relations and to take note of those aspects of their internal social and political character which influence the formation and execution of their foreign policies.

EGYPT

Egypt is by far the most important and influential of the Arab states. It has one-third the population of the Arab world, an economy larger and more diversified than that of any other Arab state, and a level of economic, technical, and industrial development matched only in certain areas by Lebanon and Syria. Egypt has had a longer experience as a national state and better established governmental institutions. Its local educational system is more advanced than those of other Arab countries. Its secular universities have eighty thousand students, whereas there are only twenty thousand in all other Arab institutions of higher education. Its thirty thousand students in teacher training courses are almost three times as numerous as those in all other Arab states. Al Azhar University, the oldest and most influential institution of Muslim learning, has thirty-seven thousand students, drawn from all parts of the Muslim world. Graduates of Egyptian universities and Egyptian teachers are to be found in schools throughout the area, even where there are political differences between local governments and the Egyptian regime. Egyptian radio, the daily and weekly press, and Egyptian films command an audience throughout the Arab area, while the communications media of other states are essentially local in character.

Geography separates Egypt from the Arabs of Asia and of North Africa, and over the course of history Egyptian association with the areas to the northeast and the west has been sporadic. The Pharaohs of ancient Egypt turned their attention now to Palestine and Syria in the northeast and again to the upper Nile almost as the seasons came and went. The sweep of Muslim conquest in the century after Mohammed brought Egypt into a great empire, but through most of Islamic history Egypt has been a separate satrapy, province, or state. In the nineteenth century Muhammad Ali and later the British occupation influenced the development of an Egypt largely independent of the Ottoman Empire and of neighboring Muslim lands. In the period of the British occupation it was Egyptian rather than Arab nationalism that formed the attitudes and policies of Egyptians. After independence, the most important external objective of Egyptians was the unity of the Nile valley, or the establishment of Egyptian hegemony over the Sudan. Most Egyptians who concerned themselves with international affairs and policy thought of Egypt as a Mediterranean nation and, very like the Turks after the Young Turk Revolution, turned away from the Arabs of Asia and planned to make their country a part of Europe. Occasionally the idea of capitalizing on

Egypt's position as the largest independent state in the Arab area occurred to an Egyptian politician, but with little consequence. Egypt's entrance into the Arab League in 1945 was largely a maneuver to prevent the establishment of a Fertile Crescent union under Iraqi leadership and was handled so as to ensure the sovereign independence of the several Arab states.

The argument over whether Egypt is an African or an Arab state goes on. Concern over the waters of the Nile, the attraction of Libyan oil, and the political opportunities in an emerging Africa will all draw Egypt's attention to the west and south from time to time, but strong and persistent attractions are likely still to come from the northeast. Israel, Suez, and Arab nationalism have made Egypt Arab. The events of the last fifteen years have emphasized Egypt's weakness and the advantage of association with a larger area. Until the defeat of the Arab states by Israel, Egypt remained relatively remote from the Palestine issue; once Israel was established, Egypt was tied to the other Arabs by a common humiliation and a common cause, a cause which became more compelling as the nationalist revival which it evoked gathered momentum and heat.

Another force pushing Egypt into association with the other Arab states is its basic poverty. Despite its relative economic advancement, its relative lack of natural wealth makes access to outside economic resources a necessity if Egypt is not to smother under the weight of its own population. The idea of some kind of association with neighboring states, some kind of economic community which would permit an exchange between Egypt's human resources and the natural resources of the lands to the east, west, and south occurs naturally to any Egyptian who addresses himself to his country's problems. Such ideas naturally evoke fears and suspicions on the part of other Arabs who do not wish to sacrifice their own advantages for the sake of Egypt. Egypt's position in the Arab world today is a paradox. On the one hand, its geographic location, its size and relative development, and its political leadership constitute undeniable claims to leadership. On the other hand, because of its very size and strength, combined with pressing economic needs, and the sweeping vision of the future of the Arab world which its leader proclaims, it is feared in all the other states by those who have most to lose.

Egypt's most important economic resource is cotton, which for years has exceeded in value all other exports and provided the foreign exchange to pay for imported manufactures and foodstuffs. In order to avoid the economic and political results of too great dependence on Western markets, Nasser has endeavored to build up trade with the Soviet bloc and with the uncommitted nations. The decline in Western demand for Egyptian cotton coinciding with rising demand for this commodity in the Soviet Union has facilitated the new trade policy, which has its dangers in too great a dependence on the other side. The Suez Canal, an important economic asset which yields substantial revenues in hard currencies, also imposes serious responsibilities and pressures of an international character.

Egypt's homogeneous population renders the task of government simpler than in Syria and Iraq where the community is split by religious and sectional conflicts. In Egypt, the European minority group has lost its special position and privileges. The large community of Coptic Christians, although it suffers increasing discrimination, supports in general Nasser's policies of nationalism and nonalignment. It has few associations with the outside world and no foreign protector.

After the 1952 revolution, the old-line parliamentary parties, which seldom had distinguishable principles or policies, being made up of the followers of outstanding political leaders, were outlawed. The new regime's showdown with the Muslim Brotherhood, and then with the Communist party, came in 1954 when after a few days of street fighting those two organizations were overcome by the forces of the police, the army, and certain labor unions. The Communist party, never very successful in recruiting Muslims, was made up largely of members of the European community and Egyptian intellectuals to whom Marxism had a strong appeal. Severely harassed by the police, it has exerted since 1954 little influence on government policy or on public opinion. The revolutionary regime's attempt to replace the old parliamentary parties with a single party, the Liberation Rally, was at first unsuccessful. Later, in 1959–60, profiting by the increased interest in politics resulting from the Suez affair, and the union of Egypt and Syria in the United Arab Republic, the government with some difficulty was able to organize the National Union, as a successor to the Rally.

The regime remains, basically, an authoritarian one intolerant of criticism. The press in the interwar period enjoyed considerable freedom, with several journals taking a strongly independent line. After 1952 it came more and more under the domination of the government, and early in 1960 all media of communication and expression of opinion were either brought under direct government control, subjected to censorship, or otherwise made to reflect the government line.

Egypt's geographic position and its material and cultural resources make it the center of a sub-area of the Arab East which includes Libya to the west, the Sudan to the south, and—though the connection here is less close—the eastern shore of the Red Sea. Egypt's geographic proximity to these other territories, however, has little political significance or potential at the moment, except to stiffen the determination of their governments to maintain their independence of their larger neighbor. Egypt's long-held assumption that the Sudan would join with it after the withdrawal of the British was rudely shocked by the Sudanese election of independence. Since then Egypt's conception of its role in the Arab area has emphasized a wider influence over the area as a whole, and particularly in the more advanced areas, rather than the idea of the mechanical extension of its boundaries outward.

Egypt's military forces, plentifully supplied with Soviet armor, aircraft, and submarines, are a key factor in the internal security of the country and could be used with relative ease in the Sudan and Libya. They are primarily designed, however, to face the Israeli border and to provide a counter to the Israeli defense force. Operations east of the Red Sea present to the Egyptians such formidable problems, political as well as logistic and military, that it was generally expected they would continue to exercise their influence and seek to gain their ends by primarily political means. The injection of Egyptian military force into Yemen in 1962 has proved that such operations are feasible. It may presage more such adventures on behalf of Arab revolutionaries and against their enemies despite the financial burdens and the dangers of over-extension and involvement with the powers.

SYRIA

Syria has existed for centuries; the boundaries of the present state, smaller than historic Syria, were drawn by the treaty makers at the end of World War I. They encompass the northern half of the fertile strip of plains and mountains running in a belt fifty miles wide along the eastern coast of the Mediterranean—minus the bite taken out to make Lebanon—and a triangular wedge of desert and steppeland behind it. The coast and its hinterland constitute physically distinct regions. Some of the inhabitants have for centuries been grouped around the major cities—Aleppo, Homs, Hama, Damascus, Beirut, Jerusalem, Haifa. Others live in communities like those of the Alawites in the northern coastal hills, the Druses in the mountains south of Damascus, and the Maronites on Mount Lebanon. Under the Ottomans, and later under the British and French mandates, no part of the area developed the institutions or the sense of statehood. Nevertheless, an ancient sense of community, plus the rise of Arab nationalism, united a large proportion of the people in the conviction that ultimately the area would come under a single Arab authority.

Syrians have neither succeeded in establishing a stable state of their own nor have they accepted the division of the area imposed at the end of the First World War. Although divided and almost ungovernable themselves, many Syrians nevertheless persist in thinking of their country as the logical center around which the Arab nation must eventually coalesce. Damascus, they point out, was the first capital of the Arab empire, and in the nineteenth century Pan Arabist ideas had their first vigorous growth in Syria and Lebanon.

The notion that present-day Syria, Lebanon, Jordan, and Palestine are a natural entity which should be joined in a Greater Syria has long been popular in Syria. Syrians regard Lebanon as a temporary arrangement set up by the French to provide autonomy for the Christians of the Mount Lebanon, at the expense of the

Muslims of the Beqaa' and the northern and southern ends of the small state. Jordan, another Western creation, which in their opinion has long since outlived any past justification, they look upon as logically part of south Syria; Palestine, they consider Syrian and Arab territory now largely under foreign (Israeli) occupation.

The Syrians are much more addicted than the Egyptians to the kind of political activity that expresses itself in political parties, and are more adept at it. The People's party centered in Aleppo and the National party centered in Damascus have represented regional interests. The political significance of minority groups like the Druses, the Alawites, and the Christians is probably decreasing under the impact of social and economic change. For some time, socialism has appealed to Syrian intellectuals who in the Arab Socialist Resurrection (Baath) party and the Syrian Socialist Nationalist party (S.S.N.P.) have elaborated Pan Arabist doctrines. The Syrians have also one of the best organized and led Communist parties in the Arab world. Its most prominent figure is the able theorist and organizer, Khalid Baqdash, a Syrian Kurd.

The series of military *coups d'état* which took place after Syria won independence in 1945, and the complex interplay of political forces which led to union with Egypt in 1958 and have continued after its dissolution, demonstrate the inherent instability of Syrian politics. The agreement to merge the country with Egypt and to accept Nasser's leadership reflected an awareness of the dangers into which Syria's unresolved political tangle had brought the country. A condition of union stipulated by Nasser was the elimination of political parties. The old nationalist parties melted away, as the Wafd had done in Egypt. The Communist party came under the same systematic pressures as the Communist party in Egypt and was harassed into apparent ineffectiveness. The Baath, whose leaders had assumed high ministerial posts immediately after the union, sought refuge in Lebanon or became inactive after their unsuccessful bid for greater power in December 1959. Since the dissolution of the U.A.R. they have jockeyed for position in the uncertain political arena of independent Syria.

Politically, the years of union seem to have changed Syria hardly at all. The Baath group which took the initiative in calling for the union, having failed to realize the hope of assuming a dominant position in it, lost its hold in Syria as well. Other political groupings were on hand to claim their former place in the new Syrian government. Once again Syria seems destined to be governed by a coalition—or to have a coalition government; no single party, or leader, will be able to command enough support to stay in power. Gradually, Syria seems to be drifting back to the position in which it found itself in 1958, unable to resolve its political problems without some form of association with Egypt.

Syria's focus of interest remains in the Levant, the fertile strip that runs the length of the eastern shore of the Mediterranean. Like other states in that area, it looks westward to the Mediterranean rather than eastward. Both Egypt and Iraq are to a degree alien, but Iraq with its inland and Asian focus is the farther away and the harder for Syrians to understand. It is conceivable that Syria might in some future rearrangement of the balance of Arab political forces turn toward Iraq in the search for Arab unity, but at present there is little apparent inclination to do so.

With a relatively small population in proportion to available land, Syria, despite the lack of significant oil reserves or other mineral riches, has a potentially bright economic future. Since it is still predominantly agricultural, however, a series of bad crop years have slowed its economic progress. But Syria is not likely to be pressed by economic need to seek territorial expansion.

The Syrian military, though sufficiently strong to handle internal security problems and provide some measure of defense on the borders with Israel, has little potential as an instrument of international policy.

LEBANON

The territory included in the modern state of Lebanon is the center of the Levant. Perched on the coastal range of mountains and hills looking down to the sea and outward, it has been throughout historic times the home of Mediterranean traders. Geographical divisions make Lebanon a natural home for minorities. The Christian groups, about half the total population, have closer ties with Europe and the West than do their co-religionists in Egypt and Syria. Some of their leaders have advocated making Christian Lebanon into a Western state, but with the rise of Arab nationalism they have generally agreed that the future of their community lies with the Arab world. They have accepted and promulgated the belief that Christians can be as good Arabs, politically, as Muslims can.

Present-day Lebanon was created by the French mandatory power after the First World War, in accordance with its conception of responsibility for protecting the Christian population. Around the territory occupied by the largest concentration of Maronite, Greek Orthodox, Greek Catholic, and other Christians in the neighborhood of Mount Lebanon a line was drawn so as to include as much territory in the new state as possible without making the Muslims a majority. But this gerrymander proved only temporarily successful; the migration of Christians and their lower birth rate probably have now given the Muslims a majority.

The political influence of Pan Arab nationalism and the growth of the Muslim majority might eventually lead to the merger of Lebanon with a larger Arab union, but this now seems a remote possibility. Lebanon has certain unique qualities which set it aside from the rest of the area. Other Arab states include large minorities but only in Lebanon do they cluster together, lending each other mutual support. The Muslim portion of the population is not a solid unit politically. The Shi'ias and Druses who together outnumber the orthodox Sunnis, are not anxious to find themselves in a Sunni-dominated state, as they would be if Lebanon were merged in a Greater Syria or a U.A.R. Lebanon comprehends several religious communities, each with recognized rights, leadership, and representation based on an agreement known as the National Covenant. The traditional practice of giving the presidency to a Maronite, the prime minister's office to a Sunni Muslim, and the presidency of the Parliament to a Shi'ia has seldom been challenged. In Egypt and Syria this "confessionalism," inherited from earlier Islamic states and from the Ottoman Empire, is going out of use under the influence of secular, Pan Arab nationalism, but it retains wide support in Lebanon.

Lebanon has become an entrepôt through which passes much of the Arab lands' trade with the West. Hence, the prosperity of the entire country depends heavily upon keeping foreign trade free from burdensome restrictions and on maintaining good trading relations with Western nations. Merger in an Arab union would probably mean deterioration of Lebanese foreign trade.

In Lebanon, the most literate of the Arab states and probably the most sophisticated politically, modernization has proceeded as far or farther than in the urban centers of Egypt and Syria. The old upper class of landlords and community leaders has given way to a new elite of businessmen with an international outlook and professional men educated in the Western manner. Political parties and groupings reflect socialist philosophy, Pan Arabist and Greater Syria ideas, and Nasser's brand of Pan Arab neutralism, combined with a special position of neutrality in inter-Arab quarrels. The most important political divisions, however, are based on confessional groupings, with the Maronites emphasizing Lebanon's relations with the West and the Sunni Muslims stressing the area's dominant Pan Arabism.

The whole pattern of politics, including the politics of international relations, has a strongly local flavor marked by a characteristic Lebanese individualism, which is not confined to any one confessional group. An important part of the pattern is the fact that Lebanon is a free trade area for the exchange of ideas and for political activity, with an area-wide implication, as well as in the economic field. The Lebanese press, less constrained by censorship than any other in the area, includes numerous daily and weekly publications aimed at an Arab audience outside Lebanon. Lebanon is also a refuge for people from the other Arab states with political or other difficulties at home and a headquarters for political groups which cannot function in their own countries. Lebanon's attractiveness to tourists and its place in the international air traffic pattern makes it a natural meeting place for people from the other Arab states, whether their interests be politics, business, or pleasure. All these factors give an international flavor to Lebanon and draw the country's attention to the area around it.

Lebanon's international position has been subjected to an ever-changing balance of pressures, on the one side from the interests shared by most of the population in the independence of the country and its present trading pattern and, on the other, by the political force of the ideas of Pan Arab nationalism. Occasionally these pressures have produced conflict, as in 1958, but generally they have been kept in check by a middle-of-the-road policy. Lebanon has supported Arab League policy on Israel and Algeria; thousands of Lebanese traveled to Damascus to pay their respects to Gamal Abdel Nasser during the halcyon days of the U.A.R. At the same time Lebanon generally tries to avoid policies which would damage its relations with the Western powers. It maintained diplomatic relations with the British and French after the Suez attack of October-November 1956 and was one of two Arab states to accept the Eisenhower Doctrine openly and without qualification. Yet, when Syria broke away from the U.A.R., Lebanese supporters of Nasser and the Pan Arab idea protested more vigorously than like-minded groups in other Arab states.

The delicacy of the political balance in Lebanon was demonstrated most vividly in 1958 when an internal dispute brought to a head differences between the Christian and the Muslim communities and also between pro-Nasser Pan Arabs and conservative proponents of state nationalism. The recovery from the debilitating civil war and deep political wounds was remarkably rapid. But at the end of 1961 an altogether unexpected attempt against the government by the rightist S.S.N.P., a Syrian party with some Lebanese adherents, again reminded the Lebanese and their neighbors of the fragile nature of the country's political structure.

Lebanon's army, barely large enough for internal security purposes, has little international significance for foreign policy. In the conflict of 1958 it was deliberately kept out of action to avoid its being torn apart by the deeply felt issues in that struggle. After the fighting the army helped make it possible to form a new government of compromise and reconciliation under its commander, General Shehab.

JORDAN

The Kingdom of Jordan makes even less sense geographically than either Syria or Lebanon. Jordan is not a viable economic unit. Its population is divided into three groups, none of which thinks of itself as Jordanian. The nation survives in the absence of some more feasible arrangement, and because it has become a kind of keystone in the precarious arch of political forces in the Middle East.

The East Bank of the Jordan, originally Transjordan, comprises a partly arable strip of highlands and a curiously shaped piece of desert hinterland. Its population is made up of settled townsmen, village farmers, and Bedouin tribesmen, about half a million altogether. The people, little affected by modern social and economic trends, are poor, conservative, and generally loyal to the monarchy. The West Bank, the territory occupied by King Abdullah's Arab Legion during the Palestine War of 1948–49 and added to Transjordan after the war, is inhabited by about half a million Palestinian Arabs who are generally more advanced socially and economically, and more modern in their outlook, than their countrymen of the East Bank. Jordan has also some half million refugees from parts of Palestine now in Israel who are still unassimilated and are on the UN ration rolls, plus a hundred thousand who, having found places in the Jordanian economy, are self-supporting. Large numbers of West Bank Palestinians and assimilated refugees have moved to the capital, Amman, and other towns on the East Bank where they compete successfully with the less sophisticated people there for economic advantage and political position.

There is no characteristically Jordanian position on foreign policy. The West Bank residents and the refugees are primarily concerned with prospects of getting rid of Israel. The Amir Abdullah, later king, was conscious of the economic disadvantage of being cut off from the Mediterranean and anxious for a settlement which would confirm and make secure the territorial expansion that followed the Palestine War. His attempts to reach some kind of understanding with the new state of Israel were strongly opposed by the Palestinians within his own country, as by the governments of the other Arab states, and his life was finally taken in reprisal for his efforts. The West Bank Palestinians and the refugees, more aggressive in their attitude toward Israel than the monarchy, have turned for guidance and support to Egypt, Syria, and Saudi Arabia. The East Bank Arabs, though conservatively inclined and thus loyal to the establishment, think of themselves more as south Syrians than as Jordanians; some are susceptible to Syrian and

Egyptian Pan Arab propaganda and particularly to the charges that the Hashemite monarchy in Jordan is the creation of the West and that the King pays for Western economic and diplomatic support by kowtowing to Western interests.

The monarchy, having only scattered backing in public opinion, relies for support on a rather old-fashioned but shrewd upper class, which opposes Nasser's revolutionary Pan Arabism, and on the tribes of the desert. It leans heavily, also, on American and British economic, military, and diplomatic assistance, like that given by the American Sixth Fleet in the spring of 1957 and the airlift of British troops in the summer of 1958. It also makes effective use of the Bedouin elements of the army which are less influenced by foreign propaganda and more loyal to the crown than are the inhabitants of the West Bank or the town and city dwellers on the eastern side of the river.

Relations with Israel loom large on the Jordanian horizon. The three hundred mile frontier which divides many Jordanian villages from their former lands, and separates all the refugees from their former homes, encourages infiltration and border clashes. King Hussein naturally has had no enthusiasm for an Arab Palestinian government-in-exile or army, a proposal often discussed at Arab League meetings, for that would deprive Jordan of the fruits of the Palestine War. Thus, despite the common antipathy to Israel, conflict between Jordan and other Arab states over the Palestine question seems inevitable.

Jordan has to choose between its present reliance upon Western economic, military, and diplomatic support, and acceptance of the Pan Arabist line. An experiment with the latter policy in 1956–57 fizzled out. At that time the British General Glubb was dismissed from command of the Arab Legion, and the government was put in the charge of a pro-Nasser prime minister, Sulaiman Nabulsi. A joint military command was set up with Egypt and Syria, and an Arab Solidarity Agreement was signed by which Egypt, Saudi Arabia, and Syria agreed to replace the British subsidy to Jordan. This arrangement soon broke down, and the King, aware that a Pan Arabist orientation meant the end of his monarchy, again turned to the West for support. Since then he has managed to maintain, with Western help, a precarious balance of delicately interrelated forces. The 1961 truce in Jordanian relations with the U.A.R. and Iraq did not reflect any permanent change in Jordan's relations with those states. King Hussein obviously hoped that the conservative coup in Syria and the separation of that country from Egypt would make possible a closer relationship between Jordan and Syria, opening an opportunity for him to play a role in Syrian affairs. But dominant political forces in Syria would not tolerate a close relationship with Hussein.

The Jordanian army, probably the best Arab army, man for man, is too small and too short on modern armor and aircraft to exercise a significant independent role in international affairs, though it is adequate for internal security and would give a good account of itself in any action in which it was not overwhelmed by numbers. It might conceivably turn the tide in certain circumstances of political upheaval in Syria or Iraq, but its use for such a purpose would almost certainly endanger King Hussein's position and that of Jordan itself.

IRAQ

Situated in the rich Tigris-Euphrates valley and bounded by deserts and mountains, Iraq is as distinct and separate geographically as Egypt and has many of the geopolitical characteristics of that country. Its size, wealth, and location on the other side of the Levant make it another focus of power in the Arab East. However, despite its geographic unity, Iraq is far from being a demographic unit. The dominant Sunni Muslim group is less numerous than the more backward and conservative Shi'ia community of the south. The Kurdish minority in the mountains to the north and east, though Muslim, is non-Arab and is less assimilated and less tractable than the Coptic minority in Egypt. Although not so much influenced as Lebanon by divisions among its people, Iraq is far from being a consolidated state.

It is tempting to think of Iraq, as the Western powers did before 1958, as Egypt's rival, the second of two poles around which Arab political power must revolve. On almost every basis of comparison, however, Iraq is still very much less powerful and influential. It has less than one-third Egypt's population; its economic and technical development is less advanced; and its experience in self-government as an independent state has been much shorter. Its press and its schools have only a local clientele. Iraq, however, has been the source of ideas and policies different from those generated in Egypt. The two countries face a different future. Egypt seems likely to decline in relative strength, while Iraq with its resources of unused land and of oil can hope for steady growth in strength and influence.

Iraq's rivers flow into the Persian Gulf and it has looked, traditionally, toward Persia and the east, as well as to the west and south. Under the Ottomans long years of isolation from the rest of the Arab world fostered differences between the conservative valley and desert people of Iraq and the Mediterranean-oriented traders of the Levant, and the Egyptians with their strong infusion of modern secular culture from the West. But since World War I, westernization and modernization have been at work in Iraq. A sense of community of interest with other Arab states has developed. Also, in Iraq as in Egypt, Syria, and Lebanon, a new elite of educated professionals, civil servants, teachers, army officers, and technicians has arisen. Political leadership in Iraq, however, as events after the revolution of 1958 have shown, is considerably less effective and less sophisticated, although in general its political problems are similar. The older opposition parties like the Istiqlal, which were based less on political principles than on loyalty to individual politicians, faded quickly. The quasi-socialist National Democratic party and the Iraqi Baath (affiliated with the Syrian Baath) proved to have more doctrinal purpose, better organization, and better leadership. The Communists, after years of harassment under the monarchy, with the aid of ample funds and cadres of trained personnel from outside the country, quickly developed a large and effective party with "front organizations" and a large following among the mobs of "the street," until familiarity with their methods and their unfulfilled promises brought disillusionment.

Probably the most important political development in Iraq has been the rise of an amorphous and unorganized but nevertheless widespread and influential Arab nationalist movement which has stood opposed to General Kassem's government but managed an uneasy truce with it. Most of the members of the parties noted above, except the Communists, have been involved. Its platform included Arab unity, in principle, and more or less explicit recognition of President Nasser's symbolic leadership. Arab nationalism is a powerful force drawing Iraq closer to the Arab community. The revolution, however, also stimulated the strong assertion of local patriotism and resistance to the surrender of Iraqi sovereignty to Nasser or anybody else. The prolonged public controversy between General Kassem and President Nasser reflects Iraq's ambiguous position. Powerfully attracted by Pan Arab ideology, Iraq, nevertheless, is a nation in its own right with important advantages which it is reluctant to sacrifice.

Iraq's geographic position, more than that of other Arab states, produces a complex relationship with the non-Arab world. Syria has a longer border with Turkey, but Iraq has both Turkey and Iran as neighbors, and, one hundred and fifty miles from its northeast border, the Soviet Union. The long-standing differences in Turkish and Arab views on relations with the great powers, and the propinquity of their Kurdish communities, focus attention on Iraq's border with Turkey. Concern with the long, rugged border with Iran is prompted by the movement of tribes back and forth across it, and by the danger of losing access to the Persian Gulf via the Shatt el Arab which Iran is in a position to close. Moreover, the large Arab population in southwest Iran makes the Shah nervous about Iraqi influence there. The Kassem regime has shown little concern over the proximity of the Soviet border and the likelihood that any Soviet overland thrust into the Middle East would pass over Iraq. Soviet penetration in Iran or Turkey, however, or attempts in that direction, would greatly concern any Iraqi government.

On Iraq's southern border, alongside its narrow access route to the Persian Gulf, is Kuwait, with its enormous oil wealth, small population, and weak defense force. Pressures are building up to effect some change which would make its wealth available for the much needed development of the area as a whole. Iraq naturally fears that Kuwait will come under the control or influence of Egypt, thus tipping the balance of power in inter-Arab affairs away from Iraq. General Kassem's claim to Kuwait, made at the time of the announcement of its independence in the spring of 1961, and the maneuvers which it set off, probably marked the first of many duels over the future of the oil-rich sheikhdom.

Although the desert interposes a barrier to trade and travel between centers of population in Iraq and those in Syria and Jordan, Iraqi interest naturally focuses on those two countries, its most likely allies in any conflict with Egypt. The "Fertile Crescent scheme" of uniting or federating those countries has been supported by various Iraqi statesmen from time to time. In the past, Syria and Jordan have veered back and forth between Iraq and Egypt, and are likely to do so again.

Iraq has definite economic strength in any future struggle for power within the Arab world. Its oil resources bring in an impressive annual revenue—estimated at $266 million in 1960—and its interest in maintaining the flow of oil across Syria and Lebanon through the Iraq Petroleum Company's pipeline provides significant ties with these two countries as well as a link with Western powers, especially with Great Britain.

Iraq's armed forces apparently are more effective than any other Arab force except the Egyptian, though they are probably still weakened by the dismissal of large numbers of experienced officers after the 1958 revolution and by political pressures upon all ranks.

Since 1958, arms deals and trade and economic assistance agreements with the Soviet bloc have introduced a new and important factor in Iraqi international relations. Iraq now depends upon the Soviet bloc for replacements, spare parts, and ammunition for the larger part of its military equipment. However, some old British equipment remains in use, and there have been small shipments of new equipment from the United Kingdom. This ambiguous situation probably reduces efficiency but it does give the Iraqi government a certain maneuverability. On the economic side the Iraqis, with their substantial oil sales to the West, retain a balanced position. Soviet and Communist penetration, well advanced during the Iraqi Communist party's heyday in 1959, has considerably receded in the face of governmental opposition, but still has a strong potential influence.

SAUDI ARABIA

The international position of Saudi Arabia is dominated by three factors: the location of the holiest places of Islam within its boundaries; remoteness, and social, economic, and political backwardness; and its great oil wealth.

International forces draw the Saudi monarchy in several different directions. Rivalry between the Saudi and the Hashemite dynasties, dating from their contest over the Arabian Peninsula following the First World War, has led to the frequent alignment of Saudi Arabia with Egypt. The middle-class revolutionary government in Egypt, however, has in recent years promoted unpalatable social and political changes, so that the relatively conservative policies of the rival Hashemites have been more acceptable. The Saudi rulers in principle have approved Nasser's moves toward Arab solidarity but have been frightened by his growing power. Saudi Arabia has adopted a friendly attitude toward the United States because of the economic interest it shares with the Arabian American Oil Company, which holds the principal concession for the development of the country's oil resources. It has, however, sought to avoid the stigma of pro-Westernism.

Under these varied influences Saudi foreign policy has swung in a wide arc. It has consistently supported the principle of Arab solidarity, particularly in opposition to Israel. In the crises of 1955–56 King Saud generally sided with President Nasser of Egypt, but after his visit to the United States in January 1957 he took a new line. Turning away from Nasser, he associated himself with the two Hashemite kings, Hussein of Jordan and Feisal of Iraq, and sought a greater role for himself as a leader of Arab policy. This phase came to an end in the spring of 1958 when his involvement in a plot aimed at Nasser was revealed. At that time, also, a crisis arose within the royal family over the administration of the country's finances. The King surrendered the actual exercise of power temporarily to his brother Feisal, who proceeded to follow a careful policy calculated not to affront Nasser and the Arab nationalists. King Saud resumed control in December 1960, but there have been a number of subsequent changes in their relative positions. In 1962, with the monarchy again under great pressure at home and threatened by a crisis in relations with the U.A.R. over Yemen, Feisal was again in charge.

Some members of the royal family, and a small elite of educated officials, technicians, army officers, and a growing group of businessmen are the likely leaders of movements toward modernization. Apparently, the King is already convinced of the importance of rational change and is aware of the dangers of refusing to recognize the demands that are building up among workers in the oil fields and in the embryonic middle class. The sticking point is the reallocation of royal revenues so as to give greater support to economic development and public services. If such changes are not made, explosive pressures may build up that, in time, will produce a radical revolution on the Egyptian or Iraqi model.

Modernization may well take a long time, longer than in other Arab countries because in Saudi Arabia the bulk of the population is nomadic. The oil industry has built up certain cities and increased the size of the business and professional communities. But the urban population for some time will constitute only a small fraction of the population; the remainder clings to its ancient tribal system and its loyalty to the throne.

In Saudi Arabia, alone among the Arab states, the army does not provide the ultimate sanction in politics. The nomadic tribes are armed and able to fight; the King could probably withstand even a military revolt if the tribal sheikhs remained loyal. It may have been for this reason that King Saud agreed early in 1961 to the request of some of the younger men of his court for some degree of modernization of the government and a representative legislative body. The King may anticipate that a free election will return a parliament of sheikhs who will consult with him as they always have, together with members of the new elite who will take satisfaction in having a government modern in form if not in reality. Feisal, under pressure of the crisis in Yemen and defections within the royal family itself, pledged that basic changes would be made.

In its oil policy the Saudi regime has maintained good relations with the Arabian American Oil Company. It has recognized and appreciated the company's attempts to assist the development of the country and to smooth the problems of modernization. The common attitude of Saudi Arabians was expressed by one citizen who said: "We know that you run the oil industry very well and that we can't do it, but you can't blame us for wanting to do it ourselves or for being unhappy about our inability to do it."

At the same time the regime has supported the ideas of Sheikh Abdullah Tariki, the country's leading oil expert, for revision of oil concession agreements so as to give greater authority and larger revenues to the government, and greater Arab representation in the higher executive and policy-making positions in the industry. He has become the spokesman for such reforms and an advocate of plans for cooperation among the Arab states on oil policy.

Firm in its anti-Israeli posture, and having one side of the Gulf of Aqaba on its shore line, Saudi Arabia has favored making the gulf an Arab waterway, excluding Israeli traffic. It can be expected to press this issue whenever opportunity offers. Its desert frontiers with Jordan, Syria, and Iraq have caused no incidents or policy problems of significance. The badly defined borders with the political entities that rim the Arabian Peninsula, on the other hand, have been and are continuing sources of dispute. Saudi Arabia has already fought and won a war with neighboring Yemen in the 1930s and found itself again involved in that country's affairs after the army revolt against the Imam in 1962. It has an unsettled dispute with the Sheikh of Abu Dhabi and the Sultan of Muscat (who are under British protection) over territory near the oasis of Buraimi in the eastern extremity of the peninsula where oil discoveries are believed likely. The resulting difficulties between Saudi Arabia and Great Britain have troubled the relations of the United States with both parties.

STATES AND TERRITORIES ON THE PERIPHERY OF THE ARABIAN PENINSULA

From Yemen at the southern end of the Red Sea around the coast of the Arabian Peninsula to Kuwait at the head of the Persian Gulf stretches a string of barren and undeveloped territories having only partially defined boundaries. The existence in some of them of tremendous oil reserves and the possibility that oil lies under the whole area focus attention on their future. The fact that, except for Yemen, all are under one form or another of British tutelage makes them a particular concern of the Pan Arab nationalist movement, which looks to their eventual "liberation."

Yemen, a highland region with a population roughly estimated at four and a half million is one of the most primitive areas of the Arab East. After several centuries of isolation it is only now coming into contact with the outside world. The late ruler, the Imam Ahmad, whose throne often had been shaken by turbulent internal forces, sought in 1958 to stabilize his position by joining his country with Nasser's U.A.R. in an association known as the United Arab States. He had also made agreements with the Soviet Union and Communist China for the purchase of modern arms and for assistance in internal development, and with the United States for economic and technical assistance on a smaller scale.

Yemen's strategic position at the southern gate to the Red Sea, its relatively large population and prospects for development, combined with its uncertain political organization and orientation, underline its potential importance. However, none of its adventures in foreign relations has borne any significant fruit. Association with the U.A.R. had little if any practical result, except briefly to identify the Imam with Nasser's Arab nationalism. In December 1961, as part of the readjustment of his position after the Syrian defection from the U.A.R., Nasser threw off the tie with Yemen, whose ruler he denounced as reactionary and out of sympathy within the Arab nationalist revolution. Ultimately, in 1962, a military coup in Yemen by army officers who looked to the Egyptian model deposed the new Imam, Ahmad's son, scarcely a week after his father's death. Abdel Nasser, taking advantage of the opportunity to extend his influence, soon sent Egyptian advisers and military forces to help the new republican regime establish itself in the face of royalist and tribal resistance supported from outside by Saudi Arabia and Jordan.

The most persistent activity of the state of Yemen in the field of foreign relations has been its claim to Britain's Aden Protectorate and Aden Colony, which it refers to as South Yemen. With the aid of the U.A.R. and other Arab states, in the United Nations and by various propaganda means, it has sought to make an international issue of this claim. It has occasionally been the cause of border disturbances.

The Pan Arab nationalist press and propaganda have drawn attention to Britain's Aden Colony, which has an important port and new oil refinery, and Aden Protectorate. Within the colony itself, which enjoys a higher level of economic welfare and social and political development than Yemen or neighboring Saudi Arabia, a growing movement favors independence and association with neighboring states. The influence of Pan Arab nationalism in the politically aware and articulate section of the Aden Arab population is significant and likely to increase.

The independent Sultanate of Muscat and Oman, which bends around the southeast corner of the peninsula, has a special relationship with Great Britain going back to the end of the eighteenth century; it was most recently renewed in a treaty of friendship, commerce, and navigation in 1951. There are British nationals in the government and British officers in the armed forces. In the eyes of the Pan Arab nationalists, and of the Saudi royal house, the Sultan is a puppet of the British.

Muscat and Oman's problems in foreign relations are two. The first arises from a dissident movement under a religious leader, the Imam in Oman, whose stronghold is the mountainous region of the Jebel Akhdar (Green Mountain) southwest of Muscat town. His cause has been taken up by the Pan Arab nationalists and is promoted by a representative in Cairo and by initiatives in the United Nations. The second problem, in which the British government has represented the Sultan, is the dispute with Saudi Arabia over the oasis of Buraimi.

The Trucial Coast, or Trucial Oman, is a group of seven sheikhdoms lining the shore from the entrance of the Persian Gulf to the Peninsula of Qatar. They are joined in treaty relationships with Great Britain and a British Political Agent directs their foreign relations. The seven sheikhs meet in the Trucial Council and contribute men to an armed force, the senior officers of which are seconded from the British army. Having few resources or wealth of its own, the Trucial Coast supplies laborers for the oil fields of other Gulf states.

Qatar, a sheikhdom occupying a peninsula halfway up the Persian Gulf, has a population of about 25,000. Its oil, which in 1960 produced revenues of $65 million, is its only claim to international significance.

The sheikhdom of Bahrain, occupying an archipelago in the Persian Gulf off the coast of Saudi Arabia, is independent, but a treaty gives the British Political Resident responsibility for the conduct of foreign relations. Bahrain's oil revenue is modest compared with that of Kuwait or even Qatar—$16 million in 1960. But its function as a trading center for the Gulf, its great oil refinery, and the importance of its port and airfield have made it one of the most advanced areas, socially and economically, in the region. As a consequence, pressures are building up for more popular participation in government, and for freeing foreign policy from British domination, in line with the Pan Arab position.

The sheikhdom of Kuwait, the most important of them all, occupies an almost featureless stretch of sand at the northwest corner of the Persian Gulf. Its one resource, oil, provided revenues for the Sheikh in 1960 of more than $415 million. Like Bahrain, Kuwait had a British Political Resident who gave advice on foreign affairs. The startling speed with which Kuwait changed from a sleepy Persian Gulf port to a booming oil center has not left much time for the emergence of political groups. Now criticism is heard of the Sheikh's family's oligarchic rule, and organizers from outside are finding some response among members of the labor force. The ruling family has sought to follow a middle course in Arab politics, announcing its support for all the resounding generalizations of Arab nationalist policies in the Arab League, but avoiding any involvement that might interfere with present business and political arrangements. Most of the great wealth of the Sheikh of Kuwait is invested in Great Britain, and very little in the capital-hungry Arab world. Ownership of the Kuwait Oil Company is half British, half American.

In 1961 Kuwait declared its independence with British approval and sought to take its place in the world community as a sovereign state. It endeavored to exchange diplomatic missions with a few countries, and to assume membership in the Arab League and in the United Nations. Prime Minister Kassem of Iraq responded by declaring that Kuwait was a part of Iraq, which had been separated from his country by the British and maintained by them as a separate entity because of their interest in its oil reserves. Without making his intentions precise, Kassem indicated that in one way or another he expected to annex Kuwait. The resulting crisis produced the extraordinary phenomenon of British cooperation with Arab states, including the U.A.R., to give Kuwait military protection against Iraqi aggression. With Iraq abstaining, the Arab League voted Kuwait into membership, and urged that its defense be left to the League. The British, and later the U.A.R., withdrew their forces, but Saudi and Jordanian troops stayed on. When toward the end of the year new gestures by Prime Minister Kassem brought British ships boiling up the Gulf, Iraq made no move, but Kassem reiterated that Kuwait would ultimately become part of Iraq.

The Kuwait crises of 1961 revealed the complex of forces that impinge on Kuwait's future. The British interest is clear enough. From the point of view of Nasser, Saud, and Hussein, Kuwait represents the largest single concentration of what the Arab nationalists like to call Arab oil—though today it is the Sheikh of Kuwait's oil. Neighboring states look forward either to getting their own hands on that oil or to seeing it become the property of an association of Arab states. The vast resources represented by the oil of Kuwait would give an important boost to a union of Arab states. No ambitious ruler would like to see his rival become its proprietor. Thus, on future scrambles for Kuwait's vast treasures may hang the prospects for successful Arab unity.

The Sheikh of Kuwait has been advised that he must devote some of his wealth to the welfare of all the Arab people if he is to avoid being overwhelmed by his greedy neighbors and fellow Arabs. In 1961 a beginning was made when a loan fund was set up with capital of $140 million. But the outlook is that the hungry wolves around Kuwait will become ever hungrier.

SUDAN

The Sudan, though a member of the Arab League, is only partly Arab. The northern two-thirds of the country is inhabited by Arabic-speaking Muslims. The southern third is peopled by Nilotic negroes who are not Muslims and do not speak Arabic. The Sudan's connection with Egypt goes back for centuries, but it is too deeply embedded in Africa and too conscious of its borders with Ethiopia, Uganda, and the Congo to think or act solely as an Arab state. Independence was inspired and stimulated by the Arab nationalist movement and by Egyptian efforts to substitute union with Egypt for British control. But the Sudan has made clear its determination, first, to remain independent and, second, to serve its African as well as its Arab interests.

The Sudan is not one of the angry new nations. Having won independence without prolonged struggle, the Sudanese feel no bitterness against the British, who left them a small but competent cadre of administrators and officials. Characteristic of the Sudan's relations with Britain was the gesture made when it was decided to remove General Gordon's statue from its prominent position in Khartoum. Instead of pulling the statue down, as happened to De Lesseps' statue in Port Said and General Maud's statue in Baghdad, the figure of Gordon was removed after appropriate ceremonies of honor and sent as a gift to Great Britain. The Sudan's international position is based on membership in the Arab League and the Afro-Asian group of nations and on a policy of nonalignment in the cold war. But it has played a middle role as between the "positive neutralists" and the West, and it has carefully avoided identification with blocs within the Arab League or the Afro-Asian group.

The Sudan's economy is principally agricultural and much of it for a long time is likely to be on a very primitive level. Cotton makes up more than half of its exports, and its economic well-being, like Egypt's, is largely dependent upon the world market for that staple.

LIBYA

Libya occupies a vast area between Egypt and Tunisia in the Maghreb. Its arable land, only 8 per cent of the total, produces a sparse living for about a million people. Having been an Italian colony, it received its independence after the Second World War. The three provinces which make up the federal state are not integrated economically or politically. The new state, restrained by its limited resources and low level of social and political development, has been occupied largely with domestic rather than foreign policy.

Libya is a member of the Arab League and has followed an "Arab policy." In the United Nations it has generally voted with the other Arab states and with the Afro-Asian group on questions on which these groups have taken a united stand. Occasionally, however, the Libyan government has shown concern over pressures and influences emanating from Egypt, its powerful eastern neighbor.

Libya's most important connections outside the Arab world have been with Britain and the United States. Britain, in return for military base rights, has provided substantial subsidies to the Libyan treasury; the United States has maintained an important airfield near Tripoli for which it has contributed about a million dollars a year. The Libyans have persistently urged increases in both subsidies, but in spite of Arab neutralist condemnation of foreign military bases they have not sought to force the Americans or the British to abandon their installations.

The discovery of oil in substantial quantities in 1958–59 has opened up new possibilities for Libya as well as for the pattern of the international oil industry. Development is proceeding rapidly, despite a world surplus of oil, because of the attractiveness to the European market of oil supplies located west of the Suez Canal. Prospects are for the emergence of Libya as a larger Kuwait. Libya's relations with its oil-poor Egyptian neighbor are full of interesting possibilities for the future.

THE ARAB LEAGUE

The Arab League is a symbol of unity, an alliance of states joined together in deference to the widespread yearning for unity among the Arab people. Having no authority of its own, its decisions bind only the states supporting them. Independence from interference in internal affairs is carefully protected in the Pact of the League, the authoritative definition of its purposes, structure, and power.[1] Arab leaders steadfastly report that their dealings within the League are always harmonious and profitable,

[1] Fayez A. Sayegh, *Arab Unity: Hope and Fulfillment* (New York: Devin-Adair, 1958), pp. 121–125.

although it is clear to the casual observer that separate national interests often dominate its affairs. Thus the League reflects the dynamics of the Arab world: a powerful, emotional commitment to unity which demands recognition but which only partially conceals the bitter political realities of clashing local interests and doctrine. As Tom Little has put it ". . . the tensions and conflicts among the Arab states were brought to the surface within the League and seemed greater by contrast with the ideals which the League was intended to achieve."[2]

The League came into being in 1945, after years of Pan Arab conferences and discussion of a formalization of the idea of the Arab community. Its establishment was influenced by the approaching independence of Syria and Lebanon and the willingness of the British government to support the idea of unity. The occasion was, however, typical not so much of the drive to unity as of the interest of individual states in turning that drive to their own advantage. The initiative came from Nuri el Said of Iraq who in 1942 set down recommendations for a Greater Syria to be united with Iraq in a league which might involve "sacrifices of sovereignty and vested interests."[3] This proposal aroused opposition in Egypt, which feared the extension of Iraqi influence through its domination of the Fertile Crescent area and the consequent diminishing of its own, and in Saudi Arabia which reacted against a scheme which would improve the position of its Hashemite rival. The Egyptian and Saudi opponents of Nuri's plan could not, however, reject the idea of a step toward the greater unity of the independent Arab states. The Egyptian Prime Minister, Mustapha Nahas Pasha, conferred with representatives of the other Arab states and of Arab Palestine and was host to a meeting in Alexandria in September and October 1944 at which a protocol was adopted which provided for the coordination of the policies of the Arab states toward the outside world and "envisaged a progressively increasing surrender of sovereignty" by those states to the common organization.[4] Between the time of the acceptance of the Alexandria Proto-

[2] Thomas Russell Little, "The Arab League: A Reassessment," *Middle East Journal,* Spring 1956, p. 138.

[3] Cecil A. Hourani, "The Arab League in Perspective," *Middle East Journal,* April 1947, p. 128.

[4] Same, pp. 132–133.

col, however, and March 1945 when the Pact on which the Arab League is based was worked out, a growing concern for the interests of the individual states became manifest. The result was that the Pact of the Arab League provided for the protection of the sovereignty of the individual states. The history of the League has reflected this emphasis and the League has been a disappointment to those Pan Arabists who hoped that it might evolve into a responsible and authoritative instrument of Arab unity.

In the Pact Egypt obtained insurance against Iraqi aspirations for Fertile Crescent unity and the dominant position in the League machinery for itself. The first Secretary-General of the League, Abdel Rahman Azzam Pasha, an Egyptian, energetically and skillfully opposed the interest of the Hashemite kingdoms of Iraq and Jordan in a closer union of the Arab states of the Fertile Crescent area. Through much of the League's history the conflict between the Hashemite interest on one side and the Egyptian-Saudi interest on the other dominated its affairs. The two great crises within the League were occasioned by the Palestine War and by Iraq's signing of the Baghdad Pact in 1955. The latter crisis was prolonged in a new form during the 1959–60 controversy between Nasser of Egypt and Kassem of Iraq. The extension of the League to include Morocco and Tunisia has not increased the inner harmony of the organization; President Bourguiba of Tunisia withdrew from League activities for a period in protest against interference in his domestic affairs by Egypt. The addition of Algeria will introduce a new force and a likely rival of Egypt for leadership.

Persistent disputes on questions of inter-Arab and external policy, and the League's complete failure to make any progress in limiting the authority of its members, have not prevented extensive activity in other fields. The League has served as the center for direction of the boycott of Israel; it has organized and directed cooperation among Arab states in social, economic, and cultural affairs, and in public health. More significant activities in these fields are in prospect and also progress toward a common market, which might eventually contribute more than all the League's political activities to make Arab unity a practical matter.

VI

LESSONS OF THE PAST

The Arabs today are an angry and resentful people. Their view of their present situation, and how they came to be in it, colors their thinking and influences their behavior toward the rest of the world. Their interpretation of history explains their fierce resentments, their deep suspicions, and their conviction that now they must take charge of their own destiny.

The Arabs' vision of their proper place in the world lies deep in the religion of Islam. History to the Muslim is the unfolding of the will of Allah.[1] The first centuries of Muslim history seemed to demonstrate in fullest measure that Islam was the only true religion. Coming onto the world stage with virtually nothing except their religion, the Arabs with breath-taking speed won rich, far-stretching lands, great wealth and power over non-Arab peoples, many of whom sought eagerly to be accepted into the Islamic fold.

Islam became a self-contained world, the Dar el Islam or the "abode of Islam," while non-Muslim territory was the Dar el Harb or "abode of war" in which the infidels lived.[2] Despite internal conflicts and bloody struggles for power, the Muslims retained, through centuries of warfare with Christians on the European continent and during the Christian invasions of Muslim lands (the

[1] See Wilfred Cantwell Smith, *Islam in Modern History* (New York: Mentor Books, 1959), Chapter 1, "Introduction: Islam and History."

[2] Ezzeldin Foda, *The Projected Arab Court of Justice: A Study in Regional Jurisdiction with Specific Reference to the Muslim Law of Nations* (The Hague: Nijhoff, 1957), Chapter 4.

Crusades), their sense of being part of a self-contained and generally victorious world, and guardians of the only true faith.

The Mongol invasions of the thirteenth century brought disaster to all of northern Islam down as far as Syria, but after the Mongols withdrew the area, though in deep decline, was Muslim. In the fifteenth century, the eastern Arabs were swept into the Ottoman realm, but the Ottoman Turks had become Muslim themselves and the empire over which they ruled was Islamic. Long accustomed and conditioned by their religion to submit to whoever held power, the Arabs accepted the Ottomans as rulers, welcoming their victories as new evidence of the conquering power of Islam and the truth of the revelations of Allah through his prophet Mohammed.

In the Ottoman Empire, the Arabs were not a humiliated, subject people. As Muslims of older lineage than the Turks, they felt that they belonged by right. Their great men participated in the councils of the Sublime Porte and held posts of influence and responsibility. In language, culture, and religion they were the teachers of the Turks. They enjoyed economic security, although their lives were bounded by a closed system in which change was shunned and improvement difficult. Thus the Arabs, through most of the modern period, lived in a state of stagnation, bogged down in their own traditions. The Turks provided not only military protection but also security from the invasion of foreign influences.

In the eighteenth and nineteenth centuries, the Turks felt the impact of the aggressive and expansive West, but most of the Arabs maintained their sheltered innocence of the world. While the Turks played the desperate game of international politics that kept the Ottoman Empire going and attempted internal reforms that would enable them better to fend off the jealous Europeans, few Arabs were stirred by the changes taking place at home and abroad. For, they believed, Islam was invincible; the infidel would soon be punished by Allah for his impertinence.

Gradually, however, evidence accumulated that Islam was not all-conquering. Napoleon's defeat of the Mamelukes was too fleeting, too quickly wiped out by Muhammad Ali's successes, to undermine the Egyptians' or the northern Arabs' sense of self-esteem or to demonstrate convincingly the military weakness of

Islam. They recognized, however, the superiority of the weapons, the techniques, and the organization which Napoleon's forces brought to Egypt, although the success of a Muslim—Muhammad Ali—in imitating them made an equally strong impression. But Muhammad Ali's plans collapsed under pressure from the European powers and meanwhile the Arabs of Syria, Iraq, and the Arabian Peninsula, still wrapped in their Ottoman provinciality, were oblivious of the new forces which were soon to challenge the foundations of their world.

The tide of Westernism began to flow first into Egypt where Muhammad Ali had laid the foundations for trade and investment; later it was sucked in by demand for cotton set off by the American Civil War, and by the Suez Canal project. Syria, where the Christian minorities in Lebanon and Palestine attracted Western interest both for religious and economic reasons, came next.

The French occupation of Algeria in the 1830s had little significance in the Arab East, except for the most sophisticated. British intervention in Egypt in 1882 and the establishment of effective British paramountcy there took place in an atmosphere of increasing westernization and exploitation of Egyptian weaknesses. Articulate and well-informed Egyptians saw that the British, in crushing what local opposition they met, had defeated a movement quite different from Muhammad Ali's drive to set up a personal empire; it was in fact the first Egyptian or Arab revolution directed against foreign domination and discrimination (in this case Turkish discrimination against army officers of Egyptian origin) and against a corrupt Egyptian administration. But the full impact of the challenge of the West to Arab Islam had not yet been felt.

The impact of the West, however, had started a debate among Arab and other Muslim intellectuals which still continues. In the last decades of the nineteenth century Islamic revivalists contended that some modernization was needed to strengthen Islam and fit it to meet the new challenges from the West; they were opposed by traditionalists who argued for adherence to the established canons of Islam.

Within the Ottoman Empire the Arabs began in the last decades of the nineteenth century to respond slowly to the impact of the

West in the political as well as the intellectual sphere, but this response remained largely in Pan Islamic terms until the end of the First World War. They looked to cooperation with the Turks to bring about a revival of Islam and the presentation of a stronger front to Western incursions.

WORLD WAR I AND AFTER

The First World War produced the shock and the turn of events that gave Arab nationalism its present direction. Great numbers of Arabs for the first time came into contact with Westerners and became aware of the Western states as great powers. The war emphasized in the minds of thoughtful Arabs the Machiavellian characteristics of Western power politics: ruthless preoccupation with military force, readiness to promise anything to further a Western cause, combined with determination to protect and advance Western interests exclusively.

The breakup of the Islamic empire presided over by the Turks opened the door to Arab nationalism as a political force. The Young Turks in the years immediately preceding World War I, in their concentration on making their country strong, had already made an end to Pan Islamic cooperation with Arabs. Between the end of the First World War and the creation of Israel in 1948 these rejected people developed the sense of being buffeted by history, of being at the mercy of non-Islamic nations much more powerful than they.

The First World War was a shattering experience for politically conscious Arabs and in its aftermath left impressions of Western policy and behavior toward the Arabs which have influenced Arab thinking profoundly. Arabs had looked for a long time to the Turks for leadership and it was against many contrary influences that the British and Sherif Hussein of Mecca were able to gain support for the Arab revolt against the Turks. The appeal of the revolt lay in the promise it gave of Arab independence. At this point the Arabs were willing, by and large, to trust the pledged word of the British that it was their intention to create an Arab kingdom in the larger part of the Arab territory to be wrested from the Turks. That the war ended with Arab lands divided into British and French spheres of influence under League of Nations mandate and with a British pledge on record to support the establishment of a "Jewish national home" in Palestine seemed to most Arabs to provide clear and incontrovertible proof of British, indeed of Western, perfidy. The fact that the secret agreement in which the British and French representatives, Sykes and Picot, divided the Arab East between their two countries was not incompatible technically with the understanding between the British and the Sherif Hussein has been incomprehensible to most Arabs.[3] The Balfour Declaration seemed perfidious, and the point that Sherif Hussein and his son Feisal had shown themselves willing to consider an understanding with the Jews has changed very few Arabs' belief that the declaration was in violation of previous agreements with the Arabs and demonstrated the willingness of the British to further their own cause by offering anything to anybody.

Probably the most significant thing about the First World War in Arab eyes, after the fact that it demonstrated the untrustworthiness of the British and French, was that it brought an end to the Ottoman Empire and thus enabled the Arabs to seek to work out their destiny in the several national states created by the peace treaties. To a growing number who called themselves Arab nationalists, however, they were not free to do so. To those the period 1918–45 became one of constant struggle against the many forms of Western domination. They learned that the signing of treaties and the promulgation of constitutions announcing independence did not necessarily bring the reality of independence. They were basically out of sympathy with the Arab political leaders of this period who had their roots in the nineteenth century, had been trained in the liberal traditions of Europe, and had passed the scrutiny of representatives of the Western powers before they took their offices. However passionately nationalist, those leaders were members of a conservative upper class, and for the most part did not believe in social and political change.

To the new breed of radical nationalists—the middle-class members of the intelligentsia, the professional men, army officers, journalists and students, and the growing group of literate but un-

[3] Elie Kedourie, *England and the Middle East: The Destruction of the Ottoman Empire, 1914–1921* (London: Bowes, 1956), pp. 36–38 and 65–66.

educated urban lower middle class and proletariat—the interwar period brought repeated disappointment, lessons bitterly learned, and heightened awareness of the forces arrayed against them. They came to recognize that revolutionary changes must take place within the Arab world, and in its relations with the Western powers, before real independence could be achieved.

Egyptian independence was proclaimed unilaterally in 1922 by the British, who had come to realize that the nationalist movement could no longer be controlled. The British, however, reserved authority to maintain security of communications, provide for defense, protect foreign interests in the country, and handle Sudan affairs. Thus, though a step forward had been taken, Egypt was far from being a free country, particularly in the all-important area of its foreign relations. A constitution, promulgated by the King in 1923, provided for an elected parliament and freedom for political party activity. Immediately demands arose for revision of the unilateral declaration of independence. Such forward motion as had been achieved in British-Egyptian relations was reversed, however, in 1924 when Sir Lee Stack, Sirdar of the Egyptian army and Governor-General of the Sudan, was murdered in Cairo. The British responded with an extremely tough ultimatum, which re-established Britain's hold on Egypt.

After 1924 the Egyptian scene was dominated by the interplay of three forces: the King, the British, and the Wafd, which was the nationalist party that commanded the support of the great majority of the politically interested populace. After long negotiations for the revision of the unilateral proclamation of independence of 1922, a compromise was effected in the treaty of 1936. It left a British force of ten thousand men and four hundred aircraft pilots in the Suez Canal Zone and gave the British Ambassador, replacing the former High Commissioner, permanent seniority rights.

In the Second World War, Egyptian nationalists—i.e., practically every Egyptian with an interest in politics—were more concerned with opportunities to complete Egyptian independence than with the course or the outcome of the war. For many Egyptian nationalists the most significant moment came in 1942 when the British Ambassador, Sir Miles Lampson, under the guns of British tanks with which he had surrounded Abdine Palace, forced the

King to choose between abdication and the appointment of the Wafd leader, Nahas Pasha, to the prime minister's office in place of Ali Maher, who refused to declare war on Italy. Near the end of the war when another Prime Minister, Ahmad Maher Pasha, appeared to read in public the royal decree declaring war on the Axis powers, he was assassinated by a nationalist student. The issues were terribly confused, but to a great many Egyptians the experience of the war added emphasis to the conclusion that Egypt was not free and that the British were still using their position in the country almost exclusively for the furtherance of their own ends.

At the end of the First World War, politically conscious Syrians looked forward to independence. When in 1918 Feisal, son of Hussein of Mecca, led a small Arab force, the spearhead of the Sherifian army, into Damascus, the local dignitaries were ready to receive them. Most Syrians accepted Feisal as representative of the Arab revolt which the British government and the exploits of Lawrence of Arabia had publicized as the means by which the Arabs would assume independent control over most Arab territory formerly under Ottoman suzerainty. The Syrians were primarily interested in independence, but rumors of French claims made Feisal and his Arabs from the Hejaz look much more attractive than they otherwise could have. The expulsion of Feisal by the French was generally regarded by the Syrians as a betrayal of the Western allies' promises to support self-determination and Arab independence. French mandatory rule in Syria was marked by a readiness to use force to secure order, as in the bombardment of Damascus and the capture of Suweida in 1926.

Prolonged maneuvers and negotiations between nationalist political groups and the French authorities finally resulted in 1936 in treaties between France and Syria and France and Lebanon providing for independence and membership in the League of Nations for those two states. The treaties, however, like those the British concluded with Iraq in 1930 and with Egypt in 1936, reserved important matters to French authority severely restricting the independence which the Syrians were to receive. France then failed to ratify its treaties, and at the outbreak of the Second World War the French military took over in Syria. This refusal to grant long-anticipated independence, plus France's cession to Turkey of Alexandretta, which the Syrians expected to incorporate in their country, brought Syria into the war period with few reasons for loyalty to the Allies.

Maneuvers and disputes over Syrian and Lebanese independence continued during the war. In June 1941 British troops took over the area from Vichy French forces. The Free French government proclaimed the independence of the two states, but failed to transfer governing power to them. A British ultimatum to General de Gaulle in May 1945 finally brought about transfer and recognition of sovereignty, but by this time Syrians and Lebanese were in no mood to feel gratitude. With little experience in government and much resentment at the way their independence had been granted, they entered upon the difficult task of making their new states work.

Iraq's experience in the interwar period was somewhat happier than that of Egypt or Syria but it, too, emerged from the Second World War resentful of the demonstrated power of the West, and particularly of the British, to influence the course of events in the Arab world. Yet Iraq, one of the most backward and remote provinces of the Ottoman Empire at the end of the First World War, had made long strides in political and economic development under the British mandate and British guidance during early years of independence.

Feisal, after his unfortunate experience in Damascus, was, in effect, placed on the throne of Iraq by the British, who by virtue of the League of Nations' mandate exercised predominant authority in military, fiscal, and political affairs. The British Ambassador enjoyed a special position in Baghdad, with access to the highest councils of the Iraqi government. He enjoyed close and cordial relations with the monarchy, which functioned as a benevolent despotism, and with the upper class of landowners and tribal chieftains. Growing manifestations of a popular, nationalist demand for more freedom resulted in 1930 in a new treaty which provided for Iraq's independence and entry in 1932 into the League of Nations. Britain was granted rights to military bases and permanent seniority for its ambassadors, and the right to be consulted in all foreign-policy matters of mutual interest. Although nationalist feeling increased, Great Britain retained an influential position. During the war the British overthrew the Rashid Ali group, which having gained control of the country by a military coup had associated itself with the Axis. This sharp reaction called attention to Britain's continued ability and willingness to intervene in Iraqi affairs when its own interests required.

After the war Iraq, like all the Arab countries, had its nationalist groups which pressed for a greater separation of the country's policies from those of the West, but the only outstanding unresolved problems that gave leverage to the nationalists' efforts were the treaty of 1930 and the British bases, and these did not pose a serious problem for the conservative ruling group around the monarchy.

In the less developed areas of the Arab East the years between the wars saw a steady increase in awareness and expectation, a steady movement toward closer contact with the outside world. The development of a flourishing oil industry in Saudi Arabia and in Kuwait and Bahrain produced great changes, and the prospect was for still greater ones in countries where conditions of life had altered very little for hundreds of years. In the Sudan, economic change proceeded slowly with the development of the Gezira cotton scheme. With British guidance its people moved slowly and uneventfully toward the day when they too would become independent and involved in the affairs of the world. Libya felt the impact of Italy's colonial effort but took few steps toward independence.

For the most part the more remote and less developed areas of the Arab East enjoyed the luxury of having very little history or even a sense of history, but the revolution of awareness was beginning with the growth of contacts, first with the Arab world and then the world beyond. Culture and religion had for centuries made them a part of the Arab world of tradition, but the radio, motor truck, and airplane brought them in the interwar years into the world of Arab nationalism.

SINCE WORLD WAR II

The Second World War saw a revival of British interest in an Arab policy which would appeal to the Arab world as a whole, for the simple reason that old methods had ceased to work. The British were also worried by the lack of sentiment among Arabs in favor of the Allied cause and the strength of sympathy for the Axis. Relieved by the circumstances of the war from the necessity of making concessions to French claims in the Levant, and from Zionist pressures, the British helped Syria and Lebanon to gain their independence, clamped down on Jewish immigration into Palestine, and supported an Iraqi plan for the association of the northern Arab states in a Fertile Crescent Union. Egyptian, Syrian-Lebanese, and Saudi opposition having blocked this scheme, the way was open for Nahas Pasha of Egypt to take the initiative in organizing in 1945 the League of Arab States. In the League the development of *state* nationalism, the most prominent feature of the interwar period, seemed to have been confirmed and institutionalized.

In Palestine, however, affairs were moving toward an event which for politically conscious Arabs was to be the single most significant development in modern history. For the postwar generation it colors the interpretation of the whole span of the Arab historical experience. In the spring of 1947, after a long and perplexing struggle to control Jewish immigration into Palestine, the British announced their intention of abandoning the mandate. The United Nations then voted by a bare two-thirds majority to recommend partition of the territory between Jewish and Arab states, but no arrangements could be agreed upon to put that resolution into effect before the British withdrew in May 1948. In the months that followed, the Arab states attacked the newly proclaimed state of Israel, but the Jews of Palestine, strengthened by an influx of money and arms and by political and diplomatic assistance from the world-wide Zionist organization, fought the combined armies of Egypt, Syria, Lebanon, Jordan, Iraq, and Saudi Arabia to a standstill and established themselves in a part of the territory of the Palestine Mandate considerably larger than had been allotted to them by the United Nations resolution.

Zionist plans for the establishment of a state in Palestine had been public knowledge since Theodor Herzl proposed them in 1894. The Balfour Declaration of 1917 in which the British government had announced its approval of the projected Jewish "national home" in Palestine had alerted the Arabs to the political skill and influence of the Zionists. During the thirties, the Zionists had amply demonstrated their determination and given evidence of their resources by sponsoring a flow of Jewish immigrants into Palestine and by their systematic purchase and development of land. The Arabs, however, preoccupied with national independence and development, and hoping against hope that some turn of events would foil the Zionist efforts, took no effective steps to prepare against the possible occupation of Palestinian territory by a Jewish armed force. An Arab revolt in Palestine, in 1936–39, was put down by the British. When the real test came after the war, the Arab states proved unable to coordinate either their political or military efforts. Faced with a determined enemy, their forces were divided by rivalries, weakened by poor leadership, and hamstrung by inadequate logistic support.

Defeat in the Palestine War profoundly shocked the Arabs in mind and soul. Impressions of the catastrophe burned themselves into the Arabs' memory. The first reaction was humiliation. The war came just as they were awakening to the importance of their association in the Arab community and to a new sense of national pride. The nationalist spirit had touched the majority of the politically aware who in the first fire of enthusiasm believed what they wanted to believe about the waxing strength of the Arabs. Their ignominious defeat contrasted brutally with their traditional conception of Arab Islam as a superior community, a people favored of God. The outcome of the war in Palestine magnified all the conflicts in the Arab personality, all of its sharpest tensions, its gnawing fears and uncertainties.

The Arabs' second reaction was to seek the causes of the disaster. Some pointed to Arab weaknesses and counseled reforms within their own house.[4] But most sought external causes. That the Jews by their own strength could have won was unthinkable for people in a state of shock; also, it was not entirely factual. Behind the Jews in Palestine was the world Zionist organization, drawing upon the resources of the Jews of America, of Britain, and of the

---

[4] Constantine K. Zurayk, *The Meaning of the Disaster,* tr. by R. Bayly Winder (Beirut: Khayat's, 1956), and Musa Alami "The Lesson of Palestine," *Middle East Journal,* October 1949, pp. 373–405.

rest of Europe, and upon the diplomatic influence and support of the United States. To most Arabs it seemed that the Palestine disaster demonstrated the West's rejection of their cause and its decision to make possible the establishment by force of a colony in the midst of the Arab lands.

Whatever may be the true historical significance of the Palestine War and the establishment of Israel, these events furnish the lens through which the present generation of Arabs view the events of the past.

THE LESSONS OF HISTORY

The Arab historical experience is tremendously important in the thinking of Arab nationalists. Like most people strongly influenced by patriotic motives and conscious of a national crisis requiring great effort, their approach to the record of the past is strongly tinged with apologetics, which Wilfred Cantwell Smith defines as "the ideological expression of the reaction against attack. With Arabism and Islam both threatened," he says, "its aim is to prove that they are both Good Things. It is the attempt to develop a system of ideas that will serve as protection against insecurity."[5] Another distinguished specialist in Muslim affairs, G. E. von Grunebaum, says, "It cannot be overemphasized that whatever the modern Near Easterner has to say about his own background and about the West is primarily a political judgement. His presentation is meant to influence rather than to describe."[6] The Arab's subjective attitude toward the events of the past may disqualify him as an historian but, in international affairs, his conception of his historical experience may prove more important than the historical experience itself.

Professor Morroe Berger has written that whereas Western historians and Orientalists seek understanding of the present-day Arab in a study of his past, Muslim and Arab students "are more apt to stress the break with the past."[7] Actually the modern Arab's

[5] Smith, cited, p. 119.

[6] G. E. von Grunebaum, *Islam: Essays in the Nature and Growth of a Cultural Tradition* (London: Routledge and Kegan Paul, 1955), p. 186.

[7] Morroe Berger, "Social and Political Change in the Moslem-Arab World," *World Politics*, July 1958, p. 636.

attitude toward his own history is ambivalent. He searches the past for evidences of Arab greatness and of the crimes committed against the Arabs which explain their present low estate. In the next breath, however, he emphasizes his commitment to a hard-headed, progressive, secular pragmatism which will enable the Arabs to throw off the burdens of traditionalism. Nasser himself, whose most important speeches are often mainly accounts of the disasters that have befallen the Arabs and the glorious victories achieved by Arab nationalism through the ages, occasionally warns his people that too much dwelling on Egypt's past tends to draw their attention away from the problems of the present.

In attempting to set down what the lessons of history are for modern Arabs, one encounters the same problems and risks as in generalizing about Arab awareness of the outside world, Arab attitudes toward the West, and Arab nationalism itself. Strong elements of difference and dissent must be recognized. Yet, there is a striking degree of uniformity in the thinking of Arabs about their history. Many politically conscious Arabs in both conserva-tive and radical circles agree on the concepts which follow:

The Long History of Arab Unity

A staple of Arab oratory, propaganda, and political writing is the idea of the unity of the Arabs from the earliest days of the Arab conquest and their acceptance of a common purpose, a kind of historic Arab nationalism. According to this reading of history, unity is the natural state of the Arabs whereas disunity came with misfortune and defeat; their future depends upon the restoration of their natural unity.

The Struggle with the West

Arabs are keenly aware that difficulties with the West did not start with nineteenth-century colonialism. They refer frequently to the prolonged struggle between Christianity and Islam for control of the Mediterranean, and to the great Christian-Muslim conflicts at the time of the Crusades in Palestine, and in Spain and the Balkans. Of particular interest is the comparison between the Crusader kingdoms and Israel. Few Arabs today recognize the active cul-tural exchanges in the past between the Arab world and the West or their significant cultural compatibility, which contrasts with the wide gap that separates both from the culture of the Far East. On the contrary, the present-day account of the history of Arab relations with the West emphasizes conflict and misunderstanding. The claim is made that the West has penetrated and perverted Arab culture.

The Competition of the Western Powers over the Middle East

Soviet-Western rivalry in the Middle East, so important in the Arab nationalists' current analysis of their position in world politics, is no new phenomenon to an Arab who recalls British-French conflicts over Muhammad Ali and the Ottoman Empire, and their rivalries in the Middle East in the late nineteenth century and through the period of the two world wars. Farther back in the past are the long conflicts between Great Britain and Russia in the eighteenth and nineteenth centuries and between France and the Hapsburgs in the sixteenth and seventeenth. The lessons drawn from these events are that the Middle East has a fascination for the Western powers, but that although they sometimes join forces they are usually involved in bitter rivalries. This fact Arabs agree should not be overlooked in planning their strategy.

The Machiavellian Character of Western Powers

The ability to make use of available resources for the furtherance of one's own interests is a quality which human beings are prone to admire in themselves and deplore in others. Arabs have been more impressed by the Western powers' use of military and economic power to acquire and defend interests in the Middle East than by the missionary and educational efforts which contributed substantially to the Arab awakening. The fact that the West has always been very much the dominant partner in enterprises in which Western and Arab states have been involved has provided the basis for the common assumption that the West regards Arabs as people to be used, not dealt with on equal terms. The capitulatory regimes that exempted Westerners from local law, their exploitation of trading opportunities in Arab lands where military and political authority of Western countries gave their nationals special protection and opportunities, the carving up of the Arab lands and their division between Britain and France at the end of the First World War—these and many other experiences have taught Arabs that the behavior of the Western powers in the Arab world is guided by considerations of Western interest and not by Arab rights or claims.

The Untrustworthiness of Western Promises

The Arab reading of history since the First World War strongly emphasizes the emptiness of Western promises. The standard Arab version begins with British promises to the Sherif Hussein of an Arab kingdom in return for his revolt against the Ottoman Turks, and the contradiction of this agreement in the Balfour Declaration approving the establishment of a Jewish national home in Palestine and the division between Britain and France of the newly freed Arab area. It also includes President Wilson's proclamation of the principle of self-determination and the visit of the American King-Crane Commission to the Levant to determine the political desires of its people, all of which was followed by American withdrawal from responsibility for the peace settlement.

The Second World War, in Arab eyes, begins with Roosevelt's proclamation of the Four Freedoms, the signing of the Atlantic Charter, and the call to the world to rally for a fight against tyranny and against the Nazi and Japanese idealization of brute force. It ends with the establishment in Palestine by military force of a state made up of colonists from the West. The fact that these colonists were themselves refugees from Western (i.e., Nazi) brutality in no way mitigates in Arab eyes the lack of regard for Arab interests, or weakens the Arab opinion that the establishment of Israel was a betrayal.

The Identification of the United States with the Western Colonialists

From Wilson's time many Arabs cherished the hope that the United States, with no obnoxious colonial record and with a reputation of concern for human rights, would prove different from the other Western powers in its Middle East policies. This hope has been disappointed by American support for Israel, American participation in plans for Middle East defense with control over local military bases and forces, American support for the European powers on "colonial issues" in the United Nations, the Eisenhower Doctrine offering aid and support only to those countries willing to stand up and be counted on the side of the West and, last but not least, America's preference for conservative regimes and its identification with the *status quo* in the Arab area. Despite the American stand against Britain, France, and Israel in the Suez crisis, the more extreme nationalists equate the United States with the other Western powers, no matter what differences it may occasionally have with them.

The Role of Russia

The Arabs claim to have had long experience with Russian attempts to compete with the Western powers in the Middle East. To them, Russia is just another great power with which they will deal on the same terms as with the others. In the past few years Arab attitudes toward Russia and Communist China have fluctuated in response to circumstance, being warm and friendly when they were supporting Arab causes and reserved when the Russians were putting pressures on them. It seems clear, however, there is a double standard in Arab treatment of the Communist powers and the West. Historical experience has conditioned the Arabs to an automatic, defensive reaction to Western initiatives, whereas, regardless of what they say, they are ready to believe better of the Communist bloc. This attitude may be attributed to the absence of a Russian record of domination of Arab lands, the Communist support of "Arab causes" in recent years, and to the belief that it is easier to get away with abusive treatment of the West than of the Soviets.

The Rise of the New Asia and Africa

Whereas Arabs read the history of the nineteenth and early twentieth centuries as a story of the oppression of Arab and other Asian and African peoples by the Western powers, they see in recent history evidence of a great upsurge of downtrodden peoples. The present age is one of self-determination and liberation, and they are very conscious of the powerful historical forces working for their cause and binding them to all other peoples who have suffered under imperialism's sway. This concept of current historical reality gives a certain continuity and direction to Arab behavior in international affairs and adds a powerful stimulus to self-confidence.

The characteristic feature of Arab interpretation of history is its repetitious emphasis upon Western turpitude and Western responsibility for Arab woes. Why the facts of history are viewed in this manner is a question to which no simple answer will suffice. In any event, the interpretation itself is of importance to everyone concerned about Western-Arab relations. That was made obvious by the tumultuous course of events in the 1950s.

VII

ARABS STEER THEIR OWN COURSE:
From the Palestine War to Suez

Step by step the bars to Arab independence were removed in the period between the end of the First World War and the end of the Second. But the foreign policies of the Arab states and their ability to pursue them in the arena of international politics lagged behind. It was not until after their humiliating defeat in Palestine that the Arabs began to take hold of the direction of their own affairs. An examination of the main events in which the Arabs have been involved since the Palestine War reveals Arab nationalism in action. Over and over, the major international events of this period have demonstrated the waning power of outside forces to determine the outcome of events in the Arab area and the growing capability of the Arabs to make Arab nationalism a reality in international politics.[1]

MIDDLE EAST DEFENSE

In 1950, Britain, France, and the United States issued a Tripartite Declaration guaranteeing the borders between Israel and the neighboring Arab states against aggression from either side and serving notice that they would limit arms shipments to the area to

[1] For a useful account of this period see George F. Hourani, "A Decade of Revolution: Social and Political Changes, 1949–1959," in Tibor Kerekes, ed., *The Arab Middle East and Muslim Africa* (New York: Praeger, 1961), pp. 27–45.

levels required for internal security.[2] The Declaration was primarily directed toward maintaining stability within the region and not to the matter with which the Western powers were becoming principally concerned: the defense of the area against attack from the Soviet Union. Here the situation seemed to call not for a Western declaration but rather for a direct proposal for the co-operation of the Arab states with the West. The proffered redrawing of the Anglo-Iraqi treaty having been rejected by Iraq, and the Egyptian government having shown no willingness to accept a renegotiation of the Anglo-Egyptian treaty of 1936, the British government, with American agreement and cooperation, devised the idea of a regional defense organization. Thus they hoped to satisfy the preoccupation of the Arab states with safeguarding their sovereignty and independence. Great Britain, the United States, France, Turkey, and the principal Arab states were to combine their resources for defense. The British base at Suez would become by agreement with Egypt an "Allied" base under a new Middle East Command. The Arab states were to provide bases and facilities and put their armies at the disposal of the organization; the Western powers were to supply troops, equipment, and the high command. It was the word "command" that immediately struck the Arab eye.

Because of Egypt's size and influence and the strategic importance of the Suez base, the Western allies planned to seek Egypt's approval of the Middle East Command first. At this time, however, negotiations for revision of the Anglo-Egyptian treaty of 1936 broke down and on October 10, 1951, the Egyptian Parliament approved the abrogation of the treaty. On October 15, two days after it was proposed, the government rejected the invitation to join the MEC. Looking back, it is difficult to comprehend how the British and their allies could have believed that the Egyptians would accept a defense agreement based on a Western and Turkish view of the Middle East's military requirements. After the Palestine War and the founding of Israel, the Egyptians were not content to move a step at a time toward the goal of full independence.

[2] Text in J. C. Hurewitz, ed., *Diplomacy in the Near and Middle East,* v. 2: *A Documentary Record: 1914–1956* (Princeton: Van Nostrand, 1956), pp. 308–309.

They rejected the British offer to abandon the treaty of 1936 on condition that they join MEC. They did so not so much because they disagreed with the idea of MEC as because of its implications for Egyptian independence. First, Egypt had to be independent, fully and completely, without foreign troops on its soil. Then, but not until then, it might consider a defense agreement.

THE NEW EGYPTIAN REGIME

After Egypt's rejection of the proposed Middle East Command, friction over the British position in the Suez Base area increased, building up to a situation of extreme tension. Ultimately, a British attack on an Egyptian police establishment, resulting in the death of forty policemen, touched off the Black Saturday riots of January 26, 1952, in Cairo. Aimed at the symbols of Western status and privilege—Shepheard's Hotel, the exclusive Turf Club, banks, bars, restaurants, cinemas, and department stores—the riots revealed both the force of anti-Western sentiment and the impotence of the Egyptian government. Six months later a group of young army and air force officers, almost without opposition, seized the country in a revolution dedicated to the reform of the army, to wiping out corruption, and to eliminating "feudalism" from within and "imperialism" from without.

In foreign policy the revolutionary junta at first sought simply to end the privileged position of the British. Tough and adroit negotiators, they showed that they knew how to compromise on some matters—such as a referendum on future status of the Sudan —but dug in their heels on their demand for British withdrawal from the Suez Base. The Egyptians' willingness to compromise persuaded British officials, and American diplomats, that they were faced with a new kind of regime with which the West might be able to do business. As a result, agreements on the Sudan were concluded in 1953 and on the Suez Base in 1954. In the latter the British were probably influenced by increasing evidence that even the strongest military base had questionable value if surrounded by a bitterly hostile population.

Some time was to pass before it became clear that the interpretations of the Suez Base agreement, by the British and the Americans on their side and by the Egyptians on theirs, were quite different. The British and the Americans saw the agreement, which granted Egypt sovereign rights over the base area, as a gesture of recognition on their part of the changed situation in the Middle East. They hoped and believed that the Egyptian leaders would respond by cooperating with the West for the defense and security of the Middle East, and that they would feel bound by the clauses in the treaty providing for the return of British forces in the event of an attack on Turkey. In Western eyes the agreement was a new formulation of the alliance idea. For the revolutionary regime in Egypt, however, the agreement was simply a means of getting British forces out of the Canal Zone. At this point the idea of an alliance with the West had apparently not been unconditionally rejected, but if there was to be such an alliance it would have to be on terms acceptable to independent Egypt.

The revolutionary regime did not come to power with a ready-made foreign policy. Its brand of nationalism was not notably different from that of its predecessors except in degree, but to independence from the toils of "imperialism" it added the goal of social reform. The youth and the middle-class origins of its leaders, and their determined break with all that the corrupt monarchy stood for, gave a sense of imminent new departures in Egyptian policy which had a wide appeal to the Arab public. By the end of its second year, with General Naguib removed from his position as front man, the regime was beginning to develop its own style and doctrine under the leadership of Gamal Abdel Nasser, the young army officer who had patiently built up the Free Officers group which had carried off the revolution.

THE BAGHDAD PACT

On January 12, 1955, the Iraqi government announced its decision to conclude an alliance with Turkey, a country which already had a treaty with Pakistan, thus bringing close to realization an alliance of the states of the Middle East's "northern tier." Later this alliance came to be known as the Baghdad Pact. The Baghdad Pact was the lineal descendent of the proposed Middle East Defense Organization and the Middle East Command which had been rejected by the Egyptian government in 1951. After the negotiations for the Suez Base agreement between the British and

Egyptian governments in 1954, on terms which did not provide a basis for an area defense arrangement, the British and American governments had continued to search for a formula which would provide this all-important objective of Western policy in the Middle East. The conclusion arrived at was that since the governments of Turkey and Pakistan were alive to the danger of a Soviet military thrust into the area and willing to enter into a regional defense arrangement, and since other neighboring states appeared to be willing to join with them, it might be possible to form a "northern tier" defense pact and leave the Arabs to their own devices, or possibly draw them in at a later date. Adding Iraq would bring in a strategically important section of the "northern tier" and also would break the Arab League's solid resistance to area defense in association with the West; other Arab states then might see advantages in joining. Iraq's adherence, it was clear, would be a challenge to Egyptian leadership in the Arab League, but the British and Americans, and apparently the veteran Iraqi Prime Minister, Nuri el Said, were ready, perhaps even anxious, to force the issue and accept the risks.

Iraq's association in the Baghdad Pact had explosive consequences which shaped the subsequent pattern of Arab affairs and external relations. The Egyptian regime, which by this time had domestic opposition under control, responded with an all-out campaign to rally Arab nationalist sentiment against Nuri's policy. All the resources of Egyptian propaganda, diplomacy, clandestine contacts, and Nasser's personal prestige were thrown into a battle unlike anything that had ever been waged in the area before. It was to be the first of a series.

Nasser took the line that Iraq was violating the solidarity of the Arab League in committing itself unilaterally to outside obligations. He threatened to withdraw Egypt from the League—a move that would surely have led to its quick demise—unless Iraq accepted the decision of the entire League membership on the new alliance. Nasser's outpourings of propaganda and free advice on the widely heard Egyptian radio, his contacts with Arab nationalists throughout the area, and particularly his emphasis upon Pan Arabism and the importance of Arab solidarity against "imperialism" and Israel, soon began to affect Arab public opinion, undermining any inclination the Arab leaders in other states might have had to support Iraq. Particularly effective was the argument that the Baghdad Pact was not aimed at the real enemy of the Arabs, Israel, but was instead an alliance with Israel's creators and supporters, the Western powers.

On the issue of Arab relations with great powers, particularly the Western powers, Nasser took the position that the situation into which Iraq had stepped was tantamount to a return to the old treaty relationships which delivered the smaller country over to the power of the larger. The principal nationalist aim, he insisted, was independence, and the only way to achieve and maintain independence was by breaking ties with the great powers and binding the Arab states together into a solid bloc. He urged that the Arab League defense agreement of 1950, called the Arab League Collective Security Pact, was a satisfactory basis for the organization of area defense. If the Western powers were really interested in having independent states provide defense, let them supply weapons to the Arab League without requiring political commitments and without insisting on retaining the command function. This the Arabs themselves could provide.

Iraq stuck by its decision and answered Nasser's sallies in the propaganda battle. In some ways the conflict was a revival of the old Egyptian-Hashemite rivalry, but it contained the new element of Nasser's emerging capability to appeal to believers in Arab nationalism throughout the Arab area and to speak to them in terms of Pan Arab aspirations and goals which transcended the interests of individual states and governments.

With Iraq effectively inactive in the Arab League and with the other Arab states, tacitly at least, accepting Nasser's case against the Baghdad Pact, Nasser proceeded to try to set up his own area defense organization. After much consultation Syria and Saudi Arabia signed defense agreements with Egypt in October of 1955. Two months later the Chief of the British Imperial General Staff, Sir Gerald Templer, arrived in Amman with the apparent purpose of persuading the Jordanian government to follow Iraq into the Baghdad Pact. The Jordanian public, particularly the West Bank Palestinians, responded with violent demonstrations against the Western powers and against Prime Minister Majalli, who spoke in favor of Jordan's adherence to the Baghdad Pact. The public demonstrations brought about the fall of the Majalli government, and there was widespread expression of approval of the replacement of Jordan's tie with Great Britain with a new association with Egypt, Saudi Arabia, and Syria. The King managed to ride out the storm without giving way to demands for a pro-Nasser government, but in March he moved to assuage public feeling by dismissing General John Bagot Glubb, the long-time British commander of Jordan's army, known as the Arab Legion.

Thus the West's second try at an area defense organization, though it did provide the substance of a defense agreement in the north, touched off a struggle in the Arab area which stimulated Arab solidarity and the organization of opposition to alliances and alignments with the Western powers. The contest was by no means a decisive one, since Nasser's attempts to organize an Arab counterpart of the Baghdad Pact had little real consequence, but it did demonstrate the popular appeal of Pan Arabism and Nasser's ability to manipulate it as a political instrument.

THE ARMS DEAL AND "POSITIVE NEUTRALISM"

On February 28, 1955, Israeli armed forces attacked Egyptian military installations in the Gaza strip, killing thirty-eight persons and wounding thirty-one. Beginning with an attack on the Jordanian village of Kibya in October 1953, Israel had made a series of reprisal raids into Arab territory; the Gaza episode was the first invasion of Egyptian-controlled territory. It would certainly be wrong to conclude that this particular raid was solely responsible for the Egyptian decision to approach the Soviets about purchases of arms and the subsequent arms deal which was announced in September 1955. The Baghdad Pact was probably an important factor. Also involved were Egyptian unwillingness to sign the agreement required for participation in the American Mutual Security program, the high price of American arms and the requirement of dollar payments, and a variety of influences pushing the Egyptians in the direction of neutralism. All these contributed to an Egyptian decision which might have been made even if the Gaza raid had not taken place. The raid, however, gave emphasis to certain problems confronting the Egyptian leader and called for a dramatic response.

A principal effect of the Gaza raid was that it exposed the weakness of the Egyptian armed forces. The army officer corps which had made the Egyptian revolution had accepted the regime's initial emphasis upon social and economic reform. Now it demanded more arms, and it was doubtful whether the army's loyalty could be counted upon if it did not receive more and better weapons.

Nasser needed arms quickly with which to strengthen his defenses and bolster the loyalty of his army. But arms were not available from traditional Western sources. He tried the Americans and found that the price of the arms he needed, outside the terms of the regular Mutual Security Program, would cost more dollars than he had in the Egyptian treasury. His thoughts on the problem of satisfying his needs for arms apparently led him into an examination of the whole question of Egypt's relations with the great powers.

One month after the Gaza raid, and a little more than two months before going first to the American and then to the Soviet Ambassador, Prime Minister Nasser, in a speech before the Cairo Officers' Club and in other public statements during the following weeks, outlined the basic concepts of the foreign policy which later came to be known as "positive neutralism." He noted the importance for small nations of keeping themselves free from domination by great powers and the necessity of avoiding alignments with them. The most significant fact of the world situation, he pointed out, was the struggle between the two great-power agglomerations, the West under U.S. leadership and the Communist bloc under Russian leadership. He argued that their approximate equality in military potential was advantageous to small nations, and especially to the Arab states. Neither the U.S.S.R. nor the United States could permit the other to occupy an area of such strategic significance. Obviously, in this situation, the best course for the Arab states, if they wished to escape involvement in the cold war, was to avoid dependence upon either antagonist. Nasser pointed out that Egypt was heavily involved with the West in the economic sphere. For years the great bulk of the cotton crop, the source of most of its foreign exchange, had been sold in Western markets. While the Western market for Egyptian cotton was shrinking, there were prospects for increased demand for Egyptian cotton in the Soviet bloc and in the uncommitted nations of Asia. Furthermore, the Soviet bloc countries were now producing more and more of the manufactured goods which Egypt needed. Therefore, he concluded, the way was clear for Egypt to balance its economic relations between the West and the Soviet bloc. Ultimately it would be desirable to develop Egypt's trade with the uncommitted nations, thus splitting its external trade and economic commitments three ways.[3]

Coming between the Gaza raid and the approaches to the American and Soviet ambassadors for arms, Nasser's speech reflected his thinking at a critical moment in the development of an Arab approach to foreign-policy problems—an approach which has dominated Arab-Western relations ever since.

During the spring and summer of 1955 Nasser progressively developed the doctrine of neutralism, fitting it into the frame of Arab nationalism. In April he left Egypt for the first time—except for his military service in Palestine and the Sudan—to go to the conference of African and Asian states at Bandung, Indonesia. On the way he conferred with Nehru, the originator of Asian neutralism. Bandung apparently provided a moving and stimulating experience. He discovered that leaders of emerging states all over the Afro-Asian world shared many of his ideas, his fears of involvement in the great-power struggle, and his hopes for some formula by which the new nations could find the way to economic and social development and begin to play a role in shaping world affairs. This group listened to him respectfully as the spokesman of an Arab point of view, as an Arab and not merely an Egyptian leader. Also significant must have been his contact with the representative of the Chinese Peoples' Republic, Chou En-lai, who skillfully impressed the conference with China's interest in the welfare of the emerging Asian and African states, convincing many of their

[3] The gist of Egyptian thinking on political and military strategy, in somewhat garbled form, appeared in 1956 in an undated supplement to *The Egyptian Economic and Political Review* entitled "The Strategy of Egyptian Defense." The editor says that the article was prepared with the cooperation of the Public Affairs Administration of the Egyptian armed forces.

leaders of Communist sympathy and willingness to assist in their struggles against the efforts of the Western "imperialists" to reimpose control. It has been said that Chou at Bandung suggested to Nasser that the Soviets might be responsive to a request for arms.

The Egyptian-Czech arms deal, arranged by Nasser and the Soviet Ambassador,[4] and announced on September 27, 1955, ended the dependence of Egypt on the West for its weapons, a dependence which had been a feature of the Arab situation since the Arabs had begun to build modern armies. It was immediately clear that this was an historic change of great though unpredictable significance. Dismay was the first reaction of the Western powers, followed by an anxious search for some way to reverse the momentous change in Egypt's historic policy. But it soon became clear that there were no means, at least none which they were prepared to use, to undo the damage. The West was still in the process of adjusting its thinking to the new development when a roar of approval rose up from every Arab state. Almost to a man, politically conscious Arabs saw the arms deal as a master stroke by which Nasser had broken the West's monopoly of arms, thus asserting Arab independence. So long as the West apportioned its arms sales to maintain approximate equality between Israel and all the Arab states taken together, Israel had an advantage because of its single command and interior lines of communication. Nasser had found a way out. Not only "Nasserist" radicals gave their approval but also westernized, upper-class Arabs in every country, including many who were basically well disposed to the West and hopeful that Western influence would predominate in their countries. In their view, and that of most Arabs, Nasser had outwitted the Western powers; he had found a clever way to play off the East and West against each other. For once an Arab leader had carried off a coup, winning a great victory in international politics. Little concern was felt about opening the door to Russian influence. Nasser's contention that the Russians and the West would deter each other was gladly accepted. Besides, few believed that the Western powers could not and would not protect the Middle East

---

[4] Daniel Solod, who in a subsequent post was declared *persona non grata* by the government of Guinea in December of 1961 because of interference in Guinean domestic affairs.

from the Soviets, if it came to that. The Arab welcome for Nasser's move gave vent to feelings built up during decades of frustration at Western superiority and condescension compounded by the deep humiliation of defeat in Palestine and the existence of an alien state, Israel, on Arab territory.

When, in December of the same year, the United States and Great Britain, in conjunction with the World Bank, offered to assist Egypt in constructing the Aswan High Dam, the great symbol of Nasser's internal development program, most people believed that Nasser's policy had proved sound. He could indeed get help from both sides.

Meantime, as Soviet arms flowed into Egypt, British troops were being evacuated from the Canal Zone in accordance with the Suez Base Agreement of 1954. The completion of the evacuation was celebrated in June 1956 with an immense parade of Egyptian troops displaying great quantities of new Soviet weapons. To make it an all-Arab triumph, units from the armed forces of other Arab states—Sudanese desert soldiers on camels, a smart Arab Legion company from Jordan, and a Lebanese ski-trooper outfit with its white uniforms dazzling in the Cairo sun—marched with the Egyptians. Dmitri Shepilov, the new Soviet Foreign Minister, was conspicuous in the place of honor in the reviewing stand. An enormous, bearlike figure with an unruly mop of hair—he looked very Russian indeed and seemed to be taking all the bows as the Stalin tanks rumbled by and the MIGs roared overhead. The Western military attachés in their trim uniforms managed to appear detached even as they strained to keep count of every Soviet weapon which the Egyptians proudly displayed and Shepilov gleefully acknowledged. Seldom has a parade had such historic significance. For the first time since 1882 the Egyptian army—not British forces—was the final source of authority and power in Egypt. To Western eyes the parade pointed up the possibility that Egypt had exchanged its old relationship with Great Britain for a new and more demanding dependence upon the Soviet Union. To Mr. Shepilov the scene must have foreshadowed the decline of Western prestige and closer and closer ties between the Arabs and the Soviet bloc. To Nasser, apparently, the ceremony bore testimony to the efficacy of his neutralist policy in freeing Egypt from its past bonds and providing it with the strength to run its own show in its own way. As the Stalin tanks rumbled past the reviewing stand in front of Farouk's old palace, one could not say which of these interpretations was to prove correct.

THE SUEZ CRISIS

On July 19, 1956, Secretary of State John Foster Dulles withdrew the United States' offer of assistance to Egypt for the construction of the Aswan High Dam. In his statement he said that developments within the seven months since the offer was made "have not been favorable to the success of the project." Egypt, he noted, had not reached agreement with the other states through whose territories the Nile flows, and said that "the ability of Egypt to devote adequate resources to assure the project's success has become more uncertain than at the time the offer was made."[5] The next day Great Britain withdrew its offer of assistance, and on July 23 the International Bank announced that its offer of a loan had automatically expired with the withdrawal of the American and British offers.

At this time President Nasser was in Brioni, Marshal Tito's island retreat on Yugoslavia's Adriatic coast, engaging in talks with Tito and Prime Minister Nehru of India which he hoped would build up his image as a member of a neutralist high policy board. Quickly returning to Egypt on July 26, the anniversary of King Farouk's abdication and departure from Egypt, he gave a memorable speech before a large audience in Alexandria.[6] He told how the Arab states had been dominated by the Western powers. But, he said,

Today—since our political freedom has been achieved after the announcement of our principles, after our cooperation, and after the establishment of a united national front of all the sons of this people against imperialism, against despotism, against domination and arbitrary rule, against exploitation and against foreign interference—they take us into account. And they know that we are a nation with self-

[5] Noble Frankland and Vera King, eds., *Documents on International Affairs, 1956* (London: Oxford University Press, for the Royal Institute of International Affairs, 1959), pp. 69–70.
[6] Same, pp. 77–113.

esteem which can do what it pleases. Today the importance of Egypt in the international field has grown and the importance of the Arab nation in the international field has grown and become great.[7]

He spoke of the Brioni conference at which he had conferred on world problems—"the German problem in Europe; the Chinese problem in Asia; and the Palestine and Algerian Arab problems which concern us as an Arab Nation and an Arab people." He said, "the viewpoint of President Tito and Premier Nehru was in line with the Arab view. In this way the Arab viewpoint was able to capture another stronghold and assert its existence in the world."

Nasser then reviewed recent relations between Egypt and the Western powers, making the point that the West was still seeking every opportunity to subordinate and control Egypt and the Arab states and to limit their freedom of action. He cited the West's attempts to bring Egypt into a defense alliance in which it would be "an appendage and subordinate." The West, he said, had provided Israel, "a nation of a million," with equal or greater amounts of arms than it allowed the Arabs, a people of seventy million, and vastly greater amounts of economic assistance. Reviewing negotiations for the construction of the Aswan High Dam, he claimed to see in the conditions which Great Britain, the United States, and the International Bank sought to attach to their participation a return to the techniques by which in the past Egypt had been made financially dependent upon the Western bankers.

"This is what happened in the last century," said the Egyptian President. "Will history repeat itself in deception and misrepresentation?" The answer to this question was: "We shall never allow history to repeat itself." Then came the startling announcement that the Suez Canal Company, a "state within a state" and a hangover from the "imperialist" past, was to be nationalized and the control of the canal, which was "the property of the Egyptian people," was to be taken over by Egypt.

Though unexpected, both Mr. Dulles' withdrawal of his government's offer of assistance and President Nasser's angry reaction fitted into the pattern of Western-Egyptian relations which had been developing since the arms deal of the previous autumn.

[7] Same, pp. 80–81.

Egypt's relations with the West in the first half of 1956 had become increasingly tense. The Voice of the Arabs program on the Egyptian state radio stepped up its attacks on Western "imperialism," and Moscow radio gave a steady chorus of approval. The Egyptian radio and many friends and supporters of Egypt, as well as official representatives, strongly opposed the Jordanian government during the disturbances of December 1955 and January 1956. Tensions increased between Israel and the Arabs; in the spring of 1956 there was a considerable step-up of raids by Arab commandos (*fedayeen*), most of them Palestinians trained in Egypt and directed from Egypt. In May, Egypt had recognized Communist China.

Negotiations on the High Dam project had never gone well. The Western powers' decision to assist the project had been strongly influenced by their desire to prevent the Russians from taking over the whole show in Egypt. They had wanted to demonstrate that they, too, were willing to offer assistance "without strings attached." During the negotiations, however, the Western representatives had shown increasing concern about the economic soundness of the scheme and began to ask for guarantees with respect to Egypt's financial policies, external as well as internal, during the period of the project. On the Egyptian side, the High Dam project was an important feature of domestic policy, but by no means so important as to override every other political consideration. After the heady excitement of the duels with the Western powers over the Baghdad Pact and the Soviet arms deal, Nasser was unprepared to trim his sails in the interest of this or any other economic project.

Mr. Dulles' withdrawal of American assistance reversed the decision made in the previous autumn to accept Nasser on his own terms, and to work with him in one field while the Russians worked with him in others. His action was apparently prompted by the fear that Congress would not provide the necessary funds. However, the decision to make an open announcement of withdrawal rather than to allow the whole project to die a diplomatic death was a policy decision, a decision openly to challenge Nasser and his policies.

Nasser's reaction reflected the whole pattern of foreign-policy ideas which he had been developing since coming to power. He reacted quickly and violently, standing up to all the Western powers, and making the point that the Arabs now count for something in the world. Not long after the nationalization of the Canal Company he said publicly that he had done it not just for the sake of the canal but in order to arouse Arab nationalism. The decision to nationalize the Canal Company, along with all other major foreign enterprises and institutions, had doubtless been made early in the history of the regime, but this particular gesture was made at this time in the knowledge that it was a challenge not just to a company, not just to a single nation, but to the whole system by which the Western powers and their allies had once dominated many of the affairs of the world. In effect, it was a challenge to the international community which had been developed in the great period of Western hegemony and, what made the challenge more defiant, it was based on the principle of the sovereignty of a relatively new and weak nation. Although it was the United States that had initiated the withdrawal, Nasser struck back at Western "imperialism," which to him meant principally Great Britain and France. He did so knowing full well the dangers involved, but he had a doctrine which provided an explanation of how things would work out. Great Britain and France would almost certainly seek to use force against him, he believed and his principal advisers agreed, but the United States would restrain them. The United States would do so both because it was less "imperialist" than they, less convinced that the former Western position could be restored by force, and also because it would be aware that Western intervention would risk war with the Soviet Union.

The American reaction was indeed quite different from that of its British and French allies, although that fact was not always apparent. Whereas they both very soon referred to the possibility of using force, the American government never did so. The French attitude was much the harshest. Nasser was described as "a permanent menace to the peace" and as a military dictator whom the international community would have to find means of checking. From the beginning the French government was impatient at the delays involved in attempts to negotiate an agreement on the canal

with Nasser. The British Prime Minister, Sir Anthony Eden, de-
cried "Nasser's arbitrary action in breach of solemn undertakings,"[8] and joined with the United States and France in recommending some kind of international administration of the canal.
A facility of such vital interest to so many nations, he argued,
could not be left to the responsibility of a single state, certainly
not to a state run by a man like Nasser.

The drama that was played out over the operation of the Suez
Canal by Egyptians was symbolic of the crisis as a whole. As
pressures built up, officers of the Suez Canal Company explained
to the world that they could not make their highly skilled pilots
work for the Egyptians, that the pilots would be bound to get fed
up and leave, and that the Egyptians could not possibly manage
the complicated problems of operating the canal. After the first
few pilots left, those that remained complained loudly to attentive
newsmen about the weight of the burden they carried. Threatened
with the withdrawal of the remaining company pilots, the Egyptians refused to cave in, and saw most of them leave. The whole
world watched the progress of convoys through the canal, and, in
the West at least, waited for the Egyptians to fail. Gradually it
became apparent that with very little outside help the Egyptians
were operating the canal efficiently and well. Two things were
clear: that many Westerners expected the Egyptians to fail because they were Egyptians, and that the famous French-run Suez
Canal Company had been profitably deceiving everybody for years,
possibly including itself, about the difficulty of its task.

The Western formula for the solution of the problem created by
the nationalization of the Suez Canal Company was worked out
at a twenty-two nation conference held in London in August. Its
recommendation, supported by eighteen of its members, was the
establishment of an international authority for the operation of the
canal, of which Egypt would be a participating member. The canal,
it was argued, was an international facility which "should be detached from politics, and the management of its operations should
be placed on such a basis as to secure the maximum of international confidence and co-operation."[9]

[8] Same, p. 128.
[9] Same, p. 187.

Nasser described the recommendations as "collective colonial-ism," the imposition of the authority of a group of nations over Egypt. He denounced the various pressures, including threats of force and economic restrictions, that had been applied. The inter-national character of the Suez Canal, he asserted, was guaranteed by the Constantinople Convention of 1888 of which Egypt was a signatory and which Egypt was willing to reaffirm. He challenged the claim that nationalization had in any way affected the security of the canal, pointing out that the company had never had au-thority in that regard. Security had always been afforded by the government of Egypt—he did not mention the presence of British forces in the Canal Zone until June of that year—and by the Constantinople Convention. Nationalization according to Nasser meant only that a foreign company, which while operating under Egyptian license had for years sent its immense profits abroad, had had its license removed. Henceforth, an Egyptian company would perform the same functions; the Egyptian government would guarantee the compensation of the company's stockholders, the technical efficiency of canal operations, and adequate main-tenance and development of canal facilities. It would continue to be bound by the terms of the Constantinople Convention to pre-serve the international character of the canal.

There was little or no argument about the right of the Egyptian government to nationalize the company, but there was much dis-cussion of the willingness of the maritime nations to trust the operation of the canal to a single country. When the Egyptians pointed out that the United States operated the Panama Canal without an international advisory board, the answer in effect was that Egypt was not the United States. The Western maritime na-tions were unwilling to trust Egypt with the operation of the Suez Canal because it was Egypt and because Gamal Abdel Nasser was its president.

This was the main issue. The British and the French were de-termined not to let Nasser "get away with" the sudden ousting of the Canal Company; his action challenged the international system which they had built up over the years. The American government appeared to have had many of the same worries but could not see how the use of force could resolve the problem. As this difference in attitudes became more and more clear, the British and French began to suspect that Mr. Dulles' various proposals, such as the Canal Users' Association, were devices for delaying their resort to force rather than serious attempts to force Nasser to change his position.

Nasser, for his part, was vastly encouraged and strengthened in his position by the support of the Arab public and the governments of the Arab states (including somewhat reluctant support from Iraq). Most of the Afro-Asian states registered their approval, by which he set great store, and so did the states of the Soviet bloc. The British Labor party expressed its opposition to the use of force, an attitude which was shared by much of the British public. Nasser took great care to represent Egypt as fighting the battle of all the small and uncommitted nations against the pressures and the outmoded conventions by which the great powers had long exercised their control.

Once he had challenged the West with his decision to nationalize, Nasser had little to do with the course of the world crisis which he had precipitated. He stood firm while the British and French, by attacking him in conjunction with the Israelis, made him the hero of the Arab world. He watched the United States, backed by the Afro-Asian states, the U.S.S.R., and much of world opinion, force the British, French, and Israelis to accept a cease-fire and ultimately agree to the withdrawal of their forces from Egyptian territory. Despite the misadventures of his army in the Sinai Peninsula, despite the inability of his air force or army to offer effective resistance to the British and French at Port Said, Nasser had won. Nasser's leadership and his neutralist policy seemed to have been vindicated and glorified in Arab eyes and in the eyes of many others throughout the world.

VIII

ARABS STEER THEIR OWN COURSE:

From Suez to the

Breakup of the U.A.R.

The main significance of the Suez crisis, as seen by many Arabs, was the changed posture of the United States. For the first time the greatest of the Western states had openly broken with its allies over a "colonial issue" and in doing so had jeopardized the Western alliance, a thing which few Afro-Asians had ever expected to see. To many this opened up possibilities of a completely new course of American policy, in which the United States would cooperate with the emergent states in their efforts to free themselves of their colonial inheritance. Nasser's public statements at the height of the crisis had recognized the assistance he had received from both the Soviet Union and the United States. However, room was left for the conclusion that it was the Soviet threat of force against Britain and France that finally brought their acceptance of the cease-fire. Nevertheless, it was the future potential of a U.S. policy freed of dependence upon "imperialist" counsels that seemed most significant to Nasser and his entourage and to many Arab nationalists. They saw visions of their great day dawning, with the United States and the Soviet Union vying with each other to help them along their way.

But events soon demonstrated that these hopes were illusory. Suez changed a great many things, even possibly certain American attitudes and ideas about the Middle East, but the United States had not seen the light of Arab nationalism, as some of its adherents briefly hoped.

Disillusionment started when the United States failed to respond to requests for shipments of wheat and drugs. It was compounded when the first ship entering Alexandria harbor after the crisis proved to be Russian. It brought wheat which was soon followed by Soviet pharmaceuticals. The U.S. refusal to release frozen Egyptian funds pending determination of compensation for Suez Canal Company shareholders added to the feeling that the United States was imposing an economic blockade. The last straw was the Eisenhower Doctrine for the Middle East, which the President proposed to Congress on January 5, 1957, and which led to the Joint Congressional Resolution approved on March 9.

THE EISENHOWER DOCTRINE

President Eisenhower proposed that Congress authorize him to offer to cooperate with any nation or group of nations in the Middle East in developing its economic and military strength, and to provide assistance and cooperation, including the use of the armed forces of the United States, to nations requesting aid "against overt armed aggression from any nation controlled by International Communism."[1] This was neither a return to the unequal treaties of the post-World War I period nor another Middle East Command or Baghdad Pact. Nevertheless, it had the effect of dissipating much of the credit the United States had won by its rejection of gunboat diplomacy in the Suez crisis. Like the Baghdad Pact, the Eisenhower Doctrine split the Arab states and set them quarreling again over Western influence and Nasser's policy of nonalignment.

The proposals of the American President rang strangely in many Arab ears. They followed and purported to respond to the Suez crisis in which Great Britain, France, and Israel had wrongly, according to the UN resolutions supported by the United States, attacked Egypt, but their emphasis was all on "international communism" and the danger of overt Soviet aggression in the Middle East. Bound up in the problems of the Middle East and almost oblivious of events in Hungary, even the most sophisticated Arabs could hardly look on proposals for defense against Soviet aggres-

[1] Paul E. Zinner, ed., *Documents on American Foreign Relations, 1957* (New York: Harper, for the Council on Foreign Relations, 1958), p. 201.

sion at this time as anything but a red herring. A second reason for the unfavorable reception of the Eisenhower Doctrine was that Nasser himself took the initiative against it. Why did he do so? In the background were certainly the sense of invulnerability which the Suez crisis had generated and his susceptibility to every scrap of evidence that the unreconstructed "imperialists" were seeking new ways to accomplish their old aim of dominating the Middle East. He may have listened to clever Soviet propaganda which had broadcast that the American role in the Suez crisis had been planned by the Western powers from the start, in order that the United States might deal with the Arabs in case the British-French-Israeli attack failed. President Eisenhower had proposed to assist the Arab states against "aggression from any nation controlled by International Communism." Nasser quickly concluded that this meant him, and that the Eisenhower Doctrine actually was another Baghdad Pact in a more insidious form. The American purpose, he believed, was to isolate him from the other Arab states and to bring into close relations with the United States the Arab leaders who opposed and feared him and the neutralist Arab nationalism which he symbolized.

In the Arab states there was a mixed reaction to the Eisenhower Doctrine and to Ambassador James P. Richards, the special representative of the President, who was sent to explain it. Only Lebanon and Libya accepted the American proposal without public reservation. Iraq joined with the other Middle East members of the Baghdad Pact in a favorable response, but in public statements later the Iraqi government avoided identifying itself with the doctrine. Saudi Arabia, after a visit to the United States by King Saud, gave partial support without specific mention of the doctrine itself. Jordan and the Sudan did not reply to the invitation, and Egypt, Syria, and Yemen rejected it. In April, King Hussein of Jordan accepted some much needed aid from the United States at a time when his relations with Nasser were extremely bad, but he took pains to state publicly that the aid was not provided under the terms of the Eisenhower Doctrine. By the end of the year Iraq and Saudi Arabia were avoiding all mention of their originally favorable attitude. An act of the Lebanese Parliament accepted the U.S. offer, but only in principle. President Chamoun's apparent willing-

ness to invoke the doctrine aroused opposition in the spring of
1958. After his fall the statute was repealed.

In the meantime, however, a contest had developed in which
Nasser and his supporters all over the area were pitted against
the governments of Iraq, Saudi Arabia, and Jordan. Here the
Eisenhower Doctrine was buried under the broader issues of Nasser's neutralism and his growing capability for speaking to, and
in the name of, the politically conscious sector of the Arab population. Worried by these developments, Arab leaders took steps
which soon led them into a head-on clash with Nasser.

In Jordan, before the Suez crisis, internal and external pressures
were building up against the special relationship with Britain.
Britain's participation in the attack on Egypt, which aroused a
great wave of Arab feeling against the "aggressors," led to a meeting in Cairo in January 1957 of Nasser, King Saud, Syrian Premier
Sabri el Asali, and King Hussein. There it was agreed to substitute
an Arab subsidy for the British payments upon which the Jordanian treasury had been dependent, and to allow the Anglo-
Jordanian treaty to lapse. This agreement, added to the military
alliance which already bound the four Arab states together, looked
like the basis of some form of Arab union more effective and
binding than the Arab League. Very soon, however, such prospects
began to fade. At the end of January, King Saud returned from a
visit to the United States apparently convinced that he should play
a much more active role in the Arab area, and that the United
States considered him a wiser and better influence than President
Nasser. In the weeks that followed, a crisis in Jordan was to test
both his and Nasser's influence, finding something wanting in each.
King Hussein discovered that his Prime Minister, Sulaiman Nabulsi, and his army Chief of Staff, Ali Abu Nuwar, were both looking to Cairo for guidance and that his own position in Jordan was
increasingly dependent upon his willingness to follow the lead of
President Nasser, who wielded great influence over the Jordanian
populace, particularly the former Palestinians. Hussein dismissed
Nabulsi and Abu Nuwar, but only by going at great personal risk
to the scene of an incipient army revolt at Zerqa was he able to
keep the army from turning against him.

The crisis in Jordan brought the U.S. Sixth Fleet into the Eastern Mediterranean and gave rise to Soviet warnings of impending American aggression in the Middle East. Amman charged Egypt with intervention by clandestine means on a massive scale, and Cairo warned of "imperialist" and world Zionist efforts to isolate Egypt and destroy Arab nationalism. The leader of this campaign was the United States, according to Nasser.[2] The crisis brought Hussein and Saud closer together; Saudi Arabia actually paid its share of the promised subsidy for a time. Hussein and King Feisal of Iraq joined together in condemning interference by Arab states in each other's affairs.

A significant consequence of the Jordanian crisis was the multiplication of clandestine activities throughout the Middle East. Nasser's activities were the most conspicuous, probably because they were the most successful. His many willing and eager followers everywhere occasionally embarrassed him by going off on their own. King Saud, who had plenty of money and who was used to spending it in order to get his own way, appeared to have a hand in quite a number of things. The "imperialists" were accused of sponsoring the nine clandestine radios which Nasser said were attacking him at one time. Henceforth, covert activities were a factor of increasing importance in the Arab situation.

The Jordanian crisis of 1957 showed Nasser's great strength among the populations of other Arab countries. But even with clandestine assistance, this did not prove to be enough to topple a king who, even though he was identified with the old regime, proved to be brave, determined, and lucky.

THE SYRIAN CRISIS AND THE FORMATION OF THE UNITED ARAB REPUBLIC

During the latter stages of the Jordanian crisis in the spring of 1957, events in Syria began moving toward a climax that again focused the attention of the world on the Arab area. During the summer, relations between Syria and the West worsened. People and ideas sympathetic to Nasser came into increasing favor and power. A political crisis put in power an uneasy coalition which included some Baath party leaders, a group of army officers whose political background was unknown except that they seemed to

[2] Speech of July 26, 1957.

have connections with the Baath party, and an old-line politician of sinister reputation, Khalid el Azm. One of the army officers, the chief of Army Intelligence, Abdel Hamid Serraj, exercised power and influence in the army and throughout the country far beyond that which normally attached to his office. Khalid Baqdash, the chief of the Syrian-Lebanese Communist party, was said to be very close to the coalition, and the new Chief of the Army Staff, Afif el Bizri, was a Communist or had, at the least, very close Communist connections. Syrian military and economic missions were in Moscow discussing agreements on arms and on economic assistance and, it was widely rumored, much closer ties between the two countries. There were also widespread reports of impending Syrian-Egyptian union. On August 13, in an atmosphere of increasing suspicion and tension between Syria and the West, three members of the American Embassy staff in Damascus, including the military attaché, were declared *personae non gratae* on charges of plotting against the regime.

Later in August, Loy Henderson, a Deputy Under Secretary of State and a senior Middle East expert, flew to a Baghdad Pact meeting at Ankara where he discussed Communist gains in Syria with Prime Minister Menderes of Turkey, King Feisal of Iraq, and King Hussein of Jordan. Turkish troops were mobilized on the Syrian border. The Soviet Union seized the opportunity to accuse the United States of preparing to intervene with force in Syria, and threatened dire consequences. Syria and Egypt joined the chorus of accusation.

Tension over Syria persisted through the autumn. The United States, the Baghdad Pact members, and King Hussein of Jordan warned of a Soviet-Egyptian takeover and, on their side, the Soviets and Egyptians warned of the imminence of "imperialist" aggression. Syrian and Egyptian missions busily traveled the road to Moscow. On November 20, Cairo announced an Egyptian-Soviet aid agreement (which did not, however, bar deals with the West), and another agreement shortly thereafter with Czechoslovakia. Syrian economic and military delegations continued to negotiate with the Russians.

Meantime an Egyptian parliamentary delegation in joint session with the Syrian Parliament voted in favor of the union of Syria and Egypt. So many previous indications of this possibility had come to the public attention that there was little response to this particular event. However, after only a few days of goings and comings between Damascus and Cairo in the last two weeks of January 1958, the union of Syria and Egypt was announced. The question in people's minds was what finally had brought about this long-anticipated but still surprising move and what the terms of the union actually were.

Only gradually did the evidence come out that it had been the Syrians who had pressed for the union and in the end had won over a reluctant Nasser with the argument that if he did not accept the presidency of Syria there was danger that the Communist elements in the Syrian coalition would turn the state over to the Soviets. From a variety of sources involved in the transaction, and never contradicted by anyone in a position to know, has come a story of growing conflict within the Syrian coalition in the last weeks of 1957. Khalid el Azm, who hoped to reach the heights of power in Syria by making a deal with the Russians, and Afif el Bizri apparently sought to bring Syria into a close relationship with the Soviet Union. Others in the coalition, led by the Baath party people, fought to avoid the trap. The Baathis, fervent believers in Arab unity to start with, became convinced that Nasser, whose stature as an area leader they thought would enable him to sway the Syrian public and whose commitment to independence they trusted, would be able to save the country from the plotting of the Russians and Azm, Bizri, and Baqdash. That this should have happened while many voices in the West and in the Baghdad Pact countries, as well as in Jordan and Saudi Arabia, were warning of collusion between the Egyptians and the Communists for a takeover in Syria is one of the great ironies of the recent history of the Arab East.

The proclamation in February 1958 of the merging of Egypt and Syria in the United Arab Republic (U.A.R.) electrified the Middle East. Popular enthusiasm in Syria and Egypt seemed practically unanimous. In every Arab state the popular response was strongly favorable. The great outpouring of verbiage on the in-

evitability of Arab unity which had filled the air and covered countless printed pages for so many years seemed at last to be vindicated. Arabs, who had long acknowledged unity as a moral and
political principle without any conception of how or when it might
take practical form, suddenly were confronted with what seemed
to be proof of the validity of the idea. Many non-Arabs, who had
questioned the practical significance of the idea, now changed their
minds and predicted that the remaining Arab states would soon
be attracted into the union.

At the time it seemed that the prediction would prove accurate.
The Imam of Yemen, autocratic ruler of the most remote and
traditional of the Arab states, moved to join his state in a loose
federation with the U.A.R. His motive seemed not so much anticipation of the benefits of economic and political integration as the
hope that association with Nasser's name would strengthen his own
position at home. Yemen's joining the new U.A.R. also announced
the Imam's approval, in general, of Nasser's foreign policy.

The formation of the Arab Union by Iraq and Jordan seemed
only to underline the significance of the Egyptian-Syrian merger,
which it followed so precipitously. Certainly the union showed that
the Iraqi and Jordanian regimes feared that, without some extraordinary effort on their part, their countries might be unable to resist
the magnetic attraction of unity centered on Nasser's Egypt. Until
the Iraqi revolution made an end to the union, only the most per-
functory and half-hearted measures were taken to make it a
reality. The U.A.R., on the other hand, quite rapidly began to
function, if not as a unitary state, at least under a single top authority.

During the months following the union of Egypt and Syria a
great sense of confidence and hopefulness was apparent in President Nasser's entourage. It was as though history, as in the Suez
crisis, had proved his policies sound and was providing solutions
to his problems that he himself could not have planned. That history was on the side of the Arab nationalist movement, and that it
had bigger things in store for the entire "Arab nation," was a commonly expressed belief among Nasser's advisers and admirers, and
the feeling spread to Arab groups throughout the Middle East.

CRISIS IN LEBANON[3]

Signs of strain on the traditional truce between the Christian and Muslim communities in Lebanon began to appear after the Suez crisis as a result of President Chamoun's treatment of his political opposition and his too obvious and consistent pro-Western policy. He provoked only occasional murmurs of protest, however, until the Syrian crisis at the end of 1957 crystallized the conflict between Arab nationalism and Western power and pressure. Lebanese Muslims, usually as conscious as the Christians of the advantages of Lebanon's special position, began to feel the pull of the larger Muslim community around them. Clashes between Muslims and Christians became more numerous. Assistance from Syria began to flow into the Lebanon. President Chamoun not only stuck to his policies but also announced his intention of running for the presidency for a third time, something that no president had done before. At this, tension built up rapidly between his followers and the Muslim groups which looked increasingly to Gamal Abdel Nasser for leadership.

The assassination in Beirut on May 8, 1958, of Nasib al Matni, a pro-Nasser journalist, was the spark that kindled the awaiting fuel. Lebanon found itself involved in a struggle that was almost but not quite a civil war, and at the same time was more than that. On May 13, President Chamoun told the British, French, and American ambassadors that Lebanon was under foreign attack, meaning that his Muslim opponents were receiving arms, money, and men from Syria, and propaganda assistance from Egypt.

The basic question was whether the country was, in fact, involved only in a civil war, i.e., a conflict between Lebanese factions. To the Christian Lebanese, to the West, and to the Arab governments in Baghdad, Amman, and Riyadh, it looked as though Nasser were assisting the Muslim half of the Lebanese population to upset the traditional balance and bring the country into line with the foreign policy of the U.A.R. They thought he might ac-

[3] See Fahim I. Qubain, *Crisis in Lebanon* (Washington: Middle East Institute, 1961), for a judicious and informed account of the Lebanese crisis of 1958, particularly Chapter 10, "Summary and Conclusion."

tually destroy Lebanon as an independent state. To the Muslim Lebanese—or at any rate to the Sunnis who are the largest single group—President Chamoun, a Christian, appeared to be leaning on the Western powers for support for a policy of which the Muslim population disapproved. By persisting in this policy in defiance of Muslim wishes, he seemed to be breaking the traditional compact between Christians and Muslims. When the disorders produced extensive armed conflict, the President publicly stated that he might call for the assistance of American armed forces under the Eisenhower Doctrine. Then the issue was clearly drawn between the Christian Lebanese, supported by the West, and the Muslims, supported by Nasser and the nationalist element in the larger Arab community.

In the United Nations the Lebanese government charged the United Arab Republic with "indirect aggression." A UN inspection team was sent to Lebanon to determine whether the U.A.R. was, as charged, providing military and other assistance to the rebels. The point proved more difficult to establish than had been anticipated. The UN team reported early in July that it had found no evidence of Syrian infiltration and little evidence of arms smuggling.[4] There seems to be no room for doubt that Lebanese rebels found sympathy and eager support in Syria and that they were able to make purchases of arms and to recruit some personnel there, with the knowledge and assistance of government authorities. It is probable that Syrian assistance went even further. But the evidence does not indicate a planned campaign for the subversion and domination of the Lebanese government.

A more likely explanation is that, as a Lebanese civil war developed, Syrians and Egyptians lent assistance both officially and unofficially to the Lebanese rebels with whom they sympathized.

In any event the situation was transformed by developments outside Lebanon and the U.A.R. On July 14, 1958, an army revolution in Iraq overthrew and killed the King and the Prime Minister and established a government which announced itself as sympathetic with the Nasser regime in Cairo. The immediate con-

[4] Later in the month the United States delegation to the UN presented a bundle of unevaluated reports of U.A.R. assistance to the Lebanese rebels. *The New York Times,* July 17, 1958.

clusion of many in Western capitals and in Arab governments fearful of Nasser's growing power was that the Iraqi revolution was either engineered by Nasser or was the result of his influence. In any event, they thought, its success was likely to set off a surge of Arab nationalist revolutionary enthusiasm which might topple Chamoun in Beirut and King Hussein in Amman. Chamoun lost no time in appealing for American troops, and Hussein was not far behind him.

Summoned by the legitimate governments of Lebanon and Jordan to which it was obligated by explicit and repeated commitments, the United States sent troops into Lebanon on the 15th of July, and agreed with the government of Great Britain on the dispatch of British troops to Jordan. The troops apparently had orders to do nothing but protect the governments of the two countries. They made no forays and were attacked by no one, aside from a few snipers. The Soviets made the air crackle with charges of invasion and intervention and demands for withdrawal, and the U.A.R. broadcasting stations and press played the same theme. But nothing happened until in due course the representatives of the Arab League states, including Lebanon, Jordan, and the U.A.R., presented a resolution to the United Nations General Assembly in which they expressed their confidence in each other and their wish that the Secretary-General would "facilitate the early withdrawal of the foreign troops from the two countries.[5]

The expeditions to Lebanon and Jordan demonstrated that the United States and Great Britain would intervene in local situations and at the behest of local governments undeterred by the threat of Soviet reprisal. Beyond that it is far from clear what the troop landings showed. Attacks on the two governments might have taken place and one or the other might have been overthrown had not the armed forces been present. Actually, political activities went on as usual. Chamoun was forced to yield the presidency in due course to the army Chief of Staff, Fuad Shehab, whose only interest was in reviving Lebanon's traditional political compromise. The Prime Minister was replaced by the Mayor of Tripoli, who had been the principal rebel leader in that strongest Muslim and

[5] *Yearbook of the United Nations, 1958* (New York: Columbia University Press, 1959), p. 47.

most pro-Nasser Lebanese city. In Jordan the King was left with essentially the same problems and essentially the same situation that faced him before the British troops arrived.

Nasser characteristically described the American and British landings as an attempt of the "imperialists" to return to the Middle East. He learned of the landings and of the Iraqi revolution on his way home by sea from a second meeting in Yugoslavia with Marshal Tito. Returning to Yugoslavia immediately, he then went to Moscow in a special Soviet plane to discuss the crisis with Premier Khrushchev. Apparently he anticipated from the events in Lebanon much wider repercussions than actually occurred: Western intervention in Iraq, for example, or attempts on the part of the American forces in Lebanon to exterminate the rebels which might lead to border clashes spilling over into Syria. He seemingly was convinced that another major conflict with the West, including the United States, was at hand. So he sought to bring Soviet weight into the balance, although he did not then ask for Soviet military support and apparently was offered none. Nasser then turned to the task of bringing about the withdrawal of United States and British troops from Arab soil.

The lesson of the Lebanese crisis for Nasser, as for others, must have been that, despite their very considerable conflicts and disagreements, the Arab states had the final say in their internal affairs and that external force could not divert general trends or dictate events. It also demonstrated that the Soviets were not in every circumstance prepared to counter Western initiatives in the Arab area. But while these lessons were being digested the revolution in Iraq was introducing new factors into the Arab situation.

THE IRAQI REVOLUTION

While American and British troops were streaming into Lebanon and Jordan, the Iraqi revolutionaries were seeking their footing in the midst of a flood of brutality and terror quite different from the calm with which the revolution had been received in Egypt in 1952. Nevertheless, there were similarities between the two revolutions. In Iraq, a small group of military leaders went about the task of setting up a government in ways reminiscent of the Egyptian military regime in its early days. Exchanges between the two regimes emphasized their mutual regard, their dedication to Arab nationalism, and their intent to cooperate. The new Iraqi Foreign Minister stated in effect that Iraqi foreign policy would be the same as that of the U.A.R.

Quite soon, however, serious differences arose between Brigadier Abdel Karim Kassem, the new Prime Minister and senior member of the military regime, and his second in command, Colonel Abdel Salaam Aref. Aref wanted to establish some direct connection with the U.A.R., while Kassem was determined to retain Iraq's separate and independent status. In September, Aref was removed from his post as assistant commander in chief of the armed forces and not long thereafter was put under arrest after an attempted revolt by a small group within the army that sympathized with his position.

In Iraq, Communist activity was more evident than it had been in the Egyptian revolution. Large numbers of Iraqi Communists who had been forced into exile under the monarchy came hurrying back, many from the Soviet bloc, and soon set up the country's most effective and determined political organization. They quickly got some of their own people into a position to advise the Prime Minister, and these advisers apparently warned him against Nasser's ambitions and influence, as well as against the designs of the Western "imperialists."

The revolutionary regime in Iraq had, by all accounts, even less in the way of ready-made plans and policies than the Egyptian revolutionaries had had on coming to power six years before, and they certainly had a more chaotic situation to deal with in a less united country. In this situation the Communists moved with frightening speed to organize the country for their own purposes. From Kassem they got toleration and a certain amount of cooperation, probably because they appeared to him to be his only trustworthy allies against the pro-Nasser elements in the army and the public, and because in the early months of the revolution they provided a degree of stability in the country by organizing various elements of the population. First the Communists organized the Popular Resistance Force, a militia designed to provide means of controlling the "enemies of the revolution" but which also gave the Communists themselves a quasi-military force they could use for their own purposes. Then they proceeded to organize farmers, teachers, government officials, and professional groups on a national basis. By the spring of 1959 these Communist-organized groups very nearly amounted to a second governmental system with a potential for taking authority and control away from the regular government agencies which controlled agricultural marketing and food distribution, education, the courts, and many other areas of government activity.

The trend of affairs in Iraq led to the formation of nuclei of resistance to Prime Minister Kassem's regime and to the strengthening of those elements which identified themselves with Arab nationalism, that is, with the wider Arab nationalist movement rather than Kassem's particular Communist-influenced blend of Iraqi nationalism. The friendly relations between Nasser and Kassem's regime had long since given way to mutual suspicions and recriminations, and Nasser's Cairo radio was appealing to the Arab nationalist forces within Iraq. Kassem's radio was, meanwhile, accusing Nasser of interference in Iraqi affairs and of plotting with Iraqi dissidents against the regime.

On March 8, an incident in Mosul, in northern Iraq, transformed the breach between Nasser and Kassem into a bitter feud which dominated Arab affairs for many months. A contingent of the Communist-controlled Popular Resistance Force, sent to Mosul in anticipation of anti-regime demonstrations, attacked Arab nationalist groups. This apparently triggered an army revolt already planned but set for a later date. A bloody battle resulted between the Communist-led PRF and the pro-Kassem military, on one side, and the anti-Kassem army group and other anti-Kassem elements, on the other. Bitter fighting between Kurds and Arabs, only vaguely related to the main political issues, also contributed to the bloodshed.

The Mosul uprising gave the signal for a new and significant turn in Nasser's policy. In December 1958, in a speech at Port Said, he had denounced the Syrian Communist party for its attempts to sabotage Arab nationalism and the U.A.R.[6] After the March revolt he attacked both Kassem, as an enemy of Arab na-

[6] *Nasser's Speeches*, 1958, pp. 353–355.

tionalism, and the Communists, who "have led demonstrations in Baghdad and levelled invective against us." These Communists, he said, "are agents who neither believe in the liberty of their land or their nation, but only do the bidding of outsiders."[7] This was the beginning of a vigorous two months' campaign warning of the danger of international communism, led by Nasser himself in a series of dramatic speeches and supported by his press and radio.

This kind of talk soon provoked a response from Premier Khrushchev; addressing an Iraqi delegation in Moscow, he warned Nasser of taking on more than he could handle, jokingly suggesting that he was likely to strain himself. Following this lead, professors in Soviet bloc universities lectured Arab students on Nasser's foolhardiness, the Soviet press and radio chided and warned Nasser, and Khalid Baqdash, the Syrian Communist leader then in exile, denounced Nasser before a Communist party conference in Warsaw.

Nasser's warnings of "imperialist and Zionist" dangers slackened, and his attacks against the Soviets for a time replaced the accustomed salvoes against the West. In due course, however, the dispute with Khrushchev was patched up and Nasser announced that the Soviet Premier had given him "renewed assurances" of respect for the integrity of the Arab states. Nevertheless, things had been said on both sides which were hard to forget and which emphasized for both parties to the U.A.R.-Soviet relationship its conditional character, and for everyone the fact that under certain circumstances Nasser's neutralism was capable of talking back to the Soviet Union as vigorously as to the West.

ARAB SOLIDARITY

After a long period of tension, culminating in October 1959 in a nearly successful attempt to assassinate Prime Minister Kassem, the Communists' drive in Iraq diminished in force. A widespread popular reaction had set in against them and Kassem had taken steps to curtail their activities. Kassem and his able Foreign Minister, Hashim Jawad, gradually returned to a foreign policy similar

[7] Same, p. 123.

to that of the U.A.R., emphasizing Arab nationalism, Arab unity, and "positive neutralism." The policy, however, was carefully devised to protect Iraq's sovereignty and to revive the Arab League principle as the basis for relations among the Arab states.

Other developments after the Lebanon crisis and the Iraqi revolution of 1958 modified the expectation, so widespread after the Suez crisis and the union of Egypt and Syria, that the logical next step would be unification of the Arab world under Nasser. Instead, 1960 and 1961 saw a return to the idea of solidarity among independent states as an alternative to union.

Nasser remained the most influential Arab leader, the only one capable of evoking response in every Arab country. His ideas and activities set the tone of much of Arab thinking about foreign policy. His preoccupation with African affairs and his attempts to play a role in the Congo crisis had limited appeal in the Arab world to the north and east of Suez, but they marked him as the Arab leader with a world view and a place on the world stage. Nasser, however, soon received a heavy blow to his personal prestige which put an end to the brief period when cooperation and solidarity had been the keynote of Arab state relations.

THE BREAKUP OF THE U.A.R.

Before the momentum given the Egyptian-Syrian union by the tremendous enthusiasm of the Arab public began to flag, it had received a stimulus from developments in Iraq. There, uncontrolled public disturbances and the ominous growth of Communist power gave Nasser and the Syrians good reason to seek mutual protection against whatever contagion Iraq had contracted. Whenever Nasser visited the "Northern Region" (Syria) his personal popularity and influence were demonstrated anew.

By 1960, however, it was clear that the union was not working out well. Those—and there were many—who had believed that once political union was accomplished all kinds of good things would follow, were soon disappointed. The more practical minded had counted on the union's making some economic problems easier, adding to Arab strength by merging the two armies, and developing a form of government satisfactory to both Egyptians and Syrians. But they also were disappointed.

A setback in economic conditions dampened much of the enthusiasm for the union. After a period of agricultural prosperity, Syria suffered three seasons of drought which, by turning the country from an exporter to an importer of wheat, adversely affected the whole economy. The Syrian business community was, however, perhaps even more concerned about the encroachment of Egypt's system of centralized economic controls upon the traditionally free Syrian economy. Moreover, the armies, which Arab nationalist publicists had been saying for years would get along like brothers, proved to be suspicious of each other and jealous of their own prerogatives, as brothers sometimes are. There were rumors of the highhanded behavior of Egyptian officers assigned to the First Army in the Northern Region. Before long it was mutually agreed that each army would tend to its own area, with a minimum of mixing of personnel.

Difficulties were greatest in the field of government. The Syrian leaders who made the agreement with Egypt had accepted the abolition of parties as a condition of union but they were never reconciled to the sacrifice. Accepting Nasser as a symbol of the Arab nationalism in which they believed, they signed away their own political freedom because they felt that the alternative was a Communist takeover. Anyhow, they were confident that they, the originators of the idea of Arab unity and the most adroit politicians of the Arab world, would soon be running the union. But Nasser was determined to safeguard the union by the same means which he had used to protect the revolution in Egypt. Hence, the joint National Assembly of the U.A.R. and the union cabinet with its two executive boards never had a chance to become vital political entities. The National Union failed in Syria, as in Egypt, because it offered a debating society as a substitute for the give and take, the rewards and punishments, of real politics.

The enemies of the U.A.R. and of Nasser predicted that Syria would be Egyptianized, that it would become a satrapy with Egyptians in every post of power. But Nasser and his advisers soon discovered that they had neither the flair nor the personnel for governing a province, and, when the union dissolved, it was remarkable how few Egyptians were in Syria and how little they had to do with what went on there. In fact, the worst thing the

Egyptians did to Syria was to leave it without a government. It was the government in Cairo which ran the U.A.R., and, as time passed, fewer and fewer Syrians occupied positions of importance in it. Many Syrians who had been given positions with important-sounding titles discovered that they had been brought to Cairo not to participate in government but to be kept away from Damascus. The most important Syrian remaining in Damascus was Abdel Hamid Serraj, former omniscient G-2 commandant who served as the minister of interior for the Northern Region. He did his job ruthlessly and too well. In harassing the enemies of the U.A.R. he built up a tremendous resentment against it. Attempts by Nasser's chief lieutenants, culminating in a long mission by Abdel Hakim Amir, failed to get things moving in Syria and by mid-1961 the only questions were when, and by which of the high contracting parties, the union would be broken asunder.

In July, during the ceremonies celebrating the 1952 revolution, Nasser announced a series of decrees implementing its social and economic policies. Among the more important were one which nationalized a number of companies and another which imposed a stringent income tax. Both applied to Syria as well as to Egypt. This was a clear challenge to Syria's conservative business community and to all who had hoped that Syria would be exempted from the onward march of socialism in Egypt. Still there was no open break; Syria remained loyal to the union, perhaps because it had no outstanding political leaders of its own and no feasible alternative policy.

The occasion for separation was provided by Abdel Hamid Serraj and the Egyptians themselves. In a cabinet reshuffle following Nasser's July decrees Serraj was appointed a vice-president and ordered to Cairo where he became involved in a dispute with Abdel Hakim Amir, Nasser's deputy for Syrian affairs. When Serraj returned hastily to Damascus, apparently without authority, the Egyptians arrested his principal lieutenants. With the Syrian security apparatus thus immobilized, a group of army officers moved with their troops during the night of September 27–28 to seize key points in Damascus.

Early on September 28, representatives of the dissident army group presented their demands to Abdel Hakim Amir. It was announced that they were not asking dissolution of the union but only certain privileges for Syria and the Syrian army. At first it was reported that the Egyptians had accepted their demands but then word came from Cairo that Nasser refused to compromise. In a speech the next day he said he could not "bargain over our republic" with a "separatist, reactionary, imperialist movement." There followed a period of confusion during which Cairo radio reported demonstrations against the dissident army group in all the large cities of Syria while Damascus radio reported enthusiastic response to Syria's liberation from the Egyptians.

For a time it seemed that Egypt might take military measures to preserve the union with Syria. Paratroopers were landed in Latakia, ships were requisitioned in Alexandria, and the Egyptian navy was reported to be on its way to Syria. But on the 29th, Nasser said that he had asked himself whether ". . . one Arab's blood should be shed by another, whether Arabs should fight each other, and in the interests of whom will be shed this blood and in the interests of whom do we fight each other while there are enemies lying in wait?" So, he said, he had ordered the Egyptian paratroopers not to fire on Syrians but only to offer their services to those loyal to the U.A.R. When the one hundred and twenty that went in were promptly taken prisoner, he ordered the others not to land and ordered his navy back to Alexandria. In Syria there had been some demonstrations hostile to the coup and friendly to Nasser and the union, but more in favor of the separation of Syria from Egypt. Inevitably, a few old scores were paid off in the hours after the coup. Also a considerable change took place in the prison population, as Serraj and his men went in and those whom they had imprisoned went out. In the course of the exchange there were some casualties. On the whole, however, it was remarkable that the U.A.R., which came into being with so much fanfare and such obviously genuine popular support, should come apart so quietly and with so little popular protest.

Syria and Egypt

The new group in control in Syria was soon identified as conservative. Nasser's propaganda machine denounced it as reactionary and as being in league with "imperialist" forces. It named as the principal supporters of the separatist movement the British, King Hussein of Jordan, and the Khamasiya, a textile manufacturing enterprise in which five wealthy Syrian families were involved. The Syrian Arab Revolutionary Command (SARC), the small group of army officers responsible for the actual seizure of power, kept in the background, avoiding publicity. But Cairo identified them, particularly Lt. Colonel Haider el Khuzbari, cousin of the interim premier, as representatives of the most powerful conservative families of Damascus. Khuzbari and SARC quickly made friendly gestures to the West and were reported to be in close contact with King Hussein. At the same time, however, friendly exchanges took place between the new Syrian government and Prime Minister Kassem in Baghdad. In December a generally conservative Parliament was elected. The Communist leader Khalid Baqdash was refused permission to return to Syria, although General Afif el Bizri, who since his expulsion in 1958 had spent much of his time in the Soviet bloc, was allowed to return. Perhaps more important than its conservative character was the representation in the new Syrian assembly of all the traditional elements in Syrian politics. Nasserites and extreme leftists were the only groups not openly represented.

However opposed to Egyptian rule in Syria they might be, the new men in power in Syria found it necessary to avow their loyalty to the ideals of Arab nationalism and Arab unity. But they did not state whether they intended to reverse the social and economic revolution which Nasser's decrees had initiated. In a "ministerial statement" read over Damascus radio on September 29, Premier Mahmun el Khuzbari said that Syria ". . . once again asserts to the Arabs and Arabism that it was and still is the fortified stronghold of Arabism and its pulsating heart. . . ." The next day the new Minister of State for Propaganda, Information, Radio, and Television, Dr. Mustapha al Barudi, said: "The objective in the past is the same as that of today. It has not changed at all. The Arab people of Syria have never deviated from unity nor from its objective. . . . Our aim is the liberation of all parts of the Arab homeland—its liberation from imperialism and the foreigner, its liberation from internal oppression." Both officials explained the break with Egypt as Syria's rejection not of the principle of unity but of Egyptian pride and greed. Egypt had deviated from the true path of unity which Syria by its sacrifice of sovereignty in 1958 had sought to follow.

Discussion of socialism the new Syrian leaders found more difficult. Speaking before members of the trade-union federation on October 1, Khuzbari said: "All the members of the cabinet support a genuinely socialist policy—socialist, and based on principles of justice, equality and genuine socialist safeguards which aim at giving the worker his full and unabridged rights and not one which takes with the left hand what it gives with the right hand." The military members of the new government (SARC) listed "the realization of true socialism" as one of three aims of the revolution, along with protecting Arab nationalism and establishing a true democracy. Two things seemed clear: (1) the political equilibrium in Syria was maintained by a complex and uneasy combination of disparate elements, and (2) Nasser's Arab socialism with its social and economic reforms had left its mark in Syria; it could not be blotted out by the new regime. Events in the spring of 1962 continued to testify to the increment of "Nasserism" which remained in Syria, and all signs pointed to confused but steady movement in the direction of Arab nationalist and "Arab socialist" formulas.

The Syrian revolt made Nasser in effect president only of Egypt rather than of a union of Arab states, though the name has not been changed and Egypt is still officially the United Arab Republic. His people, who had been nourished for years on the promise of a great role in the coming Arab unity, became again only Egyptians. When Nasser explained to his Cairo audience on September 29 his decision "not to agree to turn unity into a military operation" and asked his listeners to accept for the moment the turn of events in Syria, he made clear how difficult he found his position. "I know," he said, "that the stab of the enemy may wound the body, but will not wound the heart. But the stab of a friend tears the heart more than it tears the body. I know this because I have felt it." He went on to ask Egyptians to maintain their faith in eventual Arab unity and to believe that in the sweep of history the dissolution of the U.A.R. would be looked on as a momentary reverse in the fortunes of the united Arab world. The reactionary elements in Syria which had allied themselves with the traditional enemies of Arab nationalism were mentioned, but no serious search was made for foreign enemies on whom to fix the blame.

For a change, attention was turned to what the Arab nationalists, and particularly the Egyptians, had done wrong. Nasser told a rally of Cairo University students on October 2 that Egyptians must have the courage to look at their own mistakes. The first mistake he identified was in being deceived by "reaction," in making a truce with the internal enemies of Arab nationalism. He named King Hussein as an example, though the Syrian conservatives were obviously also in his mind. The second mistake was in being overcome by conceit. "Because we were overcome by conceit," he said, "we believed that the struggle for Arab nationalism had come to an end."

Nasser had every reason to interpret the Syrian coup as a rejection of the social and economic phase of the Egyptian revolution. Accepting the challenge, he pushed ahead even more vigorously with plans for Arab socialism. The great mistake in Syria, he believed, was not in trying to extend the social and economic revolution to Syria. The mistake was in waiting so long to do so.

After the Syrian coup, Nasser nationalized still more enterprises, sequestered the property of hundreds of persons believed unsympathetic to the revolution, and introduced more socialist reforms. Apparently he genuinely feared that a conservative coup might take place in Cairo like that in Syria; his socialist measures deprived what was left of the old upper class of power to act against him. Experience had shown, so he believed, that there was no point in compromising with the conservatives, either within his own country or in other Arab countries. The nationalist revolution in Egypt, he apparently felt, would have to be complete to be successful; once successful it would appeal to the masses in all the Arab countries over the heads of the ruling conservatives.

A minor incident in the Arab drama after the Syrian coup illustrated Nasser's determination not to compromise. The Imam of Yemen, who had associated himself and his country with the U.A.R. in 1958, after the Syrian coup apparently thought Nasser's name no longer sacrosanct, so he wrote a poem in classical Arabic poking fun at Nasser's socialism and declaring it to be incom-

patible with Islam. Nasser's reply, a roar of contemptuous denunciation of the backward-looking and decadent regime in
Yemen, included the announcement that he was severing the tie
that joined the U.A.R. with Yemen in the United Arab States.
Nasser now stood an avowed opponent of the old order and a
devotee of revolution, social and economic as well as political.

These developments seemed to indicate revival of Egyptian nationalism, abandonment of the Pan Arab idea, and declining interest in the politics of Afro-Asia and of nonalignment. But before
long Nasser arranged another conference of the big three of neutralism by inviting Marshal Tito to Cairo as Nehru was passing
through on his way back from a visit to the United States. Thus
he announced that his status as neutralist statesman remained unaffected. Despite the loss of Syria, Nasser's basic orientation in international politics was unchanged, and he continued to be identified with the ideas of Arab nationalism and unity.

Reactions and Implications

Many Syrians were glad to see the Egyptians go and to feel that
Syria was again independent. Some blamed the union for economic
losses; others, with good reason, hated the oppressive regime of
Abdel Hamid Serraj; others felt deprived of a role in their own
country's affairs by Nasser's application to Syria of the ban on
political activities which he enforced in Egypt. Most Syrians heart-
ily approved the foreign policies of the U.A.R. and continued to
support the ideas of Arab nationalism and the goal of Arab unity.
But they were Syrians as well as Arabs. Opposition to the union
was for the most part a matter of injured pride, the feeling that
Syria and Syrians were not given a major role.

On the surface, the reaction of the Egyptian public to the Syrian
break-away was one of relief, combined with resentment that the
Syrians, who had imposed themselves on Egypt and who had
gotten more out of union than they gave, should have taken their
leave with talk of regaining their independence.

Thus the long-anticipated union of Arab states broke up without
any popular outcry, but the lack of demonstrations, for once in the
Arab world, masked feelings of great significance. In both countries
a deep sense of unease expressed itself in stout reaffirmation of the

principle of Arab unity. In both countries the ordinary people, who did not pretend to understand the issues that had led to the rupture of the union, were saddened. They felt that a blow had been dealt to an ideal which was important to them and to the whole Arab community. More sophisticated persons, including many who accepted and approved the break, regretted that the union should have failed. The majority of the politically involved felt that the failure of the U.A.R., whatever the reasons, represented a setback to a development to which the Arabs were inevitably committed.

Disappointment was particularly strong among Arabs who had been less directly involved than the Syrians and the Egyptians. The West Bank Palestinians in Jordan, who had looked to Nasser and to the union as a source of leadership for the whole Arab world and for common action to resolve the Arab-Israeli problem, were deeply disturbed. The Muslim Arabs of Lebanon also were disappointed. Many of them had hoped that Nasser and the U.A.R. might create an Arab community in which they could have a place. They engaged in pro-Nasser demonstrations more vigorous than any in Syria or Egypt. Some despairing young Arab intellectuals blamed Nasser for not fighting harder to prevent the destruction of the union, for not sending troops against the separatists in Syria who, they persisted in believing, represented only a small group of opponents of Arab nationalist unity. Many felt that Arab nationalism had suffered a defeat, as it had on the battlefields of Palestine in 1948, and that it would be forced again to withdraw for a time from active politics to re-examine its creed and to forge a new program. They hoped that it would rise from this defeat, as it had in the early fifties, stronger and more determined than before.

The period following the Palestine War and the Egyptian revolution saw Arab nationalism develop policies and techniques which made it a force to be reckoned with in international politics. It saw Arab nationalists for the first time in modern history determining the course of events in Arab lands, often against the will of the powers which had long dictated the shape of things in the area. One of the most striking aspects of the period was the unanimity with which Arabs had stood together on the major issues of the time. The Syrian coup in September 1961 brought to a close, however, an era in which many Arabs had come to believe that Arab unity and the creation of a great Arab state were just around the corner. Once more it brought into high relief the disparities and rivalries within the Arab world and within the Arab nationalist movement itself.

Of at least equal importance was the fact that in Nasser's mind and in the minds of his closest followers the breakup of the union with Syria confirmed a belief in the necessity of social and economic revolution. Thus ideas of compromise and cooperation among the disparate Arab governments were thrust aside, and Nasser turned his attention to the basic changes in his own country and to the perfection of "Arab socialism," which he hoped would inspire the peoples of the other Arab states to cast aside their traditional governments. They would be replaced, he believed, by governments which shared his social and economic as well as his international policies and would join Egypt in a more viable union than that with Syria had proved to be.

IX

THE ARAB-ISRAEL CONFLICT

The Arab-Israel conflict, which is involved in almost every aspect of Arab foreign relations and foreign policy, is a great historical tragedy, a clash of cultures, of aspirations, of irreconcilable hopes, and of the most bitter hatreds. Hundreds of proposals for compromise, offers of mediation, efforts to promote understanding or to create an atmosphere conducive to settlement have fallen on barren ground. Their failure suggests that it may be a mistake to think of this as the kind of problem for which a solution can be found, except in the processes of history.

Myriads of written and spoken words have failed to make clear the roles played by the several actors in this tragic drama, or to ascribe praise and blame to the satisfaction of anyone but the partisans of one or the other of the antagonists. And the partisans have become more extreme and uncompromising with the passage of time. Of the many persons who have set themselves, or have been assigned, the task of finding a way through the impasse between the Arabs and Israelis—scholars, diplomats, government officials, and representatives of the United Nations and of various religious, humanitarian, and charitable foundations—almost all have in time become disillusioned or embittered. Very few have won the confidence of both sides, and some of the most objective have been most vigorously attacked.

Conventional procedures involving attempts to break the problem down into its elements, to find a basis for compromise on some of them and, by introducing outside resources and rewards, to induce opposing parties to accept new arrangements, have repeatedly failed. Both parties are seeking control of territory in Palestine, but no scheme for dividing it between them is acceptable. Each pursues psychological, as well as material, goals which it considers vital, but which are irreconcilable with the realization of the other's endeavor.

This is the heart of the conflict. A body of Jews reacting to the horror of Hitler's effort to eliminate their race and religion in Europe, sought to achieve some command over their own fate by pushing through to completion the long-cherished scheme of establishing a Jewish state. They established it on territory which Arabs had occupied for centuries, and at the precise moment when the Arabs were re-emerging as a people in search of the means to control their own lands and destiny. Thus Jewish and Arab nationalisms clashed head-on in Palestine. The Zionists, as the Jews who sought to create the new state called themselves, had selected Palestine as its site almost without considering that the territory was inhabited principally by Arabs. They chose Palestine because, some hundreds of years before, it had been the site of the last Jewish state, and because it contained their holy places. The Arabs, on their part, did not choose Palestine as an issue between themselves and the Jews, or as the issue which would stimulate the Arab nationalist movement and provide its divergent elements with a common enemy and a common purpose. They ignored Zionism and evaded its implications for years, but once their defeat in the Palestine War was a fact, and once Israel was established in their midst, the Arabs almost unanimously accepted Zionism as the most vivid symbol of the things that they must oppose and overcome.

For the Zionists and, after the creation of the state, the Israelis, establishing a viable state and guaranteeing its security were objectives on which they could make no compromise. For the Arabs, the establishment of Israel and, perhaps equally important, their having to accept it, meant defeat, humiliation, and failure to reach their most cherished objective—command of their own land and destiny. But the Israelis, starting at the end of the Palestine War with a fragment of territory not clearly suitable for the establishment of a viable state, could not regard any concession they might win from the Arabs as adequate compensation for the sacrifice of any part of the land they had succeeded in occupying. On their side, the Arabs could not regard any concession that the Israelis might make to them as satisfactory compensation for their acceptance of Israel as a state.

For both the contestants, the Palestine question was fraught with the deepest emotions. Each regarded its rights as elemental, firmly based on reason, law, morality, and the will of God, and was convinced that any means to achieve its purpose were justifiable. As passions rose, ruthless brutality and irrationality became commonplace on both sides. Desperate deed has been heaped upon desperate deed until there is no unsorting of right and wrong, of guilt and responsibility. Each side has done things without number which the other can never forgive nor forget.

THE ARAB IMAGE OF THE ISRAELIS

The conflict between Arabs and Israelis is greatly influenced by the image which each has of the other. Each image is strongly tinged with misunderstanding and fear, but because each has a basis of fact it is not likely to change quickly.

The Arabs credit Israel with dogged determination, immense energy and skill, and single-minded devotion to its objectives. The Arabs were acquainted with the Jewish colonies in Middle Eastern lands which had long accepted their minority status and were Oriental, not Western, in culture and outlook. Only in the thirties, when the influx of refugees from Nazi persecution began, did the more perceptive Arabs recognize another kind of Jew. It was not until the Jewish underground forces began to clean up Arab resistance in Palestine, in the last weeks before the British withdrawal, that the Arabs realized what daring, skill, and ruthlessness they were up against. Arab diplomats and political leaders had for some time been learning about the skill of the Zionists in their fields, but it was only after the Palestine War that they fully recognized the quality of their antagonists. Both the Jews and the Arabs engaged in terrorism and in political maneuver, but the Jews were overwhelmingly more effective. The Arab reaction was naturally one of fear, and was marked by a tendency to exaggerate the deviousness and cleverness of their enemies. The image of the almost superhumanly clever and able Jew helps to explain the

Arabs' reluctance to negotiate, and their fear of accepting normal commercial relations with Israel.

Another important element in the Arab image of Israel is that country's relationship with the Western powers, particularly the United States. The Arabs have been impressed by the numerous instances of British cooperation with the Zionist and Israeli Jews, extending from the Balfour Declaration to the Anglo-French-Israeli invasion of Egypt in 1956. They have forgotten, or explained away, the equally numerous instances of British disagreement with the Zionists and the unhappy efforts of the British government, at great cost to its prestige in many quarters, to carry out its obligations under the Balfour Declaration and the Mandate for Palestine to restrict Jewish immigration. Even when British policy became manifestly pro-Arab and anti-Zionist, the Arabs either took it for granted or discounted it as a devious plot. French support for Israel, particularly in the crisis of 1956 and throughout France's long struggle with the nationalist rebellion in Algeria, was obvious. As for the United States, the Arabs have been impressed by its hurried recognition of the state of Israel, by the vast sums of money collected from American Zionists, and by the American government's assistance to Israel which from 1945 to 1960 exceeded that given all the Arab states together. The Arabs noted, also, the outspokenness of certain American congressmen on Israel's behalf and the talk of the Jewish vote—assumed even by many Americans to be solidly pro-Israel and frequently reported to exert effective pressure upon the American government on Israel's behalf. Arab conclusions about the measure of American support for Israel have also been affected by the vastly disproportionate attention given Israel in the American press and on radio and television and the sympathetic point of view of these media, so strikingly in contrast with treatment given the Arab cause.

The Arabs consequently view Israel as the darling of the Western powers, sustained and protected by them. They see it as a force that cannot be dealt with in terms of its actual size, population, or resources, but only as an extension of the Western powers. Thus they have come to think of Israel as a colony of the West, a bridgehead for Western interests, an instrument of Western policy. This concept makes it all the more difficult for the Arabs, preoccupied with their struggle against colonialism and outside interference in their affairs, to consider a settlement with Israel. The Arab pictures Israel as a branch of a world community of sixteen million people which will ultimately seek to move into the Middle East through its present bridgehead in Palestine, extending the boundaries of the Jewish state from the Nile to the Euphrates in accordance with Biblical prophecy.

For this apprehension, Israeli and Zionist leaders bear much responsibility. They emphasize the ability of the Jewish state to draw upon the resources of Jewish communities throughout the world, and to influence the governments of various states in their behalf. Walter Eytan, long the Director General of the Israeli Ministry of Foreign Affairs and then Ambassador to France, has written: "It is a commonplace of our [Israel's] Foreign Service that every Envoy Extraordinary and Minister Plenipotentiary of Israel has a dual function. He is Minister Plenipotentiary to the country to which he is accredited—and Envoy Extraordinary to its Jews."[1] The idea that all Jews are associated with Israel and that Israel draws strength from the world Jewish community was expressed by David Ben Gurion's Independence Day message in 1957. He said: "The ingathering of Israel's exiled and scattered sons is the common task of all sections of the Jewish people wherever they may live. Everything that has been created in this country is the common possession of the Jews of all lands."[2] Eytan compares the relation between Israel and Jews living outside Israel with the relationship between France and the French citizens in Italy, or between Great Britain and the British community in Peru, or between the Americans of Swedish, Irish, English, or Italian origin and their "home countries."[3] But he is mistaken. The difference, actually, is considerable. Most Swedes in Japan or English in Peru retain their Swedish and British passports; they are still Swedes and Englishmen although living abroad. The Jews in the United States or Argentina, however, carry American or Argentinian passports, being born or naturalized citizens of those countries.

---

[1] Walter Eytan, *The First Ten Years: A Diplomatic History of Israel* (New York: Simon and Schuster, 1958), p. 192.

[2] As quoted in same, p. 195.

[3] Same, p. 194.

The relationship of most naturalized Americans to their home countries, moreover, is quite different from that of the American Jew to Israel. The American whose parents or grandparents came from Norway may send money to relatives and may go "home" on a sentimental visit, but he is under no obligation to return to Norway to live there or to aid others to return, and he has no legal status in Norway except as an American citizen. The Israeli Law of Return, however, makes every Jew automatically a citizen of Israel once he sets foot in the country. This and the Israeli emphasis upon immigration give the Arabs great concern, because of the implication of expansion at Arab expense. David Ben Gurion assured the American Jewish Committee in 1950, and again in 1961, that the emigration of Jews to Israel is at their own "free discretion."[4] Yet through all the strands of Zionist argument runs the strong threat of rejection of the idea that any Jew can be assimilated anywhere in a country other than Israel, that his ultimate obligation is to the state of Israel, to expanding its strength, either by immigration or by support.

At the Ideological Conference sponsored in Jerusalem in 1957 by the World Zionist Organization, Nahum Goldmann, its president, expressed his vision of the kind of state Israel should become in order to avoid domination by the surrounding Arab world: ". . . backed by the Jewish people of the world, Israel will no longer be merely a tiny part of the Middle East, but will represent forces and influences spread all over the world which will make it, as was once said, a small great country. . . . Zionism has never wanted just a state which would be of a few million Jews on the Mediterranean. It wanted a state which would be commensurate with the uniqueness and greatness of Jewish history; a state which would play quite a different role from that which a normal state of a few million people ordinarily plays."[5] He claimed for Israel a "vital partnership" with Zionists of other countries. His conception was supported by some representatives of the Jewish Diaspora (the Jewish communities outside Palestine) but it was rejected

[4] Irving Spiegel, "Ben Gurion Gives View on U.S. Jews," *The New York Times,* May 1, 1961.

[5] *Forum for the Problems of Zionism, Jewry and the State of Israel: Proceedings of the Jerusalem Ideological Conference* (Jerusalem: World Zionist Organization, 1959), pp. 126–127.

and attacked by others, particularly the representatives of the Israeli majority. Premier Ben Gurion criticized Goldmann's conception of a Zionism whose supporters accepted residence outside Israel. "My Zionism," he said, ". . . was built on the conviction that we did not form a part of the peoples among whom we lived, that we had no intention of remaining in exile, and that our deepest aspiration was to return personally to Zion."[6]

In his main address to the conference Premier Ben Gurion expressed his concern at the increased assimilation of American Jews, which he saw weakening their ties and obligations to Israel. The Russians, he hoped, would ultimately arrive at the "only real solution" of the Jewish problem in Russia: "the opening of the gates for the *aliya* (migration) of the Jews to Israel."[7] The emphasis was upon immigration: "The survival and the peace of the State of Israel will be safe-guarded by one thing and one thing alone—large-scale immigration. For the safe-guarding of its security the State requires an addition of at least two million Jews in the coming period." And further on: ". . . we are still at the beginning of the process of the ingathering of the exiles. None of us can foretell the potential scope of the ingathering of the exiles."[8]

It is thus not only Israel's connections with the Western powers and its ability to call on the support of Jewish communities all over the world that frighten the Arabs, but also the prospect of waves of immigration which could not be contained within the present boundaries of Israel. They have seen the Zionists proceed from plans for agricultural settlements in Palestine to the idea of a Jewish homeland, enshrined in the words of the Balfour Declaration, which was not to "prejudice the civil and religious rights of existing non-Jewish communities in Palestine." They have seen them move on to plans for the establishment of a state which looked upon the thirteen or fourteen millions of Jews outside its border as "colonies" and potential citizens.[9] The Arabs were im-

[6] Same, p. 149.

[7] Same, p. 123.

[8] Same, p. 119.

[9] See Michael Ionides, *Divide and Lose: The Arab Revolt of 1955–1958* (London: Geoffrey Bles, 1960), pp. 82–85, for a description of how Zionist aspirations and Zionist arguments have adapted themselves progressively to opportunities.

pressed also by Israel's constant efforts—as in the Eichmann trial of 1961—to bind the Jews of the world to it and to convince them that nowhere else can they live whole and secure lives.

Israel's image in Arab minds today combines ruthless aggression with great skill and cleverness, backed by the resources of the Western powers and of world Jewry. Then to complete the picture, there is the evidence of the expansionist drive and potential of the state of Israel.

THE ISRAELI IMAGE OF THE ARABS

Over the centuries the Jews of the Middle East have adjusted to living with an Arab Muslim majority, often in a relatively peaceful relationship. But the great majority of Zionists have not been Middle Eastern Jews. The originators and early supporters of the movement came for the most part from Russia and Eastern Europe and their dreams of establishing a Jewish state in Palestine were framed almost entirely without thought of the Arab inhabitants. The possibility of Arab opposition hardly occurred to them until after the First World War.[10] The hallowed tradition of the Jews, that Palestine was the Promised Land, and their belief that under the Ottomans the land had been allowed to go to waste and was sparsely occupied by listless and backward people—these concepts were fundamental in the plan to establish a "homeland" *with the consent and cooperation of the Arabs*. After the Balfour Declaration and the beginnings of Jewish immigration under the British Mandate, when the Zionists learned that relations with the Arabs constituted a serious problem, they assigned some of their best people to learn Arabic and to specialize in Arab affairs. Some of them, particularly some Zionist members of Jewish communities in Arab countries, hoped that Zionists and Arabs could come to

[10] Rony E. Gabbay, *A Political Study of the Arab-Jewish Conflict: The Arab Refugee Problem (A Case Study)* (Geneva: E. Droz, 1959), p. 30. See Chaim Weizmann, *Trial and Error: The Autobiography of Chaim Weizmann* (New York: Harper, 1949), for a fascinating account of the forces which combined in this extraordinary man's life to produce his drive to create a Jewish state in Palestine, almost without thought of the Arab position in that country. Weizmann's story is also interesting because of the way it demonstrates how the Zionists explained their goals in ways acceptable to those from whom they were asking support, always raising their sights after each forward movement.

terms. In fact, at the end of World War I contacts between Feisal, leader of the Hashemite army and later King of Iraq, and Zionist leaders made some kind of accommodation appear possible, but on Feisal's part it depended on the establishment of the great Arab state which he believed the British had promised his father. King Abdullah of Jordan agreed to secret negotiations with Israel after the Palestine War, but his assassination in 1951 ended that initiative. Otherwise no significant Arab leader has accepted the possibility of settlement with Israel. The Arab attitude has been one of almost unrelieved hostility; consequently the Israeli image of the Arabs gives the impression of great capacity for hatred and intransigence.

The Arabs have given the Israelis ample evidence upon which to base such an impression. They have refused to confront the state of Israel directly in discussion and negotiation; they have cut off all its contacts with the Arab world and have sought in every way possible to isolate it not only from the Near East but from all of Asia and Africa. Arab sports teams refuse to meet Israeli teams in international competition, even at the cost of forfeited games. Countless incidents—for example, the widespread criticism of the Lebanese Foreign Minister, Charles Malik, for visiting the Israeli exhibit at the Brussels International Fair—have revealed the determination to deny Israel the slightest courtesy or contact which might be taken to signify acceptance or recognition. The Arab press, always violently emotional in dealing with the opponents of the Arab states, has over the years found Israel guilty of every conceivable crime and a good many that are quite inconceivable. It has seen the Israeli hand in every Arab misfortune and spotted Israeli maneuvers and intrigues in the most unlikely situations. All this has gone into the Israeli image of the Arab character.

In the years following the Palestine War, throwing the Israelis into the sea and the idea of a war of revenge were prominent themes in the Arab press and in the statements of Arab leaders. With the passage of time this approach has given way to somewhat more restrained talk of liberating Palestine and restoring the rights of the Arab refugees. In his comparatively moderate statement before the United Nations General Assembly on September 27,

1960, President Nasser discussed the Palestine question in terms of United Nations responsibility. He said:

In our part of the world, the Arab East, the United Nations has forgotten its Charter and disregarded its responsibilities towards the rights of the people of Palestine.

Have the days and the years led to a solution of the problem? Have the people of Palestine forgotten all about their country, their land and their homes? Did the Arab nation forget the tragedy of the Arab people of Palestine, against whom imperialism conspired—with a mandate from the League of Nations—taking upon itself to promise to certain groups a country belonging to another people? . . .

The only solution to Palestine . . . is that matters should be restored to normalcy and should return to the conditions prevailing before the error was committed.[11]

Even where the hatred and the desire for revenge is screened out for the United Nations forum, the Israelis see in this statement of Arab attitudes toward the question of Palestine an implacable and intractable rejection of any suggestion of accommodation. Most Israelis believe that the hatred and the desire for revenge are still there behind the disguise.

Outside the forum of the United Nations frequent belligerent statements from the Arab side support the Israeli assumption that the Arabs are waiting only for the day when they can strike. In June of 1960, President Nasser said: "The people of Palestine will return to be masters in Palestine whether the war criminal Ben Gurion announces this or not."[12] The Voice of the Arabs, on the Egyptian radio, also frequently refers to the ultimate Arab attack on Israel. For example, on August 20, 1960, Fayiz Gandil, in an attack on King Hussein of Jordan, said: "The Arab nation wishes to liberate Palestine but the Jordanian rulers wish to consider the Western Bank part of Jordan. The Arab nation prepares to leap on Israel, while the Jordanian rulers establish solid ties with Israel." Nasser has seemed to Israelis to be the spearhead of Arab opposition. They have concluded it unlikely, because of

11 Information Administration, Press Bureau, Permanent Mission of the United Arab Republic to the United Nations (New York), *Text of Statement Delivered by President Gamal Abdel Nasser to the Fifteenth Session of the General Assembly of the United Nations on September 27, 1960*, p. 9.

12 *Nasser's Speeches*, 1960 (April-June), p. 147.

what they believe to be his urge for power and for empire, that he will accept a peaceful relationship.

Frustrated by failure to persuade the Arabs to accept the *de facto* situation and sit down to a "rational" resolution of outstanding issues, many Israelis have found in what they believe to be the weaknesses of the Arabs both an explanation of their behavior and some hope that they will be unable to bring to bear effectively their advantages of population and geography. Israelis often explain the continued resistance of the Arabs to settlement by citing the venality of Arab politicians, the backwardness of their society, and their dependence upon the grievance against Israel both as an excuse for their own shortcomings at home and their inability to view the international scene objectively. The growing belief among Israelis in the immutability of the Arab character, its inherent shiftlessness, incapacity for discipline and organization, cowardice, and inconsistency, paralyzes efforts to find some common ground and leads to the conclusion that the only thing the Arab understands is force.

Thus both the Israeli image of the Arab and its counterpart create a state of mind in which a settlement based on agreement seems out of the question. Only the build-up of military and diplomatic strength vis-à-vis the other party appears a practical course of action.

APPROACHES TO THE ARAB-ISRAEL PROBLEM

Behind the Zionist movement lie profound spiritual, cultural, and emotional drives and a dream which the Jewish people have cherished over the centuries. Since the end of the nineteenth century, when Theodor Herzl wrote his book, *Der Judenstaat,* and the first Zionist Congress was held, Zionist Jews have pursued a policy of hardheaded pragmatism leading straight to their objective of a state in Palestine, utilizing every resource to the full, taking advantage of the most unlikely situations, and repeatedly converting losses into gains. The Israelis have adopted the same pragmatic approach in dealing with the Arabs since the Palestine War.

Their objectives are to consolidate their state and establish economic and political relations with the neighboring states that will enable Israel to achieve prosperity and security. They offer the

Arabs profitable trade relations, transit facilities across Israeli territory, compensation for Arab property left in Israel by the refugees, and cooperation in the commercial and industrial development of the area. The Israelis have little patience with the Arabs for refusing to negotiate on these terms; they see little point in arguing about Arab rights in Palestine. Their own rights in the area, they point out, are founded on the Balfour Declaration, the League of Nations Mandate for Palestine, and the United Nations Partition Plan of 1947. Departures from the terms of these instruments, they explain, were necessitated by the refusal or the inability of the British and of the United Nations to guarantee the Jews their legal rights, or by the refusal of the Arabs to honor them.[13] When pressed on these points, however, Israelis are likely to fall back to a pragmatic approach: Israel is a fact; it has been created as a result of a war which the Arabs started and lost; it will be to their advantage, and to the advantage of all concerned, to acknowledge defeat and accept Israel's terms.

The hard school through which Israel's leaders have come and the desperate dangers and difficulties which they have survived, and which probably they must face again, have made them disinclined to give up anything unless compelled to. Premier David Ben Gurion and those who make policy in his government follow a hard line. Stern and unyielding, they believe in making clear Israel's ability and readiness to use force in its own interest. The idea of a negotiated settlement with the Arabs, although still advanced, has actually been put on the shelf. Meanwhile, interest and effort are being channeled into an attempt to leapfrog over the Arab states, and to outmaneuver them by winning influence and markets in the nations of Africa and Asia, beyond the Arab periphery.

There has long been a group in Jewish Palestine which believed that Arabs and Jews could live side by side in peace, and that a policy for an independent Jewish state could be worked out which would be acceptable to the Arabs. Within Mapam, the Marxist labor party in Israel, and a group known as Ihud, the idea finds support that the present conflict with the Arabs is intensified by

[13] J. C. Hurewitz, "Recent Books on the Problem of Palestine," *Middle East Journal,* January 1949, pp. 87–88.

Israel's identification with the West in its foreign and domestic outlook and policies. According to this view, Israel could reach an accommodation with the Arabs if it were content to be and to behave like a small Semitic state adjusting itself to the facts of life in the Middle East, adopting in the United Nations a neutralist policy in line with that of the Arabs. But, they argue, peace with the Arabs is impossible as long as Israel is, in effect, a Western state planted in the Middle East, leaning on the Western Jews and the Western powers for support, and following an essentially Western line in international policy.[14] Some assert that only a united Arab state can make peace with Israel, hence they look with favor on steps toward Arab unity.

Few Israelis accept this general line of reasoning, and, so long as the Ben Gurion school dominates thinking in the government, it is unlikely to have much practical influence on Israeli policy. The people who run the Israeli government are highly skeptical about any real improvement in Arab-Israeli relations brought about by the means recommended by Mapam, or by any other means. They have long since given up the idea that some clever formula might be found which would resolve the difficulties between them and the Arabs. Other people all over the world continue to look for the right combination of pressures and inducements or the right mediator to bring an end to one of the world's longest established crisis situations. As they come knocking on the doors of the Arab leaders, people with ideas about the solution of the Arab-Israeli situation also go in a steady stream to Jerusalem, asking to see Premier Ben Gurion. When his aides inform him that still another self-appointed mediator wants to talk with him, Ben Gurion is likely to say, "Take him out and buy him an ice cream. I don't have the time to waste in conversation about the Arabs."

The Israeli government's position is that it is willing and ready to negotiate. Ben Gurion has said that the Arabs would be surprised at his terms if they would sit down at a table with him, but Israel appears to offer no more than the "standing terms for peace"

[14] This approach to Israel's Arab policy is ably expounded in *The New Outlook,* a magazine published in Tel Aviv with the support of many persons not members of Mapam.

put forth in 1955: Arab communication across Israel, compensation to Arab refugees for their land and property, and a unified water development program. This means, in effect, acceptance of Israel as it is. Walter Eytan, after analyzing the advantages the Arabs might have gained from peace with Israel, concludes that to them the present situation has been more attractive:

. . . by maintaining a state of near war and tension, the Arab world reaped obvious advantages. It provided itself with a grievance it could nurse to its heart's content—and in politics there are few assets more valuable than a grievance. It focused international attention on itself by becoming a power for mischief; and it reckoned that, like any group which made enough of a nuisance of itself, it might hope for the prizes of appeasement. . . . It is not cynicism to say that if Israel did not exist, the Arabs would have to invent her.[15]

Out of the shock and humiliation that followed the Palestine War, and the bitterness and recrimination it stimulated among Arab leaders, came a policy that refused to acknowledge defeat or to accept its consequences. Thus, without clear leadership from a single source, but with the consent and participation of many Arabs, the policy of nonrecognition and boycott emerged. It was a way of carrying on the war with Israel on fronts where the Arabs still had resources. Like the American refusal to recognize Communist China, it expressed a moral rejection of the idea of giving aid and comfort to an enemy. By withholding recognition and prohibiting intercourse, it was hoped, the Arabs might be able to prevent the Israelis from establishing their state and taking their place in the international community. Drawing on a deep sense of history, the Arabs find in the Crusader colonies in Arab territory many parallels with Israel. Even if Israel cannot be crushed at once, a day may come when its support from the West will diminish. Then, having failed to establish an independent existence, the Israelis, like the Crusaders, will give up and go back where they came from.

Arabs are generally unimpressed by the Israeli appeal—often repeated by Westerners—to be practical and accept the facts of the situation. They ask if there is any necessity, beyond custom, for a defeated nation to make peace with its foe. Even sober and

[15] Eytan, cited, p. 113.

thoughtful Arabs simply cannot bring themselves to go through the forms which would acknowledge Israel and the implication of Arab incapacity which its very existence bears. There is a very real psychological bloc, an involuntary shrinking from the idea, an unwillingness to accept the fact, and a sometimes shamefaced realization that many Arabs prefer delusion to the humiliating and, as they believe, unjust reality. Some serious-minded and responsible Arabs, when asked if the Arabs can forever refuse to settle with Israel, answer that they cannot bind their sons or their sons' sons. The next generation can possibly take a fresh look at the problem of Israel, but they acknowledge that they are simply incapable of doing so.

Rejection of Israel shows aspects of Arab character which are in striking contrast to the Western approach to international problems. It is probably a mistake to attribute the Arabs' unwillingness to acknowledge Israel to a lack of realism. Actually, their attitude is consistent with their understanding of political reality and of the most effective ways of dealing with it. As Gandhi used passive resistance in the struggle against British rule in India, the Arabs employ their own weapons and techniques. Like the Indian nationalists, the Arabs have not adopted the weapons and the strategy of their opponents, but have fought with the means at their disposal and with a plan of battle all their own. Arab strategy is based on the assumption that the forces opposed to colonialism in the Asian-African world and elsewhere can be rallied against the establishment of a foreign colony by force in the midst of Arab territory. The decline of imperialism and colonialism all over the world emphasizes the anachronistic character of the Israeli venture, making it possible, they believe, to rally world opinion against it. In addition, the Arabs have hoped that the great powers could be drawn to use their influence against Israel—the Soviets because of their desire to oppose a Western interest in the Middle East, and the United States because, in the Arab view, its assistance to Israel has made it vulnerable to criticism and weakened its position in important areas of the world. While rallying outside support, the Arabs have mobilized all the resources at their command to obstruct Israel's efforts to create a functioning state.

ARAB POLICIES TOWARD ISRAEL

The policy of the Arab states toward Israel is coordinated in the Arab League where Egypt plays the leading role. The objective is to maintain in the Arab area a tight boycott and blockade of Israel, and to bring all influence to bear on other Afro-Asian states to cooperate in keeping Israel from extending its trade or influence, from obtaining membership in international bodies, and from gaining recognition as a nation. How this policy will change the present situation is not made clear, but it is hoped that in due time Israel will lose the cooperation of other states and the support of the West and that its strength relative to that of the Arab states will decline.

The possibility of another clash of arms with Israel is never far from Arab thoughts and is often mentioned in the press and in political speeches. But the notion that Arab armies will eventually drive the Israelis into the sea is much less common than before the Israeli invasion of Sinai in 1956. Arab leaders are probably aware that the promise of an eventual settlement with Israel by arms has less propaganda value than it had. They are also increasingly aware that armed conflict with Israel, as in 1956, is likely to bring in the great powers, leaving the final settlement to them and the United Nations, even if the Arabs were to win a military victory.

Arabs now tend to take the position that if they continue successfully to isolate Israel from its neighbors and prevent it from putting down roots in the Middle East, meanwhile developing their own strength and influence, time will work to their advantage and a favorable solution of the Israeli problem, the nature of which cannot now be foreseen, will emerge.

The Arabs have refused to deal directly with Israel or to accept the offices of a mediator on disputed issues—boundaries, refugees, status of Jerusalem, or water development—on the ground that doing so would amount to recognition of the state of Israel, which would undermine their whole position. In connection with border disputes, however, they have utilized the services of the UN Truce Supervisor and the Mixed Armistice Commissions. Nasser has accepted, and depended upon, the UN Emergency Force which has patrolled the border between Israel and Egypt, on the Egyptian side, since the end of the Sinai conflict of 1956; and he has accepted the presence of UN troops at Sharm-el-Sheikh on Egyptian territory at the entrance to the Gulf of Aqaba. Jordan and the other Arab states have been unable to agree on the status of Jerusalem; they have allowed the division of the city into Jordanian and Israeli sectors to go unchallenged.

The Arabs have held that the refugee question could be settled only in the context of a decision on Israel's right of conquest in Arab territory. In the United Nations and in public debate during the last few years they have held that the refugees were entitled to choose between repatriation or compensation as provided in the UN resolution, but they have not offered to negotiate on those terms. Meanwhile, they have resisted all efforts to resettle the refugees, arguing that resettlement would in effect concede Israel's right to the territory it occupies, and to the former homes and property of the Arab refugees. On essentially the same ground they have refused to negotiate programs for the development of water resources. They appeared at one time to be almost ready to accept the plan put forward by Eric Johnston, President Eisenhower's special representative, but in the end rejected it on the ground that joining in the plan would constitute recognition of Israel.

The Egyptians have denied Israel access to the Suez Canal, asserting their right to take measures necessary to defend their country, which is in a continuing state of war with Israel. Nasser has justified his violation of the UN resolution on this matter on the ground that Israel was violating more of that body's resolutions than he. He has offered to respect the canal resolution if Israel would respect other UN resolutions, including the 1947 Partition Plan and the resolution on refugees.

The Arab governments make recurrent efforts to maintain the appearance of agreement on their Palestine policy, but in fact there is constant rivalry on this subject, particularly between Jordan and the other Arab states, usually led by Egypt. In early 1960, the Egyptians sent a consul to the Jordanian part of Jerusalem with credentials assigning him to "occupied" Palestine, thus challenging Jordan's absorption of the West Bank after the Palestine War of 1948–49 and implying that all Palestine ultimately belongs in an Arab Palestinian state. Prime Minister Kassem of Iraq has proposed that Palestine should be liberated by Palestinians and has offered to train a Palestine army for this purpose. His proposal involved the idea of a state on the Palestinian territory not held by Israel and designed to be the basis for an enlarged Arab Palestine. Thus Kassem challenged both Jordan's claims to the West Bank and Nasser's position in Gaza, as well as Nasser's claim to represent the Palestinian Arabs.

This quarrel over Palestinian policy was patched up at an Arab League meeting at Schtaura in Lebanon in July 1960, which set up an Arab commission for Palestine composed of representatives of U.A.R., Iraq, Jordan, Lebanon, and Saudi Arabia. The commission was charged with the task of establishing a Palestine entity with an army and representation in the United Nations, but without modifying the present status of the West Bank or Gaza. This approach may reflect a fundamental change in the Arab position which formerly was based on the claim that Israel was only an enemy bridgehead in Arab territory, a temporary incident in an unfinished war. In the past two or three years responsible Arab officials have begun to talk more realistically of the UN Partition Plan of 1947. The Arab League Committee set up at Schtaura apparently takes the position now that the Palestine entity on which they plan to base their policy has legal foundation in the 1947 Partition Plan. This change may be tactical, however, not representing a decision to accept negotiation for a general settlement, although it implies such a decision.

THE ISSUES

Like the visible part of the iceberg, the practical problems left over from the Arab-Israel war are more apparent but much less significant than the more general issues lying below the surface. A great deal of time and effort has been devoted to practical issues such as water resources development, the Arab refugees, rectification of boundaries, the status of Jerusalem, and Suez Canal transit, but while basic Arab and Israeli attitudes remain as they are, there seems little hope for the resolution of any of these problems separately. Indeed it appears that both sides have concluded that the *status quo* is as good an arrangement as they can get. In fact, except for the unsettled refugees and the possibility that mutual fears and suspicions will lead to war, the present stalemate might be from all points of view the best feasible situation. So long as Israel is unwilling to make any significant concessions, particularly on the return of Arab refugees, in exchange for Arab recognition, and while the Arabs insist on substantial territorial concessions as the price of recognition, there is little prospect for breaking the present deadlock. Besides, in the background are irreconcilable attitudes: the Israelis are convinced that the Arabs are so consumed by hatred and so venal and undisciplined as to be incapable of making peace, and the Arabs, for their part, are equally convinced that Israel is the instrument of an international conspiracy to destroy the Arab nationalist revival and to establish a Jewish empire from the Nile to the Euphrates.

Negotiations

The Israelis have repeatedly indicated their willingness to sit down with Arab representatives to discuss the settlement of outstanding problems, but they have made clear their conditions: the acceptance of the *status quo* with respect to the boundaries of Israel and the continued location of the Arab refugees outside Israel. The Arab position on face-to-face negotiation has generally been that there can be nothing to negotiate, so long as the Israelis indicate no intention of yielding on boundaries and refugee return. However, they have sought indirectly to offer the United Nations resolutions, including the Partition Plan of 1947, as a basis for formal discussion. The Israelis, partly as a consequence of their lack of room for maneuver, have refused to make any concessions in advance of a face-to-face meeting. Various attempts to provide communications between the two parties and to offer mediation have proved fruitless, largely as a result of their unwillingness to trust each other and their belief that the other's position was only tactical, representing no real interest in settlement. It has frequently been pointed out that an improvement in the general atmosphere, a relaxation of tensions, is probably an essential preliminary to negotiations. The situation itself generates tensions, however, and there appears to be little prospect that a mutual agreement to keep things quiet could have any practical consequence.

Boundaries

The Arab position on the question of boundaries has been dominated by their insistence on treating the whole present situation as temporary and illegal. They have resisted negotiation on boundaries because of the danger that doing so would tend to confirm Israel's claims to sovereignty. Israel, for its part, has concentrated on making the boundaries as permanent as possible, except in those territories—like the demilitarized zones—where opportunities offered themselves for extending the area of Israeli control. Since it became clear that no legal steps were going to be taken to rationalize and confirm the boundaries laid down in the armistice agreements, the Israelis have proceeded systematically to extend their control over the demilitarized zones and other areas not clearly in their own or Arab territory. The resulting clashes and disputes have been a principal matter of business for the United Nations Truce Supervisor. With the passage of time the legal and customary basis for the existence of the demilitarized zones—territories inside the borders of the former Palestine Mandate which were occupied by Arab armies at the time of the armistice—has become blurred. The Israelis seek to extend their authority over them and the Arabs struggle to prevent it, mostly by the generally ineffective, but dangerous, threat of force.

With respect to longer-range questions, the Israelis would probably be happy to redraw and rationalize the boundaries, so hastily drawn in the armistice agreements, giving a little territory here to restore the lands of an Arab village and taking a little there to improve the defensibility of their frontier, but ending up with roughly the same total area. Their claims are based on both the 1947 Partition Plan and upon conquest in the Palestine War. The demilitarized zones on the Syrian and Egyptian borders they claim as part of the territory granted Israel in the Partition Plan, although the zones on the Syrian border were occupied by Syrian forces at the time of the armistice. Although the Arab states bordering

Israel would benefit from a rationalization of boundaries, they are unwilling to give added force to Israel's claim to recognized statehood unless they can get some compensatory concession from Israel, such as agreement to the return of those refugees who choose to return. Although irrational and difficult to administer and patrol, the Arab-Israeli boundaries are likely to stay as they are until basic changes in the over-all situation occur.

Border Tensions and Security

Border crossings and hostile attacks on both sides have been major factors in Arab-Israel relations ever since the armistice lines were established. The initial problem was the infiltration of Israel by Arabs, principally from the West Bank in Jordan, but also from the Gaza strip on the Egyptian border and from Syria. Many refugees returned to their former lands and homes, to pick up what they could of their own property, or, failing that, to take other property in its place and to make contact with friends and relatives in Israel. Inevitably, some of them got into trouble and committed acts of violence. Eventually, as bitterness increased on both sides and the boredom of refugee life turned farmers into fighters, they came over the border in private bands or with official or semiofficial help to sabotage and disrupt life in Israel and sometimes to take Israeli lives.

These raids led the Israelis in the autumn of 1953 to initiate their policy of "active defense" with reprisals against Arab villages said to harbor infiltrators. The Israeli strikes, which were made by uniformed military units and carried out under military discipline, showed careful planning and organization. Their justification was that it was impossible to seal the long and difficult border; hence Arab infiltration could only be stopped by destroying the infiltrators' bases and by making it clear that all the Arab border villages were in danger of reprisals. This policy was based on the old and somewhat tarnished assumption that the only thing that the Arab understands is force.

But "active defense," both when its victims were villagers, including women and children as at Kibya and Kalqiliah in 1953 and 1954, and when they were soldiers as at Gaza and Khan Yunis in 1955, actually had the opposite effect. Instead of teach-

ing the Arabs that crime—at least crime practiced across the Israeli borders—did not pay, it enraged Arab public opinion and
posed a challenge which Arab governments could not ignore. The
Egyptian government went into the business of training, supplying,
and directing Palestinian raiders—now called *fedayeen*—on a
much larger scale than before. If the Israeli army was justified in
crossing the frontier in the interest of security, the Egyptians concluded they had to do the same, though they wished to maintain the
appearance of Palestinian initiative and responsibility.

Well-informed Israelis have often referred to the invasion of the
Sinai Peninsula in 1956 as a reprisal raid on a larger scale intended to clean out nests of infiltrators and to teach the Arabs
another lesson on the foolishness of causing Israel trouble. They
point to the improved situation along the borders which followed
as a demonstration of its effectiveness.[16]

Since the Sinai invasion, the presence of the United Nations
Emergency Force has greatly improved the situation along the
Egyptian-Israeli borders, reducing the amount of infiltration and
lessening the need for reprisals. On other borders fewer incidents
have occurred than before the Suez crisis. The Jordanian government, never anxious for trouble with Israel, has been less willing
to cooperate with the Egyptians and has not offered haven to
Palestinian *fedayeen* as often or as generously as it once did. The
Syrian-Israeli border, because of the nature of the terrain, the uncertain status of the demilitarized zones, and Israeli preparations
to draw water in large amounts from the Jordan River, has been
more troubled. The United Nations Truce Supervisor and his staff
continue to watch the borders, investigating complaints of viola-
tions, and reporting to the Secretary-General. The UNTSO has
probably often prevented a border incident from igniting a larger
conflagration.[17] Even if the UNTSO and UNEF were completely
effective in preventing border crossings by land, the high-speed,
French-built fighter aircraft flying about within the tiny state of
Israel and the equally high-speed Soviet-built machines of the

[16] Eytan, cited, pp. 104 ff. and 110.
[17] See Elmo H. Hutchison, *Violent Truce: A Military Observer Looks at
the Arab-Israeli Conflict, 1953–1955* (New York: Devin-Adair, 1958) for
an account of the experiences of an American member of the Truce Supervisor's staff.

Egyptian and Syrian air forces patrolling the border would find it difficult to avoid occasional contact and conflict. In any event, UNTSO and the UNEF, though they have kept frontier disturbances in check, do not have the competence or capability for dealing with the underlying causes of border tension.

The position of the Israelis and the Arabs in Jerusalem gives both sides certain practical advantages which they are reluctant to risk in a compromise settlement. The internationalization of the city which was recommended by the United Nations General Assembly in its resolution of December 9, 1949, has little appeal to either side. Israel, which controls the greater part of the new city, although the holy places are mostly on the Arab side, finds sentimental satisfaction in having its seat of government in Jerusalem. It is unlikely to give this up.[18]

Many Arabs are interested in implementing the UN resolutions on Palestine and in keeping Jerusalem, along with the rest of Palestine not now in Israeli hands, free to form an Arab state of Palestine, the "Palestine entity." Jordan, however, opposing the "Palestine entity" idea, has sought to incorporate Arab Jerusalem, along with the rest of the West Bank. And Jordan's presence in Jerusalem, not any vague idea of a Palestine entity, has been the controlling factor in the Arab position there.

The Refugees

The question of the Arab refugees has often seemed the dominant one in Arab-Israel relations. They present a tremendous human problem in which a great deal of political and psychological dynamite is wrapped up. Many who have been concerned with the Arab-Israel problem, including both impartial outsiders and those directly involved, have urged that settlement of the refugee question must take precedence over more general issues. Like every other facet of the over-all situation, however, the refugee problem has proved difficult to isolate.

The Arabs contend that the refugees should have the right to choose between compensation and return to their former homes. They accept the UN General Assembly's Resolution of December

[18] See Eytan, cited, Chapter 4 and p. 86.

11, 1948,[19] which provides "that the refugees wishing to return to their homes and live at peace with their neighbors should be permitted to do so at the earliest practicable date, and that compensation should be paid for the property of those choosing not to return and for loss of or damage to property which, under principles of international law or in equity, should be made good by the Governments or authorities responsible."

In the Israeli view, the obvious way to deal with the refugees is to settle them permanently in the Arab states. Israel has made some concessions on compensation and on the reunification of families, but otherwise its position has long been frozen. An able student of the subject has written that "any thought of an Arab return seems to have been cast aside."[20] Late in 1961 Ben Gurion confirmed this position in a speech in the Knesset. He said, "Israel categorically rejects the insidious proposal of freedom of choice for the refugees."[21]

Fulfillment of the UN resolution the Arabs regard as the only feasible rectification of the injustices inflicted upon the refugees by Israeli seizure of their country, their homes, and their property. They reject resettlement and integration, the "practical" solution, on the ground that the problem is not simply one of how to take care of the physical needs of a group of displaced people. They insist that the right of the Israelis to continue their occupation of conquered territory is also at issue.

It has been charged repeatedly that the refugees have been exploited by Arab leaders for political advantage. The leaders, as well as the great majority of politically conscious Arabs in every country and of every class, are doubtless anxious to use the refugees' claims as a means of combating the Israeli *fait accompli*. However, this does not mean that their attitude on the refugee problem has been determined solely by this political objective.

Dr. John H. Davis, Director of UNRWA, the United Nations

[19] GA Resolution 194 (III). The Assembly has repeatedly postponed recommending further action on this resolution "without prejudice."

[20] Don Peretz, *Israel and the Palestine Arabs* (Washington: Middle East Institute, 1958), p. 12.

[21] "Ben Gurion Bars Return of Arabs," *The New York Times*, October 12, 1961.

agency responsible for Palestine refugee relief and rehabilitation, has said that although political factors have had some influence in preventing a solution of the refugee problem, "economic and educational limitations have been dominant."[22] Over two-thirds of the urban refugee population, he pointed out, "almost immediately became self-supporting in other Arab countries because they possessed skills which were useful in those countries."[23] Since then almost all other refugees possessing capital or skills in demand in the Arab countries have been able to establish themselves. It is the unskilled farm laborers and their families, who make up 75 to 80 per cent of the refugee group, that still fill the refugee camps. They cannot find employment in countries that already have a surplus of unskilled agricultural workers, but where such workers have been in demand, as in Syria where new lands were being opened, large numbers of Palestine refugees have found a place in the local economy. But in a world in which there is a redundancy of unskilled labor and in which mechanization is actually decreasing the demand for it, many of these poor, unskilled people separated during long years from their lands have lost command of the simple skills they once had. Attempts are being made to provide vocational training in the camps, so as to fit some of the refugees for new jobs that are appearing in the developing countries of the Arab world. The Arab states have not opposed this training and have accepted the graduates of UNRWA's schools. To absorb the bulk of the refugees, a greatly expanded training program will be needed. To provide employment for the trainees, large-scale plans for economic development must be drawn up and set in motion.[24]

To carry out these plans will require large-scale investment. The United Nations has carefully examined the possibilities of eco-

[22] UN General Assembly (15th sess.), *Official Records: Supplement 14, Annual Report of the Director of the United Nations Relief and Works Agency for Palestine Refugees in the Near East, 1 July 1959–30 June 1960,* A/4478 (New York: Author, 1960), para. 7.

[23] Same, para. 5.

[24] This conclusion was emphasized by Dr. Joseph E. Johnson, representative of the UN Conciliation Commission for Palestine, in his report of November 24, 1961. (UN General Assembly, Conciliation Commission for Palestine, *Addendum to the Nineteenth Progress Report,* A/4921/Add. 1 [New York: Author, 1961], para. 51.)

nomic development as a solution for the refugee problem. The Arab governments, though they have accepted the resettlement of large numbers of refugees and the UNRWA vocational training programs, will not agree to any development program that denies to the refugees the right of repatriation. As the Director of UNRWA has said "Ten years of UNRWA history bear out the fact that major development projects designed with the specific purpose of resettling refugees are unacceptable to refugees and host Governments alike."[25]

The Arab Boycott

The policy of boycott extends to every area in which the Arabs can obstruct the activity of the state of Israel. This includes transit through Arab territory, economic exchange with the Arab states, participation in international conferences, and trade with third countries. The Arab policy of boycott is political and economic warfare on an extended scale. Legal justification is claimed on the basis of the fact that the Arab-Israel war has never been ended and that a state of war still exists. The Israelis, of course, argue that the Arabs enjoy the benefits of belligerency without its risks and consequences and are allowed to continue to do so because the United Nations has not taken a stronger stand and insisted that the Arabs make peace. The question of how the United Nations, or any other authority, can make a group of nations accept and have "normal" relations with another nation against their will has not yet been answered.

The policy of boycott has been most often discussed and protested in the case of Egypt's denial of the right to transit the Suez Canal to Israeli ships and goods. Egypt takes the position that it is at war with Israel and therefore cannot permit Israeli ships to cross her territory or goods to go to or from Israel which might strengthen its war potential. Israel insists that Egypt is violating the Constantinople Convention of 1888, which provides that the canal shall be open to peaceful commerce in war as in peace, while the Egyptians point out that the Convention provides that Egypt is entitled to take such action as is necessary to protect its own security.

[25] UN General Assembly, *Official Records: Supplement 14* . . . A/4478, cited, para. 11.

Israel has never tested its claim in the World Court; it has frequently challenged Egypt's refusal to comply with the United Nations resolution on this subject. Nasser's answer has been to offer to comply with the UN resolution on the freedom of transit of the Suez Canal if Israel would comply with the UN resolutions on Palestine, including the 1947 Partition Plan.

On the issue of the boycott and blockade, the contestants have taken a familiar position. Israel is seeking to normalize its situation in the Middle East; the Arabs are trying to prevent it. There seems little likelihood of any significant change on this issue without change in the total pattern of Arab-Israeli relations.

Development of Water Resources

In a serious effort to break the deadlock in the Arab-Israeli situation, President Eisenhower, represented by Eric Johnston as special ambassador, put forward a plan for the joint development of water resources. The basic ideas were (1) that development of water resources can be carried out efficiently only on a regional basis, and (2) that such development in the Jordan River basin would benefit both Israel and the adjacent Arab states—Jordan, Syria, and Lebanon. The practical advantages of the scheme, it was hoped, would overcome the reluctance of the Arabs to engage in any project in conjunction with Israel. It was also hoped that participation in the joint development program would help to ease the tension between Israel and the Arabs. Worked out in the greatest detail, with the best engineering advice, the project's advantages to all parties should have been abundantly apparent. Furthermore, it was so arranged that Arabs and Israelis need not sign the same papers, or sit down together at the same table, or work together on the development program. A central authority, acting as intermediary, would have accepted the agreements of both sides, thus minimizing overt Arab association with Israel. This plan, which the United States government was willing to support in generous measure, had a great deal of appeal on its own merits. Added to this was the extraordinary skill and energy which Ambassador Johnston brought to the task of gaining acceptance for the plan, which came to be known as the Johnston Plan.

Ambassador Johnston almost succeeded. The Israelis were sold on the project from the beginning, because of their great need for additional water which could only be obtained from the Jordan system. Furthermore, a joint Arab-Israel development program fits in with their long-established plans for bringing Israel into the economic life of the area. Also, they were eager for that measure of Arab recognition which would result from participation in a joint program.

Arab engineers and development specialists were attracted by the plan's practical merits. There was a moment when there appeared to be a possibility of acceptance. But then obstacles appeared which proved insuperable. First, the Arab governments, probably led by Egypt, came to the decision that cooperation in the plan would amount to acceptance of the state of Israel, would strengthen it and reduce the effectiveness of Arab opposition. Moreover, implementation of the plan would create a water-use system based on the present boundaries of Israel. In effect, though based on agreement, it would divide Israel from the Arab states as far as water distribution was concerned, thus confirming the separation of Israeli-occupied Palestine from Arab territory. Finally, the Arabs feared that the purpose of the plan in part was to resettle a substantial proportion of the refugee population, thus liquidating refugee rights to repatriation. In this way a major effort to bring about Arab-Israeli collaboration in a program which was obviously to their mutual benefit crashed on the rock of Arab repudiation of Israel itself.

Since the failure of efforts to gain acceptance for the Johnston Plan, the Israelis have proceeded unilaterally with a large-scale project for taking water from Lake Tiberias in a 108-inch pipe at a point near the Syrian border. They say that their project is within the terms of the Johnston Plan as it was offered for agreement. The Arabs point out that the appropriation of such a large proportion of the river's flow as could be taken by the huge Israeli pipe would adversely affect Arab projects for the use of Jordan water. The Arab League has discussed plans for thwarting the Israeli project by diverting streams within Arab territory which feed into the upper Jordan. They warn that these plans will be put into effect, reducing the amount of water which the Israelis might take from the Jordan, if the Israelis open their pipe. The Syrians are particularly agitated about Israeli plans to draw great quantities of water from the Jordan system, and there have been threats of war if the Israelis actually begin taking water from Lake Tiberias. The Israelis give every sign of determination to proceed with their plans. Thus a crisis over Jordan water is steadily approaching and may soon reach some kind of a climax. It is difficult to see how either side can back very far away from the position which it has taken. The only conceivable solution would be a revival of the Johnston Plan, but the Arabs seem no more likely to accept it now than they were in 1955.

Arms Race and Cold War

The arms race between Israel and the Arab states, which began when the Zionists first armed their settlers in Palestine, continued as their underground army was developed in the years before the British withdrawal and the showdown in the Palestine War. Since the Arab armies had been armed by their Western sponsors, the Zionists had to aim at matching the existing Arab capability for military action. Probably always inferior in the quantity of arms on hand, they have had to make up in military skill and in audacity the shortages and shortcomings of their equipment.

After the Palestine War, the Western powers promulgated the doctrine of Arab-Israel balance. In the Tripartite Declaration of May 1950, they sought to stabilize the situation by rationing arms supplies to the Arab states and Israel and by guaranteeing the existing armistice lines. For five years the aims of the Tripartite Declaration were achieved, but only because the Arabs had no alternative source of arms. In 1955, however, the whole character of the competition in armaments between the Arab states and Israel changed when the Soviets began to supply Egypt. Since the Soviet bloc shipped armaments to Arab states in quantities and of types beyond their capacity for effective utilization, the Arabs' ability to use arms became the critical factor in their military position in relation to the Israelis. With vastly greater manpower and advantages of geography, there could be no question of the Arabs' eventual capacity to destroy Israel once they developed a certain level of military skill, provided that outsiders did not intervene.

Israel, of course, built up its arms inventory in response to Arab acquisitions. The United States, hoping to avoid the repercussions in the Arab world that would have developed if it became Israel's source of arms, limited its releases of arms to Israel to commercial transactions in spare parts and minor shipments of small weapons available on the open market, but did not protest sales to Israel by Canada and France. In 1962, however, after the U.A.R. developed surface-to-surface missiles from the Bloc, the United States modified its policy and agreed to sell Hawk air defense missiles to Israel.

Both sides had their troubles—Israel because its sources of arms were less certain than the source to which the Arabs looked, and the Arabs because the Soviets, though generally careful to avoid any appearance of using the arms deals to put pressure on them, occasionally gave some hint of Arab dependence upon Soviet friendship. During and after the Nasser-Khrushchev dispute over Communist activities in Syria and Iraq, spare parts for Soviet equipment became very difficult to come by and Soviet fighter aircraft, of the latest type suitable for combat with the new French Mirage fighters which Israel had obtained, were unavailable to Egypt except at a prohibitive "commercial" price.

There can be little doubt that both sides have always kept in mind the possibility of an attack on the other. A war of annihilation, a second round, and after the Sinai campaign, a third round to push Israel into the sea, have been a popular theme of Arab oratory, muted somewhat by the evidence of Israel's strength in the Sinai war and the possibility of Western intervention.

Each side suspects the other of planning a preventive war, preparing to attack whenever circumstances appear favorable. The Israeli attack in 1956 was probably, from the Israeli point of view, a preventive war. In the preceding months Nasser apparently had been making headway in organizing the Arab states in a military alliance. While he was in trouble over the nationalization of the Suez Canal Company, the West would be unlikely to come to his aid, certainly not Britain and France which were preparing to attack him themselves. The United States, so the Israeli leaders probably thought, was preoccupied with its presidential election, and also with the uprising in Hungary. So October 1956 appeared to be an ideal moment to destroy Nasser before his build-up of Soviet arms and his military alliance gave him the opportunity to destroy Israel.

Both sides are acutely conscious of the support which the other can rely on from great powers, and their thinking about the possibility of another armed conflict is certainly influenced by calculations of the role which the great powers might play. The Arabs feel that without Western support Israel would be no military threat to them. The Israelis on their side note that the Arabs get great quantities of arms and other assistance from the Soviet bloc. They also get assistance from the West and are appeased, the Israelis say, on a variety of political issues, because of the fear that they might go into the Communist orbit. Each side occasionally argues that the cold war supports the stalemate and claims that, if left alone, it could bring about a breakthrough. But Israel is absolutely dependent upon Western financial support, the Arabs for their part need funds for economic development, and both have to find their place in between East and West. So it is difficult to understand how either the Arabs or Israelis could stand alone, independent of the great powers. It is even more difficult to conceive how the Arab-Israel conflict could be removed from the contest between the West and the Communist bloc.

News reports in December of 1960 of a secret nuclear reactor near Beersheba in southern Israel opened up new aspects of the Arab-Israel arms race. Official Israeli denials were accompanied by private suggestions that Israel must prepare itself by all possible means against the day when the Arabs become sufficiently skillful in the use of their Soviet arms to realize the advantage implicit in their greater manpower. Nasser gave the Arab reaction in a speech at Port Said on December 23. He said, "If we are sure that Israel is making an atomic bomb, this means the beginning of war between us and Israel. . . ." He suggested, however, that Israel probably was not doing so. The rumor, he said, probably ". . . indicates that the imperialist states are preparing the atmosphere to arm Israel with atomic weapons and then they will say that Israel has produced atomic weapons. . . . But at such a time," he went on, "we will obtain an atomic bomb and atomic weapons at any price."

Still other moves in the contest have followed. The successful test of an Israeli rocket in 1961, said to be part of a program of scientific experimentation, excited apprehension in Cairo. Then in the summer of 1962, just before the annual celebration of the 1952 revolution, the Egyptians fired four rockets. Their significance, or at least the significance which the Egyptians wished to have attributed to them, was made clear by Nasser's announcement that one of the two types tested has a range which would take it to a point "south of Beirut." It was the Israelis' turn to be apprehensive.

Representatives of the Israeli government have expressed willingness to participate in bilateral disarmament, following a general settlement. The Arabs have scoffed at the idea that they could trust the Israelis sufficiently to enter into such an engagement or, for that matter, reach a general settlement. In present circumstances the prospects for another major military contest between the Arabs and Israel are certainly good, although it must be clear to both sides neither of them could gain real advantage from it. On the other hand, fear of imminent attack or a situation which appeared to offer an unusual advantage to one side or the other could easily brush normal caution aside. With atomic weapons involved, the dangers would be many times multiplied. Without some basic change in the over-all situation the Arab-Israel arms race will remain a threat to world peace.

The Character of the State of Israel

One point already mentioned deserves strong re-emphasis. Behind every issue that separates the Arabs and Israel lies the question: What kind of state does Israel intend to be? Israel is clearly committed to the concept of a state with a special relationship to all the Jews of the world, which looks forward to, and will do its best to encourage, substantial additional immigration. Most Israelis insist that their nation has no expansionist aims, that it is content with, or will accept, its present boundaries, and that it can take care of additional population by industrialization. If the Arabs will permit normal opportunities for trade, Israel will be a good neighbor, contributing to the prosperity of the whole area. Few Arabs are willing to accept these assurances. Recalling how the

Zionists' goals have expanded with their opportunities, they suggest that massive immigration, plus support from world Jewry, is bound, given the aggressive attitudes of Israel's leaders and people, to lead to attempts at territorial expansion.

Israelis argue that there is no ground for discussion with Arabs because the latter have made clear their complete rejection of the state of Israel. Arabs answer that their goals for Palestine are indicated by their insistence on implementation of the United Nations resolutions. They would accept, if this answer be taken at face value, the establishment of a Jewish as well as an Arab state in Palestine, with borders as prescribed in the 1947 Partition Plan, and the return of those Arab refugees who chose repatriation to places in Palestine where they or their families lived. But very few Israelis, even if they would consider such concessions, believe that the Arabs would abandon their determination to destroy Israel. The conclusion is inescapable that there is little likelihood of narrowing the gap that divides them.

X

POLICIES AND PROSPECTS:
The Arab Area

Policy and action have always been intertwined in Gamal Abdel Nasser's conduct of external affairs and it is still not possible to separate them entirely. Though the image of the pragmatist and opportunist has always been most apparent on the surface, the folk philosophy of Arab nationalism has always provided a doctrinal base. Very early in his public career Nasser set down his own philosophy of Egypt's and of the whole Arab people's place in the world. He has never again attempted such a systematic statement, but has preferred to let his actions and numerous public speeches declare his foreign policy to his followers and to the world.

It would be a mistake to treat *The Philosophy of the Revolution* as a master plan or as the key to Nasser's foreign-policy thinking. Yet it has significance as a beginning of doctrine, much elaborated and modified in the years that have followed. It also demonstrates the striking degree of continuity in Nasser's own thinking and in Arab nationalism itself.

THE PHILOSOPHY OF THE REVOLUTION

Not long after the Revolutionary Command Council came to power in Egypt, Nasser, probably with the collaboration of his friend and adviser, the prominent Cairo journalist, Muhammad Hassanain Heikal, put together three short articles under the title, *The Philosophy of the Revolution*. The articles, which were quickly translated into English and published in book form, attracted much interest, particularly on the part of those who hoped to find a simple definition of the aims of the Egyptian revolution. Hence *The Philosophy of the Revolution* was read as closely as some newly discovered ancient text, interpreted and reinterpreted, and compared with *Mein Kampf*. Of particular interest was Nasser's description of the role in world affairs which was waiting for his generation of Egyptians.

I do not know why I always imagine that in this region in which we live there is a role wandering aimlessly about seeking an actor to play it. I know not why this role, tired of roaming about in this vast region which extends to every place around us, should at last settle down, weary and worn out, on our frontiers beckoning us to move, to dress up for it and to perform it since there is nobody else who can do so.

Here I hasten to point out that this role is not a leading one. It is one of interplay of reactions and experiments with all these factors aiming at exploding this terrific energy latent in every sphere around us and at the creation, in this region, of a tremendous power capable of lifting this region up and making it play its positive role in the construction of the future of humanity.[1]

The stage on which Egypt's role is to be played, he describes in terms of three circles. The first is ". . . an Arab circle surrounding us and . . . this circle is as much a part of us as we are part of it. . . ." "There is no doubt," he writes, "that the Arab circle is the most important and the most closely connected with us." In the Arab circle "the components of our power" are the unity of the Arab people, the strategic situation of its territory, and its oil.[2]

The second circle is the continent of Africa. "It is not in vain that our country lies in the North-east of Africa, a position from which it gives upon the dark continent wherein rages today the most violent struggle between the white colonizers and black natives for the possession of its inexhaustible resources. . . . We cannot, in any way, stand aside, even if we wish to, away from the sanguinary and dreadful struggle now raging in the heart of Africa between five million whites and two hundred million Africans.

[1] Gamal Abdel Nasser, *The Philosophy of the Revolution* (Buffalo: Smith, Keynes and Marshall, 1959), pp. 61–62.
[2] Same, pp. 59, 62, 71–72.

. . . We cannot, under any condition, relinquish our responsibility in helping, in every way possible, in diffusing the light and civilization into the farthest parts of that virgin jungle."[3]

The third circle "that goes beyond continents and oceans . . . is the circle of our brethren in faith. . . ." He envisions the integration of the Muslim world by making the pilgrimage to Mecca ". . . a regular political congress wherein the leaders of Muslim states, their public men, their pioneers in every field of knowledge, their writers, their leading industrialists, merchants and youth draw up in this universal Islamic Parliament the main lines of policy for their countries and their cooperation together until they meet again."[4]

Nasser was inspired by the idea of regional cooperation and mutual assistance on a grand scale. Pointing to "imperialism" as a danger threatening all the interlocking areas, he said, ". . . imperialism is the great force that throws around the whole region a fatal siege." But he does not call for the extinction of Israel or even for a campaign against Israel. The whole book is a plea for Afro-Asian solidarity and cooperation to bring about liberation from "colonialism" and to release "the tremendous power capable of lifting this region up. . . ."[5]

Just how his vision was to be realized, Nasser apparently did not know. He has often said that his policy, foreign as well as domestic, is an evolving one, not copied after any model, not based on a fixed set of principles or on a rigid timetable, but creative and responsive to situations as they arise. Except for the idea of making the pilgrimage to Mecca a Muslim Parliament, he had no new or practical suggestions. His critics in the West, however, have often read into the concept of the three circles a master plan for the conquest first of the Arab world, then of Africa, and finally of the Islamic countries of South Asia. He has been accused so often of having said that he aspired to take over all these areas that, like many authors before him, he has rued the day he wrote his book. When asked about it by an American journalist in 1959, he said, "After the hue and cry it raised, I decided to write no more

[3] Same, pp. 60, 74–76.
[4] Same, p. 77.
[5] Same, pp. 62, 70.

books."[6] *The Philosophy of the Revolution,* quickly put together in the early days of the revolution, contained an expression of ultimate goals, rather shadowy but real enough to have lasted over the years. Nasser has developed gradually practical means of moving toward them.

THE EVOLUTION OF POLICY

Nasser and his advisers, since the revolution in 1952, have attended a hard, demanding school where few lessons could be learned by rote and where the penalties of failure were severe. Although techniques have changed, the group has retained a style characterized by the daring and willingness to experiment which amateurs and revolutionaries often bring to the ancient arts of foreign policy and diplomacy.

In defining their objectives, Nasser and his advisers have moved slowly but with greater consistency than in the development of technique. Nasser has never been overeager to come forth with a neat and complete doctrine. He has often expressed his preference for action over theories, pointing out that he is a soldier, not a professor. In describing his domestic program he once said, ". . . we do not have a written book entitled The Socialist, Democratic, Cooperative Society." It ". . . develops as the days and years pass by."[7] Strangely combined with this pragmatic approach has always been a kind of fatalistic willingness to consign the fortunes of Egypt, the revolutionary regime, and Arab nationalism to the stream of events, to the forces of history. After the seemingly miraculous emergence of Egypt from the Suez crisis, and the crisis that preceded the union with Syria, one of Nasser's principal aides remarked, "We are constantly amazed at our successes. Two explanations suggest themselves: first, our enemies help us and defeat themselves by fighting against the stream of history; second, our strength is magnified because we are going with the current of events."

On numerous occasions the current has met obstructions, and Nasser and his advisers and friends must have wondered where it

[6] Interview with William H. Stringer of the *Christian Science Monitor, Nasser's Speeches,* 1959, p. 524.

[7] *Nasser's Speeches,* 1959, pp. 405–406.

was going. Yet an identification with forces greater than himself, his government, and his country has been consistently the foundation of Nasser's policy and a help in the definition of goals. The technical, social, and psychological revolutions in the Arab world, which combined to produce the Arab revolt for independence in the First World War, and the subsequent struggle for the realization of that independence under the impetus of the Arab defeat in the Palestine War, created a new role for a new kind of Arab leader. An important segment of the Arab public came to the conclusion that only Gamal Abdel Nasser was suited to the part; he has been laboring ever since to ascertain the full range of requirements and possibilities which the role involves. As he has done so, he has developed and refined his notions as to the proper goals of Arab foreign policy. Though still not formally systematized, they fall into a pattern very like that anticipated in *The Philosophy of the Revolution.*

EGYPT, THE INNER CIRCLE

In his public statements on foreign policy Nasser has not always talked like the president of Egypt. It is from the point of view of the "Arab Nation" and Afro-Asia that he often approaches world problems, and it is this approach which has won him an audience from far beyond the borders of Egypt. But Nasser is an Egyptian; his advisers are Egyptians; it is with the resources of the Egyptian government that he has engaged in international politics; and, though he has influence and support outside of Egypt, his whole position would cave in should he lose control in his own country. Thus, though Nasser unquestionably is a man of wide-ranging interests who is deeply involved in problems far beyond Egypt's borders, he is constantly drawn back in his thinking to considerations that are narrowly Egyptian.

Because of its situation in a valley with no other resources than the narrow lands watered by its one river, Egypt's problems have a way of turning inward to the ratio of people to land. Its population, already at a level that condemns the majority to poverty, is inexorably rising. For emigration and resettlement projects, financial assistance would be needed as well as a political arrangement, perhaps a regional federation and development plan. Emigration is not a likely solution, however; the Egyptian people, who have never been colonists, cannot bring themselves to leave their native land. The only other remedies possible are enlargement of the arable area and industrialization to utilize now redundant manpower. Internal development, however, both agricultural and industrial, would require a substantial inflow of funds from foreign investors with little prospect that they would be fully repaid.

An important interrelationship between Egyptian domestic problems and foreign policy stems from Nasser's concept of the "two revolutions," to which he is dedicated.[8] From the beginning he has talked of the struggle against the threat of "imperialism" from without and "feudalism" from within. Associated with the "feudalists" and "monopolists" at home were a large part of the European population whose activities derived substantial support from Western capital and Western enterprise. The policy of nationalization, of which the seizure of the Suez Canal Company was but one example, reflected Egyptian concern about foreign influence on domestic affairs, and also the desire to assume the responsibility for foreign-owned enterprises and gather in the profit they produced.

In the field of foreign policies, the revolutionary regime at first dealt only with matters in which strictly Egyptian interests were at issue: the removal of the British from the Suez Base and from the Sudan. Before long, however, foreign initiatives took on more than strictly Egyptian implications. The regime's successes in getting the British out of the Suez Base and the Sudan, classical objectives of nationalist policy, did not arouse great popular enthusiasm because both achievements were incomplete. The British did not leave the Canal Zone immediately, and the Sudanese chose independence in preference to union with Egypt. By contrast, the enthusiasm aroused among Egyptians, and Arabs generally, by Nasser's assault on the Baghdad Pact and by the Egyptian-Soviet arms deal made a strong impression on policy makers in Cairo. These triumphant frontal attacks on the West added to the Egyptian leader's weight in international affairs and his popularity at home. The conclusion was inescapable that vigorous anti-Western policies brought an Arab leader acclaim and support, whereas

[8] *The Philosophy of the Revolution,* cited, p. 36.

policies of cooperation with the West aroused suspicion at home and produced few concessions of practical value from the Western nations.

Commentators on Nasser's international politics have pointed out that he has followed the classic pattern of Egyptian rulers in seeking to extend power southward into the Sudan and northward into Syria, a pattern established by the Pharaohs and exemplified by Muhammad Ali in the nineteenth century. An essential difference is to be found, however, in Nasser's use of Arab nationalism and the idea of Arab unity to augment the strength he derives from control of Egypt.

It is pertinent to ask whether Nasser's Egyptian and his Pan Arab interests do not frequently come into conflict and, when they do, which dominates. Egyptians have accused him of squandering Egyptian resources on Pan Arab schemes—in Syria for example—and other Arabs have accused him of readiness always to defer to Egyptian interests in a pinch. There is a widespread failure to appreciate the efforts which Nasser and his regime have devoted to Egypt's internal development and the priority which they give to Egyptian affairs in their planning. Even in the most auspicious Pan Arab venture Nasser has proven ready to reject any course which jeopardized his hold on Egypt. Probably he would say that a conflict of Egyptian with Arab interests actually cannot exist. Egypt is part of the Arab world; its destiny is interlinked with that of the whole area.

Egypt, Nasser realizes, cannot solve its problems alone. From this grim reality springs his passionate desire that his country link itself with the other Arab states and find some way to join its resources with those of the rest of the area for the greater good of Egypt and of all the Arabs.

REFORM AND INTER-ARAB RELATIONS

In every Arab state social and economic reform—even social and economic progress—has serious political implications. Reform means destruction of institutions upon which traditional rule has been founded and it implies the creation of new institutions on which new regimes with new philosophies will establish themselves.

Nasser has made a serious and prolonged effort to carry the

revolution of July 1952 on into the transformation of the social and economic as well as the political life of his country. His symbolic role as the paramount leader of Arab nationalism has the effect of equating the social and economic reforms in Egypt with Arab nationalism itself, or at least with Nasser's own Arab nationalism. The consequence is to add new dimensions to his relations with the other Arab states and to link the problems of social and economic development to questions of foreign policy.

In a series of decrees issued in July 1961 during the period of the ninth anniversary of the Egyptian revolution, President Nasser instituted a wide-sweeping social and economic reform program. In his anniversary speech he emphasized that social revolution had been an aim of the revolutionary regime from its beginning. He said, "It was evident from the first day of the Revolution that we would not be able to achieve social justice unless we eliminated the domination of capital. From the first day the Revolution was a political and social one—a political revolution against imperialism and its stooges, and a social revolution against feudalism, monopoly, exploitation and the dictatorship of capital."[9] Muhammad Hassanain Heikal, the editor of *Al Ahram,* called the decrees "the social Suez." In explaining the need for them Heikal quoted official documents referring to new millionaires who "have amassed fortunes without the exertion of any real effort and have endeavored by all means in their power to smuggle a considerable part of their wealth out of the country," to "colossal remunerations" paid by certain companies to their directors, and to a number of men who held multiple directorships in private companies from each of which they received extravagant compensation.[10]

The effect of the decrees was to impose heavier income taxes, including confiscatory taxes on income over 10,000 Egyptian pounds, impose heavy new taxes on income from residential property in the higher rent brackets, cut in half the permitted maximum and otherwise limit the size of landholdings, forbid the holding of more than one job, set limits to the amount of stock which might be held by one individual, and increase the government interest in a long list of companies and enterprises. In addition there were

[9] *The Egyptian Gazette,* July 23, 1961, p. 2.
[10] *Al Ahram,* July 28, 1961.

decrees providing for an increased number of jobs and the reduction of the hours of work for laborers. The implications of these
decrees, for external relations as well as for the internal situation,
are numerous. The new decrees emphasized the differences between the social and economic system in the U.A.R. and in the
other Arab states, particularly the more conservative states. It is
possible that tendencies to revolution among certain segments of
the population in the other Arab states will be further stimulated
and that those members of the lower classes in Lebanon, Jordan,
and other countries who favor this kind of social change will be
further aroused against their regimes. At the same time, it is likely
that the upper classes, and particularly the independent and well-
to-do business classes in other Arab states, will be influenced to
give greater support to existing regimes. In Syria, where those
classes saw the new decrees as a threat to their existence, the effect was to bring about, or at least to hasten, the breakup of the
U.A.R. itself.

It is also likely that the degree of socialism which now exists in
the U.A.R. will considerably reduce the interest of most other Arab
governments in the possibility of union with the U.A.R. The over-
all effect would certainly seem to be to sharpen the already existing
conflict between the revolutionary regimes in the U.A.R. and
Iraq on the one hand and the other more conservative and traditional regimes. To this extent the developments in the U.A.R.
will be a factor of division and instability in the area. The U.A.R.
government has never, of course, even when its formal relations
with the other Arab governments have been most correct, denied
its revolutionary character or its belief that the ultimate spread of
social and political revolution throughout the Arab area would
lead to Arab unity under the banner of Arab nationalism. Such
periods of improvement in interstate relations in the Arab area as
occurred in the year before the July 1961 decrees may be taken
to reflect only a truce of convenience.

Whatever judgment may be passed on "Arab socialism," it has
all the earmarks of an original creation, or compilation, and can
hardly be described as evidence of Communist penetration or control of the Cairo government. The socialism being put into effect
in the U.A.R., as in Iraq, is a response in part to the chaotic and

corrupt condition of the society which the revolutionary regime inherited and in part to the felt need for the organization and direction of all the resources of the country in a national development effort. It is a native product for which the Communists openly express their contempt and distaste.

These judgments do not alter the reasons for believing that the Soviet Union is delighted to see the process of socialization going on in the U.A.R. The Soviet leaders probably believe that it will create a situation favorable to an ultimate Communist takeover. It has been observed that when the July 1961 decrees and others which have followed have been put fully into effect, the only thing that will remain to be done to make the country Communist will be to remove the top fifty members of the regime and replace them with Communists. If this were to happen, it is suggested, the general public would not experience enough change in its situation to know that a revolution had taken place. If these speculations are sound, they emphasize the narrow line between an independent Arab nationalist and socialist state and one that is Communist-controlled. They also emphasize the critical importance of the determination and ability of the Arab nationalist regimes to maintain their independence, and of their capacity to understand how precarious their positions may become.

A key question is whether similar social revolutions are likely in the other Arab states. It is often argued that Islam fosters a quality of individualism that is inimical to Communist or socialist regimentation of the individual's personal life. Since it can be argued with equal forcefulness that Islam prepares the individual to submit to the authority in power, little guidance for the future seems likely from this line of analysis. It does seem unlikely that the Arab people generally—and it is admittedly difficult to generalize about all the Arab people—would take kindly to the kind of regimentation and direction of personal life to which the Russians have so long submitted and which the Chinese people have allowed to destroy the traditions of centuries. So long as the government does not direct his personal life, however, the Arab is willing to accept a great many limitations upon it without taking counteraction.

One of the strongest forces behind the possibility of further social change in the Arab world is the growing sense of the great disparity between the lives of the well-off and those of the mass of the poor. This is coupled with an awareness both on the part of the public and on the part of governments that corruption in the business community and among high government officials is one of the gravest problems that confronts the Arab world in its endeavor to make substantial economic progress. It is significant that the issuance of the decrees of July 1961 in Cairo was linked with this problem. President Nasser in his anniversary speech dwelt at length on the subject and asked the public to write to him "reporting anyone who appoints his relatives" to government jobs or otherwise is guilty of using his official or business position to enrich himself.[11]

The demand from the lower middle and working classes and peasants for a more equitable distribution of wealth and for controls which will reduce the possibility of amassing fortunes at the public expense is likely to become stronger. The processes of reform under way in the U.A.R. and Iraq will probably continue. Syria will not repeal all the social reforms of the U.A.R. period and appears likely to restore some of those that have been abolished. Pressures for social and economic change in Lebanon are rising. It will take longer in Jordan and probably much longer in Saudi Arabia before they will make themselves felt, but they are likely to become the major problem of the conservative regimes, a problem which they can solve only by radical adjustment.

One Middle Eastern Communist has expressed the opinion that the external orientation of Arab states is strictly determined by the social orientation of the dominant class: where privileged aristocracies are in control there is an alliance with the West; where bourgeois governments are in power, neutralism is the natural foreign policy; and when the working class dominates the natural orientation of Arab states will be to the "socialist camp." This appears to be an excessively dogmatic application of Marxist theories of European origin, as the classic Marxist class struggle does not seem to be taking place or likely to take place in Arab countries.

[11] *The Egyptian Gazette,* July 23, 1961, p. 5.

The effort of middle-class revolutionaries is generally directed to the dismantling of the power of the old ruling classes and to the creation of a national front or union in which all classes collaborate. The leaders of international communism, although not entirely abandoning their local agents and apparatus, seem perfectly willing to collaborate on the international stage with such "bourgeois" national fronts, so long as it serves their purpose, and to be unimpeded by any theoretical requirement to work for the early seizure of power by the "working class."

Regional economic development has appealed both to the protagonists of Arab unity and to many who, without political motives or interests, have addressed themselves to the problem of raising living standards in the Arab world. The idea has been put forward in many ways and discussed in many forums. In 1958 President Eisenhower announced the interest of the United States in "an Arab development institution on a regional basis" which the United States would be prepared to support if the Arab states themselves made a contribution, but the offer has not been taken up.[12]

In 1957 the Economic Council of the Arab League approved the statutes for an Arab Financial Institute for Economic Development. In 1959 the Lebanese delegation to the first Arab Oil Conference in Cairo made a proposal, later expanded in a project submitted by the Lebanese government to the League Economic Council, for the utilization of a part of the royalties from the Arab oil industry for area development. This proposal, based on a plan developed by Emile Bustani, a prominent Lebanese legislator and businessman, recommended that each Arab state with oil revenues and each oil company contribute 5 per cent of its annual profits from oil, estimated at about £50 million per year, to a special oil revenue account to be held by the Arab Financial Institute. This account would be used to finance development projects in the various Arab countries. The Arab governments would set up development boards with capital contributed by them and by private investment; the boards would borrow from the oil revenue account

[12] Address to the Special Emergency Session of the UN General Assembly, August 13, 1958, *The Department of State Bulletin*, September 1, 1958, pp. 339–340.

of the Financial Institute for projects approved by the Institute.[13] No action was taken to put the proposal into practice. Even when the Arab League has sponsored plans for economic cooperation among its members, red tape and existing national boundaries have restricted or nullified their effectiveness.

There can be little doubt that over the long run the development of the area's economy as a unit would be advantageous to the majority of its inhabitants. Furthermore, such development would be likely to overcome some of the existing inequalities and parochialism which divide the area politically. Getting such area development started without some prior political change, however, appears to be so difficult as to make the prospects for significant progress dim. There are other factors in addition to the political rivalries and suspicions which limit the possibilities for area development. Above all, the existing states with their economic and communications systems do represent not only a considerable investment but may furnish, in the short run, the most efficient basis for development efforts. Obviously, development should be undertaken both within individual states and, where and as feasible, on an area-wide basis. That will involve difficult decisions for outside powers willing to help, and above all for the Arabs themselves.

Nasser has occasionally shown interest in schemes for area economic cooperation and development, but he has seldom pressed the matter. It seems clear that he believes little meaningful cooperation can take place between conservative and revolutionary regimes, and that such cooperation must await further political change and the consolidation of revolutionary Arab nationalist rule over the area.

NASSER AND THE OTHER ARAB STATES

Nasser and his cohorts in the Revolutionary Command Council began as Egyptian nationalists but soon became Pan Arabists. Egypt's need for external resources and the palpable addition to Egypt's strength and influence that came from its leader's ability to speak for and in the name of the whole Arab area were im-

[13] Emile Bustani, *March Arabesque* (London: R. Hale, 1961), p. 162 ff. For text of the memorandum by the Lebanese government to the Arab Economic Council, see p. 181 ff.

portant factors in this change. The idea of Arab unity blossomed in the atmosphere created by the youthful, energetic, and reformist regime in Cairo.

The regime had neither a policy for the achievement of unity nor a picture of the kind of community which would best fulfill its dreams. It inherited certain ideas which had been common currency among Arab nationalists for four generations: the greater Egypt idea, the Fertile Crescent scheme, the concept on which the League of Arab States had been built, an idea of a unitary Arab state to include all the Arabs of the East, and another which would include, as well, those of the West or Maghreb. Each of these ideas had encountered practical difficulties in the past and not all were suited to Egyptian leadership. The planners were hampered by the prior demands of Egypt's pressing problems. Egypt's resources were limited, and traditional interests, as well as those of rival nationalists, challenged the new leadership in Cairo. Consequently, the revolutionary leaders took their usual pragmatic position, avoiding commitment to any formula and awaiting the unfolding of opportunities.

It was not long before fundamental differences of interest and approach arose between the regime in Cairo and the more conservative regimes in the other Arab states. In view of Nasser's spectacular victories in contests with the Western powers and, more especially, his ability to dramatize them as victories for Arab nationalism, it was natural that he and his advisers should place much store by their ability to appeal to the Arab masses over the heads of their traditional rulers. They began to visualize Arab unity coming as the decrepit traditional regimes crumbled into the dust and the people rallied to Nasser's standard.

How could this process be speeded up? Saleh Salem put forward a plan for creating a parliament elected by Arabs all over the Arab world which would be attached to the Arab League and provide a Pan Arab forum. Those in Cairo who pressed for the idea believed that such a parliament would support the revolutionary nationalism represented by Nasser and would override the narrow interests of the traditional regimes. The young revolutionaries in Cairo, however, soon learned that Arab unity was not to be so easily achieved and that the established regimes were a great deal more resourceful and able in their own defense than they had anticipated.

Some of Nasser's followers, and occasionally Nasser himself, presented a vision of the great Arab state of the future extending from the Arab (Persian) Gulf to the Atlantic, with a population of eighty millions, rich in its oil resources, industrialized, well armed—a great power to be reckoned with by the other great powers which had dealt so contemptuously with the fragments of Arabdom. This idea of a unified Arab world acting as a great power has powerful rhetorical appeal, particularly at the end of a speech which has recounted all the crimes of the great powers against the defenseless Arabs. But to some Arabs it is a mistake, as well as embarrassingly bombastic, to represent the united Arab state of the future as a great power. The rest of the world would be much more willing to accept the picture, they say, if it were drawn along more realistic lines, i.e., as a state of moderate size and power, not as a great military power rivaling the United States and the U.S.S.R. The argument, of course, is academic.

The history of Nasser's Arab unity policy is a bewildering series of hopeful achievements alternating with disheartening defeats. His success in joining Saudi Arabia and Syria to Egypt in an alliance directed against the Baghdad Pact, in 1955, was followed by the discouraging proof of its lack of practical value. The spectacular evidence, in 1956 and 1957, that individuals and groups throughout the area were willing to support him in almost any kind of political action against the conservative governments was followed by a series of fiascos and exposures that showed his volunteer agents to be undisciplined and inefficient and his professionals not much better. The tremendous victory in the Suez affair, and the union with Syria which followed, seemed to have opened a road to Arab unity, but these events were followed by the rallying of all the conservative states against him. The civil war in Lebanon, in which the Muslims there declared their solidarity with Nasser's Arab nationalism, was followed by the consolidation of Lebanese separatism. And, most startling of all, the Iraqi revolution, which had been almost a copy of the Egyptian revolution, turned quickly to Iraqi nationalism and became anti-Nasser. A final blow was the revolt in Syria which destroyed its union with Egypt.

A great many people have understood these events to be a series of carefully thought out operations on Nasser's part, devised to extend his power by uniting Arab states under Egyptian leadership. This is a misinterpretation. During most of this period Nasser found himself swept up in movements which he could only vaguely understand. Naturally enough, he became convinced that historical forces were moving in the direction of Arab unity, and that they inevitably would reach that end. He sought to assist the processes of history, insofar as his resources permitted. At the same time, however, he showed reluctance to take advantage of opportunities which he thought would advance Arab unity too fast, exposing it to its enemies, or creating unsound institutions. For example, he hesitated to accept unity with Syria—a hesitancy which reflected a premonition of things to come.

Nasser's setback in Syria presumably taught him some practical lessons, but it is unlikely that he revised his emphasis on Arab unity as an ultimate goal, as a necessity for Egypt and the Arab area as a whole. His speeches still echoed the refrain of strength through unity. And to meet charges of "indirect aggression" and of aspiring to take over other Arab states by force he has increasingly emphasized that ". . . the way to Arab unity is through the Arab people."[14] He spelled this out in a speech before the General Congress of the National Union:

Our work towards unity is defined by principles that would safeguard it and preserve it. These include:

(a) Any people of the Arab nation wishing for Arab unity should do this through its free and independent choice and will.

(b) Such an Arab people must have accomplished and completed the potentialities of its national unity within the limits of its existing borders before entering into commitments outside these borders.

(c) Such a people must be determined in asking for unity. They must make sure of their wish for unity.

On these bases we believe that unity should be continuously evolving and should not take place by a coup. . . .[15]

Today Nasser's policy with respect to Arab unity appears to be just about where it was five years ago, with the difference that it

[14] Speech before a committee of the National Union General Congress, July 14, 1960.
[15] Speech of July 9, 1960.

has benefited from bitter experience and is enlightened by the knowledge that the path to unity is certain to be a long and rocky one. It is still more of an objective than a program, still more an ideal than an operation.

POLITICAL FUTURE OF THE ARAB EAST

Obstacles lie across all of the more feasible paths to Arab unity. The Arab League has never become a parliament of the Arab people but remains an assembly of the representatives of the sovereign Arab states. Iraq, Jordan, Tunisia, the Sudan, and Saudi Arabia have all been emphasizing what was once the traditional Egyptian policy of using the League to maintain the *status quo* in the Arab states system. Kuwait can be expected to join them in this line of policy. Even partial moves toward union have seemed unlikely because localism and state nationalism are still so strong. The prospect of a Fertile Crescent union has been dim while Iraq has followed a policy of support for the *status quo* and the Syrians have been generally unready to accept the uncertainties of union with Iraq. Kassem's bid for Kuwait on its gaining independence does not seem to have been so much an indication of his serious intention of taking over the sheikhdom as it was the staking out of a claim. The prospects of the early adherence of other Arab states to the U.A.R., especially since the defection of Syria, have not seemed bright.

A conclusion for the future based only on this catalogue of obstacles to unity, however, would have to rest on the assumption that things are likely to stay much as they are and that the forces driving in the direction of unity will continue to be contained. This is a dubious assumption. Early in the spring of 1962 rumblings of pro-Nasser sentiment in the Syrian army began to modify the stance of the Syrian government, and by May the Syrian Premier was speaking publicly of the desire of his government for some reformulation of the association between Syria and Egypt. Nasser kept his counsel—in public at least—but it appeared that a process of negotiation had begun. While it was apparent that the pattern of the former union appealed neither to Nasser nor to the Syrians, it seemed equally clear that the forces which had brought the union in 1958 persisted. The problem for both Egyptians and Syrians was to find a formula which would give expression to the need for solidarity and cooperation within the Arab nationalist framework and still be consonant with the political and social realities.

There are many ways in which further movement toward unity might come about in the Arab world. Most of the long-term trends —particularly that toward the modification of traditional regimes and social systems—appear likely to favor that development. The collapse or overthrow of most of the conservative regimes might produce uncertain new Arab nationalist regimes which would look to Nasser for help and possibly for some kind of association with his long-established nationalist regime. In Yemen the revolutionaries have turned to Nasser for help against the northern tribesmen, who are independent, unsympathetic to the revolution, and willing recipients of Saudi assistance. Nasser has poured troops and weapons into Yemen and has found the tribesmen tough fighters and their country rugged and difficult. The Saudi and Jordanian governments for their part have found it hard to render effective assistance to the indecisive claimants to the Imamate. They have also been hampered by the tendency of their own people, particularly the airmen, to desert to Nasser. In short, the situation is a classic Arab crisis in which almost anything could happen except a pitched battle between two organized armies. Nasser is in a difficult position because of the necessity he feels for aiding a revolution which claims to be Arab nationalist in character. Saud and Hussein, on their side, are almost equally compelled to resist the revolution and Nasser's support of it. Should the strain prove too great for one or another of the two monarchies and bring a collapse, it would throw the whole Arab equation out of balance. The fact that it did not work that way when the revolution took place in Iraq does not preclude its happening in other situations.

Another possibility is that Egypt might seek to open the way by inviting other Arab states to come together in a federation for certain limited purposes. Rather than coming in the form of an invitation which might well be rebuffed, it seems more likely that the transformation of the U.A.R. into a federation would come about in response to a request from Syria for a reformulation of its association with Egypt or to a revolution in another Arab state.

If the government in another Arab state were overthrown by middle-class revolutionaries inspired by the revolutions in Egypt and Iraq, and if the new revolutionary government were to look to the U.A.R. for support but hesitated to sacrifice its sovereignty, the government of the U.A.R. might welcome the opportunity to offer to join in a federation. It seems highly unlikely that Nasser would consider federation with any state which had not embarked on a social and economic revolution similar to that taking place in Egypt.

One revelation of the Syrian crisis that led to the union with Egypt in 1958 which should be kept in mind is the extent to which external pressure, or fear of intervention, influenced the Syrian decision to join with Egypt. Some future situation in which an individual Arab state felt itself in a position similar to that of Syria in the summer and autumn of 1957 might have similar consequences.

These calculations do not lead to the conclusion that Arab unity is a certainty, but they do emphasize the variety of ways in which the strong drift in the direction of unity might produce practical results. In the event, historical circumstance and the chance of finding means of putting the idea into effect are likely to have a great deal to do with its realization or its neglect. Nothing can change the fact that the realization of any real unity will require some central authority, yet it is also clear that a strong man like Nasser frightens many Arabs and that physical conquest of the entire Arab area or a large part of it by one Arab state seems most unlikely and impracticable within the foreseeable future.

The future of Nasser's leadership in the Arab East is anything but clear. For nearly ten years his pre-eminence has been unchallenged by any other leader, though his personal prestige has its spectacular peaks and valleys, as prospects for the kind of Arab community which he has symbolized have waxed and waned. At times it has seemed that he could do no wrong and at other times that he had taken blows from which he could never recover. Yet he remains unchallenged as a leader of the Arabs, even though other chiefs of state fear and distrust him and the Arab public finds itself unable to visualize or respond to the demands which his leadership makes upon it.

Experience has shown that spectacular *tours de force* in international affairs, however much enthusiasm they may engender, do not provide an institutional base for unity. It has also shown, particularly in the short-lived union of Egypt and Syria, that one leader's personal charisma cannot resolve the myriad political and economic problems of unity.

Nasser's attention to the domestic problems of Egypt, as in the period after the breakup of the Egyptian-Syrian union, has added to his credit and reputation for responsible statesmanship, even while his socialist policies have frightened conservatives throughout the area. As always, his achievements and his influence are at the same time a recommendation for the extension of his authority and a threat to prerogatives and privilege. In the Arab area Nasser remains, as it were, the man to beat, or the man to reckon with, depending on one's view of the Arab future.

The next generation of Arab leaders is now fairly well along in its development. The new elite in every Arab country includes most of the men who will hold power and make the important decisions in the Arab East when the present leaders have passed from the stage. The elite also includes the technicians who will perform their duties under the next governments in much the same way that they do at present. More important are the men who hold the principal offices of confidence in the presidency, or the prime minister's office, or the palace, as the case may be, men whose orientation and commitment are essentially personal and political rather than bureaucratic or technical. Particularly important are those who have direct connections with the center of authority and who hold key posts in ministries or government bureaus concerned with propaganda, intelligence, public security, development planning, and in the field which is referred to as "national guidance," including direction of political activity and organized labor. In the U.A.R., Syria, and Iraq many such men, who are now in the second echelon of the dominant revolutionary group, are a great deal more radical and extremist than the men at the top. They tend to be more anti-Western, more xenophobic, less tolerant, and generally less well disciplined than the groups that actually made the revolutions. To an important degree they are the victims of the revolutionary propaganda and the tough revolutionary stance which their superiors have considered necessary to awaken their people to the effort required of them. The generation being trained in the schools today is likely to be even less capable of balanced judgment.

In every country, including those which have had recent revolutions, there is a group of active and potential opposition leaders from whom the leadership will come in the event of revolution or counterrevolution. In the monarchies this group is scattered through the officer corps of the armed services and the educated professional class. Most of these people are likely to turn to the U.A.R., and possibly in some cases to Iraq, for guidance and support in the event that they reach power in their countries. There is also the Communist and pro-Communist intelligentsia throughout the area from which the leadership in future movements against the anti-Communist bourgeois regimes is likely to come. This group has suffered during the period when the Soviet Union has been supporting Nasser and Kassem. The potential remains great, however, for the international Communist leadership in support of new Soviet tactics to bring out presently unknown Communists and pro-Communists from the Arab lower middle and lower classes to organize an attack on the "bourgeois dictators" with the support of the "street."

Whoever they are, the next generation of Arab leaders will be scarcely less important to the West—and to the Soviets—than to the Arabs themselves. Perhaps the single most predictable thing about this group is that it will be less disposed to accept the traditional patterns of social and economic organization in the Arab area or of Arab relations with the rest of the world than the present generation.

POLITICAL PROBLEMS AND RELATIONSHIPS

It would be hard to find any basis for estimating a future for the Arab East during the next ten years which did not include warning of internal strife and upheaval in several if not all states, conflict among the states, and rearrangement of present borders. For some time the most likely candidate for upheaval has been Jordan. Nevertheless, while all the usual indicators pointed to instability and change, the state has maintained its independence and the King has become palpably stronger. This would seem to be a reminder that in the Arab East the inevitable does not necessarily happen, at least not right away. It also points to certain elements in the situation which should not be overlooked in making an estimate of the future.

Jordan lacks most of the standard geographical, economic, and political requirements of national viability. By the very nature of its situation it is bound to be at odds with the other Arab states on the question of Israel, the Arab refugees, and the future of Arab Palestine. To make up for these deficiencies it has Western economic aid and the promise of military support if needed, advantages which in slightly altered circumstances would be politically impossible burdens for the regime. It also has a determined and courageous monarch. Neither the U.A.R. nor Israel is apparently now ready to assume the obligations, burdens, and dangers involved in taking over the territory of Jordan. The prospect of Israeli, and possibly Western, intervention is a deterrent to other Arab states' ambitions or hopes with respect to Jordan. The prospect of Western intervention is equally a deterrent to Israel's seizure of the West Bank.

Conceivably, the countervailing forces which have supported Jordan over the past few years could continue in balance for years to come. To regard such a delicate balance composed of so many different elements as assurance of stability, however, would be most unreasonable. When the present balance of forces in the Arab East shifts, the consequences are likely to be an Arab-Israeli confrontation, a struggle among the other Arab states for domination of Jordan, or both mixed in a military and political tangle. Furthermore, an internal political upheaval, or even an accident to the King, could have the same result, with profound implications for the future of the Arab states.

One of the great unsolved problems of the Arab East is that of the future of Kuwait and the sheikhdoms of the Gulf. For Great Britain and the United States, prompted by their concern for the continued flow of oil from the concessionary companies, to take an inflexible stand in favor of the *status quo* and support it by appeal to Britain's treaty rights and the right of the Western powers to give military assistance to sovereign states when they request it would be to accept a commitment to a long and drawn-out battle. Furthermore, it would be a battle which there is little or no chance of winning and the prosecution of which is likely to endanger rather than guarantee the flow of oil to the West. On the other hand, Great Britain and the United States would probably sign the death warrant of the sheikhdoms and guarantee an upheaval with uncertain consequences if they too precipitately washed their hands of the *status quo* in the Gulf.

The Arab nationalists argue that the oil of the Gulf littoral is "Arab oil" and not the personal property of the sheikhs and that the sheikhdoms are anachronistic holdovers from the past kept in being in defiance of the will of the Arab people by British support of a few unrepresentative individuals. Before the principle of self-determination can be applied to Kuwait, the Gulf sheikhdoms, and the other states on the Arabian Peninsula littoral, however, with the effect which the Arab nationalists have in mind, considerable change is going to have to take place both in the political development of the people of these territories and in the political unity of the other Arab states.

Very few individuals in the oil-rich states and principalities, and certainly not the people in power, are ready to make any personal sacrifice of present or future wealth or other advantage from oil royalties for the sake of their less fortunate Arab brothers or for the ideal of Arab unity.

Furthermore, unless and until there is some kind of unity among the Arab states the implementation of the principle of Arab oil for all the Arabs will be a very difficult one to apply except by means of development banks or organizations in which oil royalties are invested. The events which followed the announcement of Kuwait's independence in the summer of 1961 illustrate the way in which rivalries among the Arab states actually tend to reinforce the sovereignty of the oil-rich sheikhdoms. Prime Minister Kassem's claims to Kuwait were balanced by U.A.R. acquiescence in British action to provide security for the Sheikh and action in the Arab League, against Iraqi opposition, to admit Kuwait as a member of the League.

The future of the states and sheikhdoms of the Arabian Penin-

sula littoral is an Arab problem which probably cannot be resolved until some broader formula for the reorganization of Arab
relations generally is put into effect. The mere proposition that
the oil wealth now controlled by a few states could make a greater
contribution to human welfare and to area stability if it were put
at the disposal of the Arab area as a whole, however reasonable,
does not provide an answer to the problem of how the promise in
this conception can be realized.

A projection of the present situation and the continuation of
present trends into the future will almost certainly lead to bitter
and dangerous clashes between the British government and the
Arab states. In such a conflict the British, supported by other
Western nations and appearing to be taking an "imperialist" position, will be lined up against Arab nationalism, supported by the
Afro-Asian and neutralist nations and loudly championed by the
Sino-Soviet bloc. This outcome appears likely even if such an enlightened approach as that outlined in the Chatham House Study
Group Report entitled *British Interests in the Mediterranean and
Middle East* were to be followed. This report begins with the rejection of the long-accepted presumption that Britain has a special
mission in the Arab Middle East, saying, "This belief does not fit
in the circumstances of today, and to follow in that direction is to
court disaster."[16] It also makes the point that attempts to maintain
the position presently based on Britain's treaty relations with the
sheikhs "may damage not only her own position and chances of
recovery but also those of her allies and associates," and "may
land us in actions which are contrary to our interests and unpalatable to our electorate."[17] It also notes that attempts to handle
local disputes in the sheikhdoms in the terms in which they
are likely to appear to the British official on the spot will, to
outside opinion, ". . . appear as the irritating and pathetic attempt of a former imperial Power to cling to the vestiges and trap-
pings of empire."[18]

The only solutions of this dilemma pointed to in the report,

[16] Royal Institute of International Affairs, *British Interests in the Mediterranean and Middle East* (London: Oxford University Press, 1958), p. 25.
[17] Same, p. 105.
[18] Same, p. 107.

however, are a redefinition of responsibilities, investigation of the possibility of an association of the Persian Gulf sheikhdoms ". . . in a league or some other semi-permanent arrangements, as if they were a Switzerland with a seaboard . . ." and a greater effort to let the world know what is going on in these hitherto closely protected "Arab Monacos and San Marinos."[19] But this will not really do, since the problem does not arise solely out of local ambition and tribal conflict, not even out of Saudi or Iraqi ambition. Arab rivalry is itself likely for a time to protect the sheikhdoms from these threats, but with the onward movement of the social revolution in the Arab world and the approach of Arab unity, whether in the form of political union, federation, or economic union, the whole issue takes on different dimensions. The prospect then will be a Western position much like that taken at the London Conference on the Suez Canal problem—an assertion that treaties and international interests override claims based on national self-determination, as against an Arab nationalist assertion of the right of the Arab community as a whole to exercise the rights of sovereignty over the oil wealth of the "Arab Monacos and San Marinos." Furthermore, this clash is likely to be accompanied by extensive public demonstrations against the governments supported by the West.

The question is how long the pursuit of the proposed solutions would actually enable the West to ". . . obtain oil under commercial conditions from the states which produce it, and then bring it to Europe by the cheapest and safest route,"[20] or how soon it will lead to a Suez or Cyprus situation. Unfortunately, agreement that what is proposed does not look promising does not lead to the conclusion that there is a feasible second course which can be adopted forthwith. The realization of Western, and indeed of Arab, interests in the oil of the Arab East without the continued exercise of British tutelage and protection of the sheikhdoms and the maintenance of a "special position" by the British in the Persian Gulf would, under the most favorable circumstances, require an evolu-

---

[19] Same, pp. 105–107.

[20] This is a definition of "Britain's first and paramount interest in the area" given in *British Interests in the Mediterranean and Middle East,* cited, p. 35.

tionary process over a period of years. It is unlikely that circumstances will allow this kind of gradual development.

The issue between the West and the Arabs on Western access to Arab oil is likely to be drawn first on the question of the status of the governments of the oil-producing countries, rather than on the question of the status of the Western companies. The latter have shown themselves to be remarkably flexible and understanding of the psychological and political as well as the engineering and economic problems of extracting oil in the Middle East. The Arab states on their part have shown an increasing awareness of the value of the services offered by the Western companies. Pressures will increase for a higher proportion of the profits for the states granting concessions and for a larger and larger proportion of Arab personnel in the upper echelons, but outright nationalization seems less a threat than it did a few years ago.

The relative increase in world-wide oil production as compared with demand has reduced the dependence of Western distributors on the Persian Gulf producers. The development of Libyan and Algerian oil fields west of Suez, together with expanded production elsewhere, is likely to slow the rate at which Persian Gulf oil production expands. Though revenues are likely to continue to increase every year, they will do so at a less rapid rate than they have in the past. These circumstances may facilitate an arrangement based on the mutual interest of the Arabs and the West in the production and distribution of Arab oil. The political glamor of nationalization, however, must not be forgotten. If some Arab government wished to declare its independence of the West—as Mosaddeq did in Iran, or as Nasser did in making the Egyptian-Soviet arms deal and in nationalizing the Suez Canal Company—economic considerations or past relations with the concessionary company might be forgotten in a moment of nationalistic fervor. Also, in the longer run the development of a sizable market for oil in Communist China might have profound consequences for the economic and political orientation of the Arab East.

ARAB-ISRAEL RELATIONS

There are no grounds for optimism on the future of Arab-Israel relations. Israel is still, in Arab eyes, an insult and an affront;

hence, maintaining a strong anti-Israel policy is a matter of personal pride and national honor. There is no open movement for compromise in the interest of peace and security. Only the most indirect hints appear in the Arab press and in Arab intellectual circles that certain Israeli groups favor seeking a modus vivendi. On the Israeli side Premier Ben Gurion's tough line is still overwhelmingly predominant in the government and among the public. The Mapam and Ihud doctrines have done very little to modify the belief that the way to handle the Arabs is to keep them frightened of Israel's military strength and determination. Hope for the future is still largely based on the conviction that the Arabs will never manage to resolve their internal rivalries or learn to master their weapons sufficiently well to conduct effective combined military operations on the scale required to defeat Israel.

The Arab-Israeli stalemate was challenged in the autumn of 1961 by yet another in the long line of able and objective men who have sought to help the Arabs and Israelis out of the strait jacket into which their incompatible interests and attitudes have forced them. Dr. Joseph E. Johnson, President of the Carnegie Endowment for International Peace, who undertook a mission for the United Nations Conciliation Commission for Palestine, observed: "It is clear that as matters now stand there is no prospect of an early resolution of the Palestine question as a whole. . . ."[21] "No one who has had an opportunity to confer at length with responsible statesmen in the area can fail to conclude that there is a large degree not only of mistrust and suspicion but of active fear on both sides." This fear, he wrote, "underlies and to a certain extent probably explains governmental policies on both sides."[22]

Regarding the refugee question, which was the principal concern of his mission, Dr. Johnson said: ". . . there are many indications that no progress can be made on the Palestine Arab refugee question apart from, or in advance of, an over-all settlement." He found some willingness—"though with much reservation and scepticism"—to consider a step-by-step process which

[21] UN General Assembly, Conciliation Commission for Palestine, *Addendum to the Nineteenth Progress Report*, A/4921/Add. 1 (New York: Author, 1961), para. 52.
[22] Same, para. 46.

might lead to action on the refugee question, provided that could be done without prejudice to the positions of the governments concerned on other issues. His conclusion therefore was not surprising: "It would be unwise to plan United Nations or national policies on any other assumption than that there will be Palestine Arab refugees for at least a decade."[23]

It is not only upon the problem of the refugees and other issues between the Arabs and Israelis that mutual fear and distrust cast a baleful influence. There is also its effect on each side's suspicions that the other may be looking toward an eventual military solution. Especially after what happened in 1956, the Arabs have been basically disinclined to take aggressive military action. On the other hand, as Arab armed forces gain increased knowledge of their Soviet arms and profit by training, they approach a point at which they should, theoretically, be able to take advantage of their vastly greater manpower and may try to do so. It is difficult to judge the combat readiness of Arab troops or their ability to coordinate separate units in large operations, but there are indications that the emphasis in Egypt has been on raising the quality of the combat forces. Prospects for coordination of Egyptian and Syrian forces and facilities—air forces and air fields being particularly important—have, of course, been greatly reduced by the breakup of the U.A.R.

The Israelis on their side have maintained their high level of military preparedness but have reached the limits imposed on them by the availability of man and woman power for the armed forces. Even in the absence of specific evidence it is hard to believe that the Israelis, faced with the impending possibility of the development of Arab military skills to a level approaching their own and possessing, as they do, great scientific resources at home and contact with Jewish scientists all over the world, are not working toward the acquisition and development of nuclear and other highly sophisticated weapons. Even without the help of France, hitherto their close ally against the Arabs, Israel certainly has the capability of producing such weapons long before the Arabs.

This situation brings closer the time at which the Arabs might

[23] Same, paras. 49, 51, 52.

decide that they have the capability of defeating Israel with non-nuclear arms, but that they have very little time before this advantage will be nullified by Israel's acquisition of tactical missiles and nuclear warheads. In this situation the Israelis will be tempted to select the time and occasion for another military round if they believe that an Arab attack is imminent and that the Arabs may have overestimated their own military capabilities. In the meantime the Egyptians have produced rockets they say are capable of reaching Israel and may be looking forward to the acquisition of a nuclear weapons capability, spurred on by Israeli experimentation with rockets and their belief that the Israelis are developing a nuclear weapon. If the Soviet Union were to supply nuclear weapons to the Arabs or assistance in developing their own, the effect would be to exaggerate the consequences of the existing U.A.R. dependence upon the Soviets for conventional weapons.

Arab-Israeli tensions continue to reflect the complexities of great-power involvement. Arab insecurity is heightened by the conviction that the Western powers regard Israel as their instrument and ally and would come to its assistance in any conflict. At the same time the Arabs probably feel that the Soviet Union, which has supported them on so many international issues, has shown an unwillingness to give them direct support against Israel. Thus it is conceivable to them that an Arab-Israel conflict could come about in such a way that Israel might have the active support of the Western powers while they did not have counterbalancing support from the Soviets. From the Israeli side the prospects for great-power involvement in an Arab-Israeli struggle look quite different. They are impressed by America's unwillingness to supply arms in needed quantities, by the American condemnation of Israel at the time of the Sinai invasion, and by the diminishing interest of France in Israel. The Israelis are afraid of the possibility of an American attempt, motivated by interest in security of the area and access to Arab oil, to resolve the Arab-Israeli problem by "appeasing" the Arabs, either in a negotiated settlement or by pressures upon Israel.

There are many factors in the situation which make a continuation of the now well-institutionalized stalemate seem likely. The Arabs, despite all their fierce resentments and occasional talk of resort to force, are not temperamentally inclined to initiate military action leading to a showdown. The words of a Chinese "military sage" quoted by the editor of *The Egyptian Economic and Political Review* in 1956—"Supreme excellence consists in breaking the enemy's resistance without attacking him"[24]—still appear to sum up the policy of the Arab leaders. The Israelis, for their part, though much more inclined by temperament and confidence in their abilities to try for a solution to their problems by military means, do not seem likely to do so in view of the risks and the uncertainty that anything would be gained. Yet it is difficult to conclude that the present situation gives assurance that another major trial at arms will be avoided.

While the factors which make for the persistence of the stalemate could continue to dominate for a long period, the factors on the other side are numerous and intractible. There does not seem to be much that can be done directly to reduce the threat of a military clash. The United Nations Emergency Force, which has remained on the Israeli-Egyptian border since the Sinai war, does reduce the likelihood of brushes between the Egyptian and Israeli forces on that frontier. A similar force on the other frontiers might be equally useful, but it is not likely that the United Nations will initiate such an extension of the UNEF or that the Arab states would accept it. It is virtually a certainty that Israel would not accept it on its side of the line.

What appears at first glance to be the most promising possibility is a great-power guarantee of the frontiers. This device has already been tried in the form of a Western guarantee in the Tripartite Declaration of June 1950, but that declaration was destroyed by the breaking of the Western arms monopoly in 1955 and the British-French attack on Egypt in 1956. The only possible effective great-power guarantee would be one participated in both by the West and the Soviet bloc, an unlikely eventuality in foreseeable circumstances. Thus there seems to be little hope for reducing the dangers implicit in the Arab-Israel conflict by measures designed to alter the nature and circumstances of the military confrontation.

[24] "The Strategy of Egyptian Defense," *The Egyptian Economic and Political Review* (Cairo), Special Supplement on the armed forces of Egypt, 1956, p. 12.

It is in the problem itself that the base of the trouble and the source of the danger lies.

Although Israel has generally shown itself to be frightened of the possibility of Arab unification, the divisions of the Arab area and the rivalry among states and leaders have generally stimulated extremist policies toward Israel. One of the principal impediments to Arab negotiation with Israel has been the fear of Arab leaders of what their rivals would do to them if they accepted the idea of negotiation or assumed less than the most extreme and intransigent attitudes toward Israel. It is difficult to imagine an Arab-Israel settlement while the Arab world remains disunited. While a united Arab world might for a time continue to follow the rigid policies of the past, its leaders would at least have the capability of reaching a settlement with Israel.

There are few signs of any breakdown of the Arab-Israel stalemate in the political and psychological area. It is hard to conceive of the basic elements in the situation changing significantly, except as a result of the use of force, for a generation at least. The basic conditions of a real change are, on the Arab side, abandonment of the conventional all-or-nothing tactics and the doctrine that just being against Israel is better than any practical improvement in the situation; and on the Israeli side, abandonment of the policies based on contempt for the Arab and acknowledgment that eventually Israel must come to some kind of settlement with the majority of the people in the area in which it is located. On balance, there is little chance that these conditions will be soon met. On the other hand, in the last few years there have been more indications of movement in the direction of meeting them than at any time since the Palestine War.

There are many signs of a modification of the Arab approach to the Palestine problem in the United Nations. Attempts to create a political entity of Arab Palestine with standing in the international community and to get discussion in the General Assembly on implementation of the outstanding UN resolution on Palestine refugees reflect some change in the Arab position. The Arab effort in 1961 to get a resolution through the General Assembly recognizing the property rights in Israel of Palestine Arabs and to appoint a UN custodian for Arab properties in Israel is also part of a new approach to the Palestine problem. It is possible that the Arabs, failing in their new initiatives, will fall back on an excuse that has been often used in the past: that the Western powers are responsible for Israel and therefore should solve the problem they have created. On the other hand, there is promise in the fact that some Arabs at least are thinking in terms of action which will lead logically to a compromise rather than to an imposed solution.

On the Israeli side there is some evidence of interest in the Mapam and Ihud approaches to the problem of relations with the Arabs. In the election campaign of the summer of 1961 the new Liberal party campaigned on a platform which included a policy of improving relations with the Arabs. These ideas are by no means a strong or influential force in Israel, but they are making themselves heard by a wider audience increasingly disposed to listen to new ideas in the atmosphere created by the Lavon affair and the clashes between Ben Gurion and American Jewry. As the likelihood of another fight with the Arabs increases, there may be more who question the soundness of Ben Gurion's tough policy toward the Arabs.

Certainly the character of the state of Israel will have a great deal to do with its Arab policy. Prime Minister Ben Gurion has had some very rough sledding with the Lavon affair but he has managed to reinforce his position in Israel and with Jews everywhere by the expedient of the Eichmann trial, pressing the idea that Jews are not safe anywhere except in their own state. But even Ben Gurion will eventually pass from the scene and other leaders take his place. What their backgrounds are and what their conception of the Jewish state is will be of greatest importance. Also important will be the relative degree of Westernism in the attachments and outlook of the Israel of the future. One development often pointed to as being likely to change the country's orientation is the increasing number of Oriental Jews and relatively smaller number of Western Jews in the total population. Some have suggested that an Israel dominated by Oriental Jews should be able to get along with the Arabs better than the Western-oriented Israel of today. Even were this the trend in Israel, and it is not, the result seems unlikely in view of the fact that most of these Oriental Jews have had the experience of living as second-class citizens in Arab states and so may well be more anti-Arab than the European Jews.

In any event it must be kept in mind that the clash between the Arabs and the Zionists has been more than a difference in policy or leadership. It has been a head-on conflict of basic national interests. As such it is not likely to be solved by formulas or devices, but only by the onward movement of history bringing changes in the nature of those interests.

XI

POLICIES AND PROSPECTS:
Afro-Asia

Some Westerners are skeptical of the Afro-Asian concept. They feel that the states of Africa and Asia have little in common and that the idea is preposterous that they are sufficiently united to constitute a meaningful force in international affairs. In the past few years, however, there have been more and more demonstrations of Afro-Asian solidarity. The Suez crisis was an event which brought out with dramatic clarity the unanimity of African and Asian attitudes on certain basic issues and contrasted them with Western attitudes. While most Westerners' attention hung on events in Hungary, and many looked on the Suez crisis only as an unfortunate accident that divided the West and distracted attention from more important issues, Asians and Africans alike saw in Suez rather than Hungary the key issues of our time.

The wife of a Pakistani diplomat stationed in Cairo expressed the common African and Asian viewpoint of the Suez crisis when she said, "All Africans and Asians look upon the attack on Egypt as a white man's assault on one of us—one who dared to claim his country's rights in defiance of the white man's rules. But Hungary means nothing to us. It is a fight between white men." To prove her point she noted how America, Australia, and other Western countries took steps immediately to take in Hungarian refugees. "Can you imagine a Western country doing that for Africans or Asians, however destitute?" she asked.

These words, spoken in the heat of the crisis in late 1956, were sincere. They came from the heart of a Western-educated woman who still respects the West, or at least certain things about the West, and whose country was allied with the West. Yet she felt that the West is arrayed against the peoples of Africa and Asia. This psychological and racial tie among all non-whites, all persons who are excluded from the privileged Western community, is one of the most important factors in the international climate of the twentieth century.

BANDUNG PRINCIPLES

Soon after he took over the reins of power in Egypt, Nasser's awareness of the relationship between Arab nationalism and the Afro-Asian revolt against colonial rule began to develop in response to many stimuli. By the spring of 1955 he had already begun to develop the basic ideas of a policy by means of which small powers could join together for mutual protection and speak with a common voice in world affairs; the Bandung Conference of Asian and African states confirmed his interest in this subject. In 1957, after the Suez crisis, in a speech at the opening of the Egyptian National Assembly, he reviewed the main events and policy decisions of the revolutionary regime. Among the various battles which the regime had waged, he said, was the "battle of defining our international personality and determining our course in this world." This battle, which was intermixed with such practical problems as beating "the arms monopoly," led to Bandung. He went on to tell the National Assembly that inasmuch as ". . . the Bandung Conference represents a way and a policy in international relations, we have deposited in the secretariat of your assembly all the communiqués and resolutions issued by international conferences in which Egypt has participated and which were inspired in one way or another by the principles of Bandung." Chief among these conferences, he said, "was the Brioni conference [July 1956] in which Yugoslavia, India, and Egypt participated, and in which these three countries—whose foreign policy is very similar—proceeded along the same path which they pursued at Bandung."[1]

[1] Speech at the opening of the Egyptian National Assembly, July 22, 1957.

Emphasis on the principles of Bandung has characterized Nasser's discussion of foreign policy since 1955. It made up the concluding section of his speech at the General Assembly of the United Nations in 1960, which he began by saying, "If I may present you now with solutions to the problems facing us, I find that the best I can offer you is a picture of our thought when we were twenty-nine Afro-Asian countries meeting in Bandung." The conference, he noted, had declared two important principles: "full support of the fundamental principles of human rights" and "full equality among peoples of all races and color." He reiterated the Bandung Conference's resolutions on colonialism, including the declaration "that colonialism in all its manifestations is an evil which should speedily be brought to an end," and "the necessity of calling upon the Powers concerned to grant freedom and independence for all such [colonial] peoples." He cited the conference's declaration favoring membership of all states in the United Nations and the necessity for disarmament and the "prohibition of the production and testing of nuclear and thermonuclear weapons." The conference, he observed, accepted the principle that the best way to achieve international security is through the United Nations, and also the "necessity for promoting social development and raising the standards of living, particularly as regards Asia and Africa."[2]

Self-determination of peoples; the end of "colonialism"; nonalignment in the cold war of the great powers; a greater role in the United Nations for the nations of Africa and Asia; and a larger role for the United Nations as the arbiter of peace, disarmament, and economic and social development for underdeveloped nations—these principles have formed the main theme of Nasser's policy since Bandung. In his view, it is not a specifically "Arab" policy, but it provides a framework within which the Arabs can best pursue their own goals. First, Nasser believes that the identification of Egypt and the Arabs with other nations in a similar situation strengthens the Arab position. In speaking to the Na-

[2] Information Administration, Press Bureau, Permanent Mission of the United Arab Republic to the United Nations (New York), *Text of Statement Delivered by President Gamal Abdel Nasser to the Fifteenth Session of the General Assembly of the United Nations of 27 September 1960*, pp. 27–28.

tional Assembly on the results of the Casablanca Conference, January 23, 1961, he said, "The Arab struggle has extended from Bandung to Casablanca, and days and experiences have proved that this broad line is the Arab safety line, also the peace line."[3] A month later at Damascus he said, "When we support African issues and independence movements elsewhere, we actually consolidate our own independence."[4]

Secondly, he understands that the same revolution of awareness which has done so much to transform the Arab area is moving like a forest fire across Africa. In June 1958, in an interview with representatives of the American press, Nasser said, "The world today is completely different from what it was ten or fifteen years ago. The peoples of Africa for example have undergone very great changes . . . The African peoples now own wireless sets. . . . They also realize that there are different standards of living and that theirs is not like that of the people of the U.S.A. They know a great deal about the modern principles of freedom and peace as well as the struggles of peoples in different places for freedom." He was not averse to giving credit to France for stimulating these changes in Algeria: "France has inculcated in the Algerians the true meaning of Freedom, Equality and Fraternity, and the Algerian people set about applying these principles in their country."[5] Nasser clearly believes not only that his country and the other Arab states have a community of interest with the African states now going through the struggle of liberation, attempting to find their "international personality," but also that the Arabs have something to offer out of their own experience.

The third influence in Nasser's Afro-Asian policy is the realization that the course which the new African states take in establishing their "international personality" is of critical importance to the future balance of international forces. He probably agrees completely with Prime Minister Nehru's statement at the Bandung

[3] Pamphlet entitled *Casablanca Conference, January 1961,* issued by the Information Department of the United Arab Republic (Cairo), p. 26.

[4] Pamphlet entitled *Speeches Delivered by President Gamal Abdel Nasser in the Northern Region on the Occasion of Celebrating the Third Anniversary of the Proclamation of the United Arab Republic, February-March 1961,* issued by the Information Department of the United Arab Republic (Cairo); Speech on February 22, 1961, at Damascus, p. 43.

[5] *Nasser's Speeches,* 1958, p. 372.

Conference that "If all the world were to be divided up between these two big power blocs . . . the inevitable result would be war. Therefore every step that takes place in reducing that area in the world which may be called the *unaligned area* is a dangerous step and leads to war."[6] Nasser would probably add that alignment not only compromises the independence of the states which accept it, but also that it narrows the area of maneuver of small independent states, thus reducing their capacity to affect the international power balance. Nasser has not dismissed the possibility that he, personally, may undertake leadership of the unaligned nations. Personal vanity may play some part in his efforts to fit into the role of leader of a third force, but it must be remembered that he conceived the role for Egypt before his own international personality had been created. The advantages, to Egypt and to the Arab community, of having a spokesman high in the councils of the neutral, or unaligned, third of the world's nations are manifest to many.

Nasser's Afro-Asian policy, like his other policies, has evolved from a few simple principles. It has used three separate though related techniques: the international conference, Afro-Asian or third-force diplomacy in the United Nations, and direct political action and propaganda.

Nasser got his start as an Afro-Asian politician at Bandung. President Sukarno's opening speech must have seemed to him an expression of his own inmost thoughts when he said, "We [the Afro-Asian nations] are united . . . by a common detestation of colonialism in whatever form it appears." Sukarno emphasized other ideas which were to become standard elements in Nasser's own thinking, e.g., that colonialism in its older forms is not the only thing that the new nations have to fear. "Colonialism," the Indonesian President said, "has also its modern dress, in the form of economic control, intellectual control, actual physical control by a small but alien community within a nation. It is a skillful and determined enemy, and it appears in many guises. It does not give up its loot easily." Nasser must have been impressed by Sukarno's emphasis upon the potential strength of the Afro-Asian nations

[6] George McTurnan Kahin, *The Asian-African Conference, Bandung, Indonesia, April 1955* (Ithaca: Cornell University Press, 1956), p. 23.

with their 1.4 billion people (if China is included); even without China they make up over a third of the world's population.[7]

At the conference Nasser introduced the Palestine issue—an initiative which led to the declaration of support for "the rights of the Arab people of Palestine"—and a resolution on French North Africa, which was also accepted. He succeeded, also, in adding a clause to the final communiqué of the conference on collective defense, which the Indians and Chou En-lai contended was directed at NATO and SEATO.[8] Nasser probably intended it to apply to the Baghdad Pact.

Having thus delivered a few good strokes for his own special interests (Palestine, Algeria, and opposition to the Baghdad Pact), Nasser proclaimed his support of self-determination, his opposition to colonialism, and his belief in the cooperation of the Afro-Asian nations. In the greatest congress of those nations, he gave the impression of one who could deal with the Afro-Asian leaders on equal terms. In a burst of enthusiasm, which doubtless reflected the feeling within the Egyptian delegation, the journalist Fikri Abaza, writing in *Al Musawwar,* said that there was now a three-nation leadership in the Afro-Asian world: India, China, and Egypt. Muhammad Hassanain Heikal, in an article in *Al Akhbar* on April 26 entitled "Moderate Resolutions," credited Nasser with moderating the tone of the final conference communiqué. It was Nasser, he wrote, who had persuaded Chou En-lai to accept the conference line, in the interest of unity. In another article, May 5, enumerating the achievements of the conference, he said that an old "psychological knot" had been untied; that whereas Egyptian statesmen had long been afraid even to look at leaders from behind the iron curtain, Nasser had met with Chou En-lai on friendly terms.

THE INTERNATIONAL CONFERENCE FAD

After the Bandung Conference Nasser's, and Egypt's, attention was fully occupied with the arms deal and events leading to the

[7] Noble Frankland and Patricia Woodcock, eds., *Documents on International Affairs, 1955* (London: Oxford University Press for the Royal Institute of International Affairs, 1958), pp. 400–402.
[8] Kahin, cited, p. 32.

Suez crisis, although Cairo Radio was already annoying the British with its broadcasts to East Africa. By 1957, however, in the atmosphere of tension created by the Suez affair and the Eisenhower Doctrine, a further venture was launched on the wider anticolonialist front. The Voice of Free Africa, appearing on the airwaves with the Voice of the Arabs, began preaching in several African languages the doctrines of anti-imperialism and anticolonialism. The broadcasts ran the gamut of warnings against the persistent evils of imperialism, descriptions of its many forms, and exhortations to rise and throw it out of Africa. They stressed the identity of interests of the Arabs and the peoples of Africa, and the relationship of the African revolution and the revolution of all suppressed peoples. Although it is impossible to measure their effect, these broadcasts undoubtedly contributed to the stirring of nationalist forces and the build-up of tensions throughout the African continent.

At the same time plans went forward for holding in Cairo a successor to the Bandung Conference, a popular and less formal meeting of representatives of the peoples of African and Asian countries rather than of their governments. According to one of Nasser's old colleagues, Anwar el Sadat, a delegation of the "Asian Solidarity Committee," presumably the Soviet-sponsored Asian and African Solidarity Committee, which called on Nasser early in 1957, suggested an Asian conference. Sadat recommended that the conference be extended to include Africa, and Nasser agreed to play the host, in order to show that "Dulles could not isolate Egypt."[9]

The Afro-Asian Peoples' Solidarity Conference, meeting in Cairo at the end of December 1957, was attended by representatives of forty-five different entities, including the U.S.S.R. which was admitted as an Asian nation, Communist China, Mongolia, and a number of dependent territories which aspired to independence. Various self-appointed representatives of states whose governments did not choose to name popular representatives were also present.

---

[9] Keith Wheelock, *Nasser's New Egypt: A Critical Analysis* (New York: Praeger, for the University of Pennsylvania Foreign Policy Research Institute, 1960), p. 254.

The conference quickly plunged into an orgy of anti-imperialism and anticolonialism, without the references to Communist imperialism which had given some balance to the discussions at Bandung. Anwar el Sadat, the conference's president, is said to have been distressed by the Soviet delegation's attempts to manipulate the conference for its own purposes. For a man with his record of suspicion of Western "imperialism" Sadat's reaction was significant. The final declaration of the conference, a more extreme version of the Bandung communiqué, was marked by more intemperate language and greater attention to opportunities for widening the breach between the Western powers and the Asian and African nations. The resolution on nuclear weapons, for example, stated: "As the U.S.S.R. Government has declared its readiness to stop nuclear weapon tests beginning from January 1958, we appeal to the U.S.A. and the U.K. governments to take the same attitude."[10]

NATO was lectured on the dangers of supplying its members with nuclear and rocket weapons, and the United States was denounced for carrying out nuclear tests at Eniwetok. Greater Afro-Asian representation in the UN was called for and membership for China and Mongolia. A long series of resolutions on imperialism demanded the liberation of Aden Colony and Protectorate and other areas on the Persian Gulf still tied to Britain. They affirmed exclusive Arab rights in the Gulf of Aqaba and endorsed the "struggle of the Arab peoples for unity, independence and freedom from foreign influence." The Baghdad Pact and the Eisenhower Doctrine were asserted to "interfere with the independence of the Arab countries." A resolution on Palestine "declares that the state of Israel is a base of imperialism which threatens the progress and security of the Middle East, and condemns its aggressive policy which is a threat to world peace."[11] Finally the conference set up in Cairo an Afro-Asian Peoples' Solidarity Council

[10] *Afro-Asian Peoples' Solidarity Conference, Cairo, December 26, 1957–January 1, 1958* (Moscow: Foreign Languages Publishing House, 1958), p. 220.

[11] Same, p. 217 ff. Also see *Afro-Asian Peoples' Conference, 26 December 1957–1st January 1958: Principal Reports Submitted to the Conference* (Cairo: Permanent Secretariat, Organization for Afro-Asian Peoples' Solidarity, 1958).

with a permanent organization and secretariat. Its task was to implement the resolutions of the conference and promote Afro-Asian solidarity. It was to have a secretary-general (an Egyptian) and eleven secretaries, including one to be selected by China and one by the U.S.S.R.[12]

The Afro-Asian Peoples' Solidarity Conference came at a time when the recent Suez "aggression" and American "pressures" on Egypt contrasted sharply with the Soviet Union's ingratiating gestures. Egypt's prominent role in the conference, and in the Council which it established, tickled the vanity of the Egyptians and fitted in with their estimate of the country's proper place among the rising nations of Asia and Africa. The conference left some doubts, however, as to the purity of Soviet motives. With the passage of time, as differences developed between Cairo and Moscow and as the Soviet and Chinese secretaries in the Council became increasingly domineering, doubts as to the sincerity of Soviet support of Egypt's role in Afro-Asia increased. Meanwhile, Nasser and his advisers were learning about the trials and tribulations of Afro-Asian politics.

Nasser's policies are not equally meaningful in all of Africa. His general stand against "imperialism" and his efforts in the United Nations and elsewhere to rally support for African liberation and development are well received by Africans. The doctrine of "positive neutralism," and more particularly the phrase itself, has been adopted by African leaders from Casablanca to Nairobi and Accra and has become a staple theme of African conferences. Nasser's evident desire to increase his own stature and to gain support for Arab policies and interests, however, evokes a response that varies from indifference to hostility. The issue of Algerian independence, of course, was one on which Africans and Arabs were able to join. The Palestine issue, on the other hand, has much less meaning to Africans. When Africans—and Asians as well—have had nothing to lose from supporting the Arab stand on Palestine, they have generally done so, though often without much enthusiasm. As the Israelis have extended technical assistance programs into Africa, proving their ability to provide skill and advice that

[12] Same, pp. 264–265.

suit local needs, few Africans have been reluctant to accept their aid, despite the Egyptians' harping on Israeli iniquities at every African conference.

The big stumbling block for Nasser has been the Africans' fear that he will inject his own authority into their affairs, trying to take leadership away from them. Nasser, having helped the Sudanese to reach the point at which they could choose their political future, saw them elect to be independent. Tunisia and Morocco have vigorously asserted their intention of maintaining their independence and have rejected the suggestion that the Maghreb in any way should become a political appendage of the Arab East. These countries will cooperate, in the United Nations and elsewhere in the diplomatic arena, for the achievement of objectives of common interest, but questions which touch on their political future, or their relations with each other, they prefer to handle themselves. Habib Bourguiba of Tunisia was naturally annoyed by what he thought were Nasser's efforts to overthrow him and did not hesitate to boycott sessions of the Arab League on that account.

Nasser's experience with the sub-Saharan states has been generally the same. They have gladly accepted assistance in achieving independence and in promoting their cause in the United Nations. They have joined in resolutions supporting self-determination, opposition to colonialism and imperialism, and the solidarity and increased international role of states of Asia and Africa. But they have chosen to halt their cooperation with Egypt at that point.

One of Nasser's handicaps in seeking a wider African role is his color. An Arab observer has suggested that because Nasser is regarded as a white man by many Africans, he is forced to be more violent than his black African rivals in his attacks on the imperialists in Africa.

Africans have become Pan Africans first and Afro-Asians second. Although willing to accept the help of the Afro-Asian community they intend that Africans shall control Africa's destiny, and by their book Egyptians do not qualify as Africans. Nasser's background differs from that of the African leaders. He is a military man of middle-class origins, a practical statesman in control of a country with rich cultural traditions and a long political history. Most of the leaders of the new states south of the Sahara are the cream of their countries' intelligentsia, their professional and bureaucratic elite. Some are highly educated and sophisticated despite the short length of their own country's history. Many, whether they lean to the left or to the right, regard Nasser as a "bourgeois dictator," which is what the Communists call him. They distrust him as a military man; they distrust the methods and the manner in which he is approaching his problems; and they sometimes fail to understand the pragmatic attitude which inspires his policies. In their view Egypt is useful neither as a patron nor as a model. They consider much of its experience to be irrelevant to their situation.

As Nasser has sought to find the role which he believes is waiting for him and for the Arab nationalists in Africa, the leaders of the new African states have also been seeking to find their place and to define the "international personality" of their raw, new states. In a series of conferences African problems have been discussed and resolutions written, debated, and voted on. It is often difficult to distinguish between those which are mere gestures and those which promise action, but the proceedings, nevertheless, throw some light on Nasser's position, both from the Arab standpoint and that of the Africans.

At the first Conference of Independent African States in Accra in April 1958, Kwame Nkrumah, the host, was much in evidence. Nasser was represented by his Foreign Minister, Mahmoud Fawzi, whose mild manner proved to be less effective in an assemblage of leaders of the new Africa than in the halls of the United Nations. He presented a series of recommendations on the Bandung model, including an affirmation of the "rights of the Arab Nation in Palestine,"[13] which made little stir in the assembly. The conference's resolutions included a mild statement on Palestine, but Nkrumah's Pan African theme obviously had far more appeal than Egypt's Afro-Asian formula.

At the first All-African Peoples' Conference held in Accra, in December 1958, with representation on a popular rather than a

[13] *Africa Awake*, April 1958, p. 140.

governmental level, the clash between Nkrumah and Nasser was sharper and more open. Communist interest and activity, also, was more evident than at the previous government-level conference. At the same time a rival show was being held in Cairo. There, on December 1, "Quit Africa Day" had been proclaimed in competition with the "Africa Freedom Day" proclaimed by the Conference of Independent African States. Also an economic conference of the Afro-Asian Peoples' Solidarity Conference was called in Cairo to begin the same day as the conference in Accra.[14] The rivalry came out in a pointed remark in Nkrumah's speech to the conference in Accra: "Do not let us also forget that colonialism and imperialism may come to us yet in a different guise [i.e., from its classic European form]—not necessarily from Europe." Most listeners interpreted his statement as referring either to Nasser or the Soviets, or to both.

There followed a series of conferences at which the African states sought to work out their relationship with each other and their positions on continental and area problems. The conference in Monrovia, Liberia, in August 1959, paid much attention to the Algerian situation but passed no resolution on Palestine. A second All-African Peoples' Conference was held in Tunis in January 1960.[15] And in April an emergency three-day "positive action" conference met in Accra to discuss peace and security. At this conference there was a clash of opinion between the Egyptians, who favored violent methods, and most of the representatives of still-dependent African territories, who preferred negotiation and discussion. At Addis Ababa, at the second meeting of the Conference of Independent African states, the U.A.R., with the largest delegation attending, pushed the Palestine issue hard but found little response among Africans who were burdened with their own problems. One delegate told *The New York Times* correspondent, "We have no stomach for the Arab-Israeli dispute."[16]

[14] Cf. *New York Herald Tribune,* November 16, 1958; *The Times* (London), November 24, 1958; *The New York Times,* November 29 and December 7, 1958.

[15] Cf. *Afro-Asian Bulletin: Special Supplement on Second All-African Peoples' Conference, Tunis* (Cairo), v.1, nos. 10–11 (February-March 1960).

[16] *The New York Times,* June 26, 1960.

CONGO CRISIS

The Congo crisis brought the main features of Nasser's African policy into sharp relief, revealing the strong differences between his approach to African problems and that of the Western nations. From the beginning Nasser saw the conflict in the Congo as a struggle of a nationalist independence movement against the forces of imperialism and neo-colonialism. He became so obsessed with the danger of the re-establishment of colonialism that he could not evaluate Soviet actions with his usual objectivity. Nasser and his advisers held no brief for Patrice Lumumba. They recognized his instability and his inexperience, but they had confidence he could be relied on to resist Communist domination as vigorously as Western domination. They pointed out that he had turned first to the United States for assistance and that he made a deal for the economic development of the entire Congo with an American businessman. Nasser did not see the Congo as a likely seedbed for communism. Nationalism in its simplest form, he believed, meant something to the Congolese, but not the complex foreign doctrines of communism. Because he doubted that the Soviets could establish a Communist stronghold in the Congo, he was willing to join with them to stop Western neo-colonialism which he considered the real and imminent threat to Congolese national independence.

Nasser saw in the Congo what for years he had been telling his listeners always happened when, after a new breach in the imperialists' domain, the fate of a new nationalist state hung in the balance. He told the United Nations General Assembly in September 1960: "Four years ago the African continent witnessed the end of one era of colonialism, and today the African continent is witnessing a new form of imperialism. The aggression on Suez was the end of unmasked imperialism, and its graveyard. Today we find the Congo presenting us with masked imperialism, which does not shrink from exploiting the United Nations itself in order to realize its hidden designs and aims."[17]

Watching the Congo situation develop, Nasser saw Belgian troops and technicians return while Moise Tshombe in Katanga

[17] *Text of Statement . . . to . . . General Assembly . . . 27 September 1960,* cited, p. 6.

province, supported by the Belgian mining interests, defied the central government. President Kasavubu and Colonel Mobutu in Léopoldville, he believed, were supported financially as well as diplomatically by the Western powers and protected by United Nations troops. At the center of the picture, as he saw it, was an Israeli technical aid mission to the Léopoldville government which had stepped up its activity in the Congo just before the crisis. The United States was treating the problem as though it involved Communist penetration. This, Nasser did not believe was taking place; he doubted that the United States believed it.

Nasser's formula was to give the African and Asian nations authority to settle the dispute in the Congo, keeping the great powers out of it. Cold war issues he thought irrelevant to the basic question of independence. If the African and Asian states were allowed to deal with the matter, they would turn to the nationalist-neutralist leaders, whom they believed represented the majority of Congolese, and let the Congo evolve independently of great-power pressures. His position probably was influenced both by his fear that Western "neo-colonialism" would set up a puppet state subject to Western influence and by his desire to make this an occasion for the Afro-Asians, including himself, to play a greater role in the settlement of a world crisis in which they had a special interest.

To Western eyes, it appeared that Nasser was cooperating with the Russians. He kept insisting that the Western powers were trying to set up a puppet government instead of a true nationalist government, and voted with the Communist bloc so long as they followed that line. His course was consistently directed toward an Afro-Asian or an African solution. He never went so far as to support the Soviet bloc in its attempts to use the Congo situation to undermine the United Nations, even though he apparently believed that the West was using the United Nations for its own ends. A key move in Nasser's Congo policy occurred on September 17, 1960, when his delegation at the United Nations joined with the other Afro-Asian states in defeating a Soviet-supported anti-UN resolution. Three days later, with the other members of the Afro-Asian bloc, it put through a resolution favoring UN action in the Congo and setting up a Conciliation Commission of Asians and

Africans to be appointed by the Secretary-General's Advisory Committee.

Disputes within the Conciliation Commission, and differences of opinion among the various African states, demonstrated that the Afro-Asian group could not unite in supporting the restoration of Lumumba, who Nasser insisted was the only popularly elected Congolese leader with backing throughout the country. The Casablanca Conference, which met in January 1961, was a meeting of pro-Lumumba states only. It reflected the split that had taken place since the Conference of Independent African States met in Accra in April 1958. The states that met at Casablanca were not only pro-Lumumba but also neutralist in outlook. Although occasioned partly by the King of Morocco's desire to obtain support for his claim to Mauretania, the meeting was significant principally as a rally of neutralist leaders. Besides the King of Morocco, those present included Nasser, Nkrumah of Ghana, Sekou Touré of Guinea, Mobito Keita of Mali, Ferhat Abbas representing the Algerian provisional government, the Foreign Minister of Libya, and the Ambassador of Ceylon to the United Arab Republic. Liberia, India, Indonesia, Sudan, and Ethiopia sent their regrets.

Included in the acts of the conference was a resolution on Palestine which not only called for the restoration of the Arab rights as had the Bandung Conference and several later conferences, but also denounced Israel as "an instrument in the service of imperialism and neo-colonialism, not only in the Middle East but also in Africa and Asia.[18] This was unexpected since Ghana, Guinea, and Mali at the time were all recipients of Israeli technical assistance.

In addition, the Casablanca Conference promulgated a formidable "African Charter" providing for an African Consultative Assembly, a political, an economic, and a cultural committee, and a joint African High Command "comprising the Chiefs of Staff of the Independent African States who will meet periodically with a view to ensuring the common defence of African cases of aggression against any part of this Continent, and with a view to safeguarding the independence of African states. . . ."[19]

The conference communiqué announced the intention of the

[18] *Casablanca Conference, January 1961,* cited, p. 19.
[19] Same, pp. 16–17.

governments represented to withdraw their troops from the United Nations force in the Congo. (Eventually the troops of the United Arab Republic, Ghana and Morocco were withdrawn.) It reaffirmed recognition of the Parliament and the legally constituted government of the Republic of the Congo which came into being on June 30, 1960 (i.e., the government which included both Lumumba and Kasavubu) and urged the United Nations to reconvene the Parliament, disarm Colonel Mobutu's "lawless bands," and eliminate from the Congo "all Belgian and other foreign military and paramilitary personnel not belonging to an United Nations' Operational Command."[20]

On Lumumba's death, Nasser quickly recognized Antoine Gizenga, Lumumba's deputy prime minister, as his successor. However, he continued to search for an African, or Afro-Asian, settlement through the United Nations. The U.A.R. co-sponsored a resolution, which was passed, asking the United Nations to use force if necessary to stop the civil war in the Congo and to reconvene the Parliament.

The series of African conferences was continued in Cairo with the third meeting of the All-Africa Peoples' Conference in April 1961, which like all the so-called popular conferences was more extremist than the conferences of government representatives. Reflecting the atmosphere created by the Congo crisis, this conference was marked by its apparently unanimous condemnation of Western "neo-colonialism." It ruled out the forms of assistance which Western free enterprise countries are best able to offer to Africa. Neo-colonialism was identified as any "economic entrenchment of the colonial power before independence and continuity of economic dependence after formal recognition of national sovereignty," meaning, of course, private investments or loans, particularly those involving continuity of interest on the part of Western private business enterprises. The conference denounced the American Peace Corps, and all regroupings or associations of African states under the influence or with the participation of "imperial," i.e., Western, powers.[21]

Meantime, during this rapid succession of conferences, the Afro-

[20] Same, pp. 10–11.
[21] *The New York Times,* April 1, 1961.

Asian Peoples' Solidarity Conference with its Permanent Secretariat in Cairo continued its activities along the lines laid down at its first meeting in December 1957. With the Soviet Union and Communist China represented on the Permanent Secretariat, with an Indian Communist, H. D. Malavia, as a member, and many other Communists and Communist sympathizers active throughout the organization, the AAPSC became a sounding board for the Communist version of "anti-imperialism." The Egyptian Secretary-General, Yusif el Sebai, and other Egyptian members of the Secretariat and members of delegations to conferences were not Communists, but the propaganda which issued from the organization and from the conferences at Conakry and Bandung became less and less distinguishable from the Communist line. The resolutions of the Conakry Conference claimed self-determination for the whole list of territories under one form or another of Western influence or control, but failed to mention Tibet or any other territory under Communist control.[22]

The succeeding conference at Bandung defined colonialism and neo-colonialism as an exclusively Western practice and concentrated its attack on "the aggressive military policy undertaken by the imperialists headed by the U.S. imperialists." It condemned "the crimes committed by American, Belgian, French, British and their allies of NATO against the Congo," and denounced the executive authorities of the UN and the International Red Cross "which refuses help extended by certain countries . . . to Congo." A series of resolutions on specific situations censored the Western powers and, with respect to Laos, Vietnam, Taiwan, and Korea, roundly criticized the activities of the United States.[23]

Examination of the records of these conferences leaves the impression that much of the honest enthusiasm for the independent development of the Asian and African states which characterized the first conference at Bandung in 1955, has vanished with the withdrawal of the more moderate Africans and Asians who cannot

[22] See *IInd Afro-Asian Peoples' Solidarity Conference, Conakry—11–15 April 1960* (Cairo: Permanent Secretariat, Organization for Afro-Asian Peoples' Solidarity, 1960).

[23] *Afro-Asian Bulletin: Supplement on the Afro-Asian Peoples' Solidarity Council Session from 10th to 13th April, 1961, in Bandung* (Cairo), v. 3, no. 3 (May-June 1961).

stomach working in an atmosphere dominated by the Communists. The Communist grip on the AAPSC has become so strong as to raise real questions about it in the minds of all Egyptians, except those few who are Communists or their uncritical sympathizers.

BELGRADE CONFERENCE

The really important event in Nasser's Afro-Asian policy in 1961, however, was not the Bandung Conference but the Belgrade Conference of nonaligned nations. The idea of joint action by the nonaligned nations had been much discussed. The purposes were: to increase their power in the United Nations and in world politics in general, to limit the weight of the Soviet bloc and of the West, to minimize tensions, to reduce armaments, and to direct resources spent on arms into the development of the less advanced nations. Out of these discussions came the resolution offered to the United Nations General Assembly in September 1960 by Nasser, Tito, Nehru, Sukarno, and Nkrumah urging a meeting of the American President and the Soviet Premier to consider the reduction of tensions.

In sponsoring a conference of nonaligned nations, Marshal Tito and President Nasser were attempting to build up the influence of these nations in the world, if not as a separate bloc then at least as a like-minded group that could act together in the United Nations and elsewhere when the occasion demanded. The conference was the first occasion in which a European nation (Yugoslavia) and a Latin American nation (Cuba) had met with the Afro-Asian neutrals. It was not really a world conference of neutrals, but a meeting of those states which subscribed to a particular kind of neutralism. This was made clear by the failure to invite the traditional European neutrals like Switzerland and Sweden and the tendency to ignore new states with Westward-leaning but effectively neutral policies. However, no dependencies of the Sino-Soviet bloc were invited, unless Cuba be put into that category, and Castro had not yet declared his adherence to Marxism-Leninism. In fact it was not neutralism, in the sense of an independent foreign policy, which inspired the conference at Belgrade, but rather Nasser's and Tito's particular brand of neutralism. At this conference the controlling considerations were those which separated one group of African states—the U.A.R., Morocco, Ghana, Guinea, and Mali—from other African states on such issues as had arisen in the Congo crisis. Tunisia had made itself eligible only as a consequence of the shift in policy reflected in the conflict with France over Bizerte. India was included, not because Prime Minister Nehru's neutralism conformed to the Nasser-Tito pattern, but because Nehru's and India's claims to representation in any grouping of nonaligned states were too strong to be ignored, and because both Nasser and Tito needed Nehru's prestige for the new effort.

The behavior of the U.S.S.R. gave the conference a unique character. During the spring and summer, the Soviets had built up pressures on Berlin and at the same time began to adopt a harsher attitude toward the Nasser-Tito neutrals. The big blow delivered on the eve of the conference was the Russian decision to lift the ban on nuclear tests, followed by the explosion of nuclear devices during the course of the meetings. The assembled leaders clearly failed to meet this challenge to their basic principles. Their behavior showed that they were stunned rather than outraged. They were unable to find the courage to do more than read off prepared speeches and offer prepared resolutions.

Tito was particularly dogmatic in his insistence that nothing striking had happened and was more than a little ready to give the Soviets benefit of every doubt. Nasser, Nkrumah, and Saab Salam of Lebanon expressed shock at the Soviet resumption of testing— Salam, according to a Damascus press report, speaking at Nasser's urging. Nehru said the Soviet move had brought war closer.

Nasser, who only recently had received a substantial credit from West Germany, is reported to have been instrumental in stopping a resolution recognizing East Germany. Nevertheless his neutralism on this occasion was more "positive," in the sense of applying the same criteria in his judgment of both sides, than that of most of his colleagues. Despite his obvious anti-Western attitude on African matters, he was not willing to follow the Kremlin's line. In addition, he was not wholly pleased with his fellow neutralists. His failure to get them to accept a resolution condemning Israel indicated the limits which the Arabs' policy of ostracizing Israel had reached.

The Belgrade Conference was a great disappointment to those in the West who had hoped for a firmer response to the Soviet action in resuming nuclear tests. Those who had always suspected the neutrals of leaning toward the Communists found their suspicions confirmed. But a strong and courageous action by the nations-in-between at Belgrade was probably too much to expect. That they are as frightened by the power of the Soviet Union as by the power of the United States cannot be doubted. Their actions appeared to be influenced by the belief that they are safest when they don't take sides.

Western condemnation of the Belgrade Conference can be seriously questioned. To Westerners who saw how vulnerable to criticism the decision to resume nuclear testing had rendered the Soviets, nothing seemed important except their condemnation. To the neutral leaders at Belgrade, however, the Soviet decision appeared only one more element in a pattern of international behavior which they had come to Belgrade to discuss and protest. The conference was much occupied with the cold war and the dangers that it holds for the entire world. Every leader talked of disarmament, of the Berlin crisis, and of ways to reduce world tensions. That the Soviets had chosen to break the nuclear test ban, the neutrals regarded as important. But this action, in their opinion, did not relieve the other nuclear powers of responsibility for the danger that threatens the world. In the back of their minds was the assumption that the United States would not be long in following the Russian example by conducting its own tests.

It has been argued that the neutrals generally followed the Soviet line on reorganization of the UN Secretariat and on condemnation of the UN role in the Congo. In fact, however, there were several expressions of opposition to the Soviet "troika" plan, and the predominant theme in discussions of reorganization was the need for greater representation in the governing bodies of the UN for the new countries. This point of view cannot be explained simply as infatuation with Soviet policy. The same may be said for the discussion at the Belgrade Conference of colonialism and the issues related to it. It is true that Soviet and Chinese colonialism were not discussed, but to most of the conferring countries the problems of Algeria, Bizerte, Palestine, the Congo, Angola, and South Africa are much closer to home than situations on the borders of China or the Soviet Union.

Since the Belgrade Conference, the obstacles on the road to Arab, African, and Afro-Asian unity have dispelled much of the enthusiasm and verve that had characterized Afro-Asian politics from the time of the first meeting of Afro-Asians at Bandung. A series of events has shown that there is a difference between the outlook of nations in the process of becoming independent and of those which have secured control of their own affairs. The search for independence apparently is conducive to association with other nations which seek the same goal. The first stage of nation-building seems to stimulate dreams of brotherhood. At a later stage, however, new nations turn their attention inward, emphasizing particularism rather than international cooperation. After the struggle against common foreign enemies has lost its unifying force, there comes a revival of internal rivalries and dissents.

The breakup of the U.A.R., which came hard on the heels of the disappointing Belgrade Conference, did not damage Nasser's status as a spokesman for emerging African and Asian nations nearly so much as his enemies assumed and hoped it would. Nevertheless, his ability to influence Afro-Asian politics was reduced, for a time at least. In the aftermath of the Syrian revolution, African leaders like Kwame Nkrumah, who themselves aspired to lead the African unity movement, were bound to feel that a strong rival had stumbled, leaving opportunities open for them.

In Africa, the road to unity was as rocky as that which the Arabs were traveling. In 1959 and 1960 the brave talk of African unity had been quieted by the apparent division of African states between the extremist Casablanca group and the more moderate Monrovia group. In this division many saw the reflection of a fundamental ideological cleavage that was dividing Africa into states with an Eastern and a Western orientation. Certainly, the revolutionary and neutralist cast of mind of the leaders of the Casablanca group contrasted strongly with the moderate and practical temperament of the leaders of the Monrovia group. But as David Williams has pointed out,[24] their differences have proba-

[24] David Williams, "How Deep the Split in West Africa?" *Foreign Affairs*, October 1961, pp. 118–127.

bly been exaggerated; too much has been read into first steps, often experimental, in the formulation of foreign policy. The structure of the relations among the new nations and their place in the international community are not going to be settled in a year or in two. For the next twenty-five years at least, states like Syria, Iraq, and the Congo will be seriously occupied with internal affairs. It may take them much longer to find their place among their neighbors and in the world at large.

Since the Belgrade Conference, developments in the Congo have considerably modified Nasser's African policy. Until then he had apparently believed that the Western powers were using the United Nations to establish a puppet government in the Congo which would look out for their interest. But when, in September 1961, the UN sought to force the integration of Katanga, all Nasser's ideas about what was going on in the Congo were overturned. He must have come to realize that Antoine Gizenga in Stanleyville had failed to obtain any kind of support as successor to Lumumba, that the Soviets were powerless to influence the situation in the Congo, and that Prime Minister Adoula in Léopoldville was steadily accumulating strength. So, by the end of 1961, Nasser had apparently concluded that his assumptions that the UN was in the hands of the Western powers and therefore incapable of serving the interests of the Congo people, and that only the heir of Lumumba could properly govern the Congo, were false. He appeared ready to cooperate with the UN and to accept a Congolese central government which had the backing of the United States, and the somewhat less enthusiastic support of Great Britain and France, and at least the temporary tolerance of the Soviet Union.

At about the same time, one of the new African leaders who had been closest to Nasser, Sekou Touré of Guinea, openly denounced the Soviet Union for seeking to undermine his government and for subverting Guinean students who had been sent to Russia and satellite countries for training. Nasser had clearly recognized the dangers of Communist subversion at home, but he had tended to doubt that black Africans would be susceptible, or that the Russians would choose them as a target for subversion, at least for some time. Developments in Guinea, as in Cuba, may not have taught Nasser anything he did not already know about Communist intentions and methods, but they must have shaken his assurance that nationalism always affords sufficient protection against communism.

An important change in Nasser's Afro-Asian policy has been reflected in the relatively less important role of the Afro-Asian Peoples' Solidarity Conference which has its seat in Cairo and of which Nasser was for a time the principal sponsor. At the fourth session of its Council at Bandung in April 1961, there were bitter clashes between the delegates of the Chinese People's Republic and those of the Soviet Union and other member states over the general question of tactics toward the West and territories still in a colonial status. Since then, the Chinese member of the Permanent Council has not returned to the headquarters in Cairo. This clash was only the climax of a prolonged dispute between the Chinese and the Soviet delegates in Cairo and between both of them and other members of the Council. There can be no doubt that responsible officials in the U.A.R. have been aware since the organization of the Council that the Communists were making a strenuous effort to dominate and use the organization for their own purposes. Some Egyptian observers have suggested that the Arab experience with the AAPSC has demonstrated that the idea of Afro-Asian solidarity, though appealing, is a difficult one to translate into political action because of the wide range of interests and the wide divergencies in points of view among Afro-Asian states. They point out that the Asian states in the organization have seldom cooperated effectively with the Arab and African states on specific issues. These considerations seem to have led naturally to greater concentration, by the U.A.R. at least, on the developing Casablanca grouping which, like the Arab League, has all the appurtenances of an alliance, including a military high command, and is not just a smaller Afro-Asian Peoples' Solidarity Conference.

Another shortcoming of the AAPSC is that, being "Afro-Asian," it has heretofore excluded neutralist nations in Europe and potentially Latin America which have followed or might follow much the same line as the U.A.R. on many international issues. Always conscious of the importance of rallying all available strength in support of a position, Nasser went to the Belgrade

Conference intent on creating an organization for the practice of the politics of nonalignment which would have advantages that the AAPSC did not have, and would also be free of some of its disadvantages.

WHAT ARE NASSER'S AFRICA POLICIES?

What do the foregoing developments tell us about Nasser's African policy? In the first place, it is clear that Nasser is operating in a vast and turbulent area without significant resources of the traditional kind. His ability to play any role at all depends on the respect which he commands as an experienced practitioner of "positive neutralism" and his command of the techniques of propaganda and conference diplomacy. Cairo Radio has had a major role in stimulating nationalist tendencies throughout Africa, in stepping up the pace of the movement toward liberation and independence, and in creating distrust and suspicion of the motives of the Western powers in Africa. Nasser has probably won many converts to the idea that a neutralist position vis-à-vis the great powers is the most profitable for new nations and that dealing with the Soviet bloc is not only good insurance against Western domination but also stimulates the flow of Western assistance. He may also have gotten across to some African leaders the idea that Soviet domination is as much to be guarded against as Western "colonialism," but at this stage of African development it is unlikely that he has had occasion to give this point anything like the emphasis that it has received in the Arab East.

Through his activities on the African scene Nasser has extended his fame as a nationalist-neutralist leader whose line is worth watching and whose advice in United Nations affairs and in international politics generally is worth listening to. He has further increased his stature, or at least his prominence, as a world leader and thereby his ability to act on behalf of Egyptian and Arab interests. His critics would say that he has maintained at a high level his nuisance value in world politics. He himself claims that he has sought "to safeguard the unity of the African march [to freedom] and not to permit imperialism to pull us into branch battles with reactionary elements that are hostile to progress," and

". . . to emphasize the gravity and realism of the African struggle to the peoples which carry its responsibility and to other peoples."[25]

One objective of Nasser's African policy has been to utilize traditional diplomatic methods, along with the new diplomacy of conferences, to organize the emerging states of Africa and gear them into the third force of Afro-Asian nations which got its start at Bandung. In this effort Nasser has run against the ambitions of black African leaders, of whom Kwame Nkrumah is the most formidable and aggressive, and against the forces which support Pan Africanism as an organizing concept opposed to the wider Afro-Asianism. He has also encountered opposition from African leaders who reject not only his personal claims to Afro-Asian leadership but also his extreme form of neutralist foreign policy. This opposition has come from Tunisia, Ethiopia, Liberia, and most of the states of the French community which form the so-called Monrovia group. In them Nasser has seen, of course, the hand of the imperialists seeking to set up a neo-colonial base to oppose neutralist nationalism which he believes is the most advantageous policy for a free African or Asian state.

Exactly what the future holds for the Casablanca grouping and the "unaligned" states, ranging from India to Cyprus, present at the Belgrade Conference is not clear, nor is it clear what the U.A.R. will try to make of them. It can be assumed, however, that as in the past every effort will be made to use them in every conceivable way to achieve a greater role and a stronger voice in world affairs for the U.A.R. and states which follow its general neutralist line.

The Casablanca grouping appears to be intended to function as a kind of Arab League, an instrument by means of which the more strongly neutralist states of North and West Africa will seek to dominate events in their area. Though it is far smaller than the Afro-Asian group, it still covers a wide area and includes member states with a wide divergence of interest. Now that Algeria is independent it is likely to play a role at least equal to and probably,

[25] Speech delivered by Gamal Abdel Nasser at the National Assembly on the Results of the Casablanca Summit Conference, *Casablanca Conference, January 1961,* cited, p. 34.

because of its geographic position, more important than that which Nasser can hope to play in Africa. It remains to be seen whether Algerian leadership will follow a policy less dogmatically neutralist than that which Nasser has followed.

Nasser must recognize that his African NATO has little substance, and that he is playing a game in which one melodramatic gesture follows another. His experience in the Middle East is not without value when vast unformed forces are moving into new patterns. In this kind of situation, as he well knows, it is not always possible, nor is it expected, that proposals be realistic or that promises be kept. The main thing is to capture the imagination and to create an enduring image. Nasser wants the African states to line up with the Afro-Asian bloc. He fears that they may be entrapped into some kind of association with the West which will weaken the Afro-Asian group and limit its capability for playing the role he envisages for it. He is less afraid of the possibility that Africa may fall into the Soviet orbit because he thinks it less likely. For the moment he probably considers that he and other leaders of new countries can use the Soviets to help avert the dangers of "neo-colonialist" control of Africa. Judging from his behavior in Middle Eastern situations, we can assume that he would be as loath to see Africa fall into the Soviet as into the Western orbit.

One of Nasser's objectives in Africa, of course, is the continuation of the struggle with Israel. Nasser's interest in Africa has certainly been greatly stimulated by Israel's extensive and successful program of technical assistance to African nations, which he views as the manifestation of a joint plan by Israel and its Western sponsors to encircle the Arab area and cut off Arab influence and trade, thus setting up a counteroffensive to his attempts to exclude Israel from the Afro-Asian community. Fear of Israeli activities in Africa is reflected in Nasser's persistent efforts to get every African conference to vote resolutions on Palestine and Israel's function as a tool of Western imperialism. The importance he attaches to this issue is reflected in the opening passages of his speech to the National Assembly in Cairo on the results of the Casablanca Conference. He said ". . . the salient point of the Casablanca Conference . . . is that it was a measure taken against imperialism and against Zionism as one of its agents and tools."[26] It is doubtful that any other person attending the conference would have summed up its significance in just that way.

Nasser's hopes for excluding Israel from Africa have been dimmed by recurrent reverses. The temporary triumph of persuading the nations gathered at the Casablanca Conference to put their names to a resolution condemning Israeli activity in Africa lost its significance when the black African leaders returned to their countries and conveniently forgot what they had done in Casablanca. Israel, furthermore, continues to build up its reputation in the new African states as a country able to provide first-rate technical assistance and specialized knowledge suited to their needs. Israeli technical advisers are in greater and greater demand in almost every new state of sub-Saharan Africa, while Egyptian advisers are few and far between. A steady stream of African leaders goes to Israel for conferences, consultation and training. Tom Mboya of Kenya even went to Israel with his bride for his honeymoon. Cairo has its appeal to Africans, but they go there more often for business and training in politics and revolution than in the fields of technical development in which Tel Aviv and Jerusalem specialize.

The future of Nasser's influence and of Arab influence in general in sub-Saharan Africa is obscure. That Nasser and the other Arab states have certain disadvantages in working in Africa is clear. No amount of propaganda and diplomacy will change the fact that the Arabs are outsiders in Central and Southern Africa, perhaps not so alien as the European, but alien nevertheless. The recent history of the Arab struggle against "imperialism" and the politics of Afro-Asian solidarity have not entirely eliminated the memory of the Arab slave trader in Africa and of Egyptian attempts, from Muhammad Ali to the Khedive Ismail, to build an African empire.

On the other hand there is the dynamic appeal of Islam. It is not yet possible to predict the political and international consequences of the spread of Islam in black Africa. So far the political impact of the many African graduates of Al Azhar University and of the religious attachés posted in every U.A.R. mission is obscure, though their potentialities cannot be dismissed. Decisions made

[26] *Casablanca Conference, January 1961,* cited, p. 25.

during the summer of 1961 to introduce courses of instruction in medicine, engineering, agriculture, and other practical and technical subjects in the greatest and oldest institution of Muslim learning may in time have an important effect upon the ability of the U.A.R. to extend its influence in the undeveloped countries of Africa, where the graduates of Al Azhar will have easy entrée and where the demand is for simple technical skills rather than for the services of the highly trained and relatively highly paid graduates of Western and Soviet universities. Though it is impossible to make a prediction, it is within the range of possibility that the Islamization of sub-Saharan Africa will prove in the next generation or two to be one of the most significant factors in the development of that vast area.

When all the irrationalities, uncertainties, and obstacles to Nasser's African policies have been added up and taken into account, and when there has been a proper amount of head-shaking about the prospects for African unity, let alone Afro-Arab or Afro-Asian unity, something remains to be said. It is proper that the concluding words on the subject should emphasize the ideas with which Nasser's African policy begins: that the experience of Arab nationalism is relevant and meaningful for the new nations of Africa; that there is an Afro-Asian community of interest; and that, despite all the practical problems that attend its formal institutionalization, it is likely to be, over the long run, an historic force of tremendous proportions.

XII

POLICIES AND PROSPECTS:

The Great Powers

Gamal Abdel Nasser has always had great respect for the realities of power. He came into his position of authority in Egypt deeply aware of the physical power with which Great Britain over the years had maintained itself in Egypt and elsewhere in the Middle East. He saw clearly the disparity between that power and the capabilities of Egypt and other Arab states for influencing the course of international events. Yet he recalled that Egyptian statesmen in the past had not been entirely at the mercy of British power; frequently they had been able to influence events by encouraging or assisting the introduction of another source of power into the situation. It had always been to Egypt's advantage when more than one European power showed an interest in its fate. In a clash between great powers the Egyptian policy maker had to pick the winner and then decide whether to back it and reap the rewards of gratitude or, what often proved more profitable, to make gestures toward one power in the hope of being bought off by another.

The interplay of British and American interest in the Suez Base negotiations must have confirmed in Nasser's mind the advantages of dealing with two powers. Later, in 1955, when America refused to meet his somewhat exaggerated expectations, the appearance of the Soviet power on the Middle East scene, ready to play a role very like the one he had mapped out for the United States, confirmed the idea that, in dealing with the great powers, force must be matched against force.

NEHRU AND TITO

In handling great powers, Nasser has profited from the example of two distinguished practitioners of the art. Prime Minister Nehru visited Cairo in June 1953 for the first time after the revolution. He has been a frequent visitor since, twice host to Nasser in India, and many times a colleague at international conferences. Marshal Tito of Yugoslavia was slower to make Nasser's acquaintance. He came to Egypt first after the completion of the Egyptian-Soviet arms deal, in January 1956, when the two chiefs of state issued a joint declaration affirming their commitment to the principle of nonalignment. The three leaders then met at Brioni in July of the same year for a conference on international affairs. The publicity given the meeting by the Egyptian press and radio indicated that Nasser wanted to give the impression that he, Nehru, and Tito constituted the high command, or big three, of neutralism, which, without actually forming an alliance or setting up an organization, would speak for and to the uncommitted third of the world. Nehru, it appeared, found these ideas presumptuous and Tito thought them a bit in advance of reality.

Though Nehru has consistently avoided becoming closely involved with Nasser in any kind of pact or even in an informal agreement, he has consulted extensively with him. Nasser has probably learned a great deal from Nehru about the importance of the United Nations in the diplomacy of weak nations and about the power of world opinion. The Egyptian leader may also have listened to lectures on the politics of the great powers, the obligation of those nations which are not great powers to make their voices heard in world councils, on the need for disarmament, on the menace of the cold war to weak nations, and on racialism as an issue in international relations.

Despite the apparent harmony in their outlook on foreign affairs, the two leaders are in many respects different. Nehru is an aristocrat and an intellectual; Nasser, a soldier of lower-middle-class origin and a man of action. Nasser, fearful of great-power intervention in his country and in neighboring states, feels that he must be constantly on the alert to thwart "imperialist" designs. Nehru, though accepting the usefulness of arms to defend Indian territory against neighboring states, has believed his neutral position to be a practical defense against great-power intervention. Unlike Nasser, who would probably like to have an effective Arab or African joint command of the sort projected at Casablanca, Nehru seems fundamentally opposed to any arrangement which would involve the uncommitted countries in the use of force.[1] Nehru's tendency toward pacifism seemed to disconcert Nasser and his followers. Much as they admired the Indian leader's adroitness in international politics, they felt that his reluctance to consider the use of force was somehow a weakness. When others identified their neutralism with Nehru's, the Egyptians often pointed out that they were not neutral in exactly the sense that Nehru was. They were "positive neutrals," i.e., neutral on cold war issues but more willing to take sides, using force if needed, on issues that directly affected their interests. Thus, when India finally invaded Goa early in 1962, Nasser and the other Arab "positive neutralists" did not share the West's outrage or accuse Nehru of abandoning his neutralist position. They cheered his willingness to act in India's national interests, and in what they believed to be the interests of the people of Goa, against the Portuguese imperialists. For the same reasons they were prepared to cheer Sukarno's use of force against the Dutch in New Guinea, seeing no conflict with neutralist principles in such action.

On communism Nasser and Nehru differ. Whereas Nehru understands Marxism intellectually and is willing to take the risk of allowing the Communists freedom of activity within the democratic system prevailing in his country, Nasser regards communism pragmatically. He considers communism too dangerous to be let loose in small and undeveloped countries. Countries the size of Egypt or Syria he may believe can more easily be subverted than a country like India.

Marshal Tito of Yugoslavia has probably been Nasser's most influential teacher. Like Nasser, a soldier and a man of action, Tito's experience and situation have admirably suited him to give Nasser practical advice on foreign policy. An old master at playing

[1] See his speech before the Political Committee of the Bandung Conference, April 22, 1955, in George McTurnan Kahin, *The Asian-African Conference, Bandung, Indonesia, April 1955* (Ithaca: Cornell University Press, 1956), p. 64 ff.

off the great powers, with demonstrated ability to get something from both sides in the cold war, he appeals to Nasser as a man who has successfully survived the kind of pressures which Nasser most fears. Whereas Nehru's neutralism is too passive and inactive for Nasser's taste, Tito's has just the right combination of practicality and aggressiveness.

Tito's solutions for Yugoslavia's domestic economic and political problems, particularly problems of organization, seem applicable in Egypt. After wrestling with the problem of transition from personal government to some kind of regime with broader popular support and participation, Nasser decided that the Egyptian people were not ready for exposure to the temptations and foreign pressures that free, multi-party political activity would bring. The Indian experience he found of little value as a model, but Yugoslavia's controlled socialist economy and limited popular participation in government he chose as a prototype for Egypt.

Tito urged weak nations to stick together and not to align themselves with any great-power bloc. Tito's views, particularly those on the helplessness of small powers alone in the face of the great-power struggle, fitted in with Nasser's beliefs and feelings and with his own experience. Tito's strategy of nonalignment did not envisage withdrawal or lack of interest in world politics. On the contrary, he wanted the unaligned nations to make themselves heard, speaking with the voice of reason to the great powers. In particular, he emphasized the gap between the rich and the poor nations of the world, the justification for the rising dissatisfaction of the have-nots, and the obligation of the great powers, in the common interest, to help provide resources without political conditions for the development of underprivileged and underdeveloped areas.

Tito's Marxism probably has little meaning for Nasser, though his long experience of dealing with the Soviets adds to his authority. As a Communist who successfully defied the central authority of the Communist power bloc, Tito was a living example of the possibility of a successful policy of nonalignment. In the whole area of foreign policy Nasser has found Tito a sympathetic and compatible colleague. Their collaboration has doubtless strengthened Nasser's own convictions by demonstrating that there are others who, even though they have different backgrounds and adhere to different ideologies, see things in the field of international affairs basically as he does. The measure of his acceptance of Tito is indicated by the fact of his willingness to overlook Yugoslavia's recognition of Israel.

POSITIVE NEUTRALISM'S APPARENT BIAS

Nasser has given his foreign policy the label "positive neutralism." Like the doctrines which bear the label of Arab nationalism, the foreign-policy doctrines which bear this name are essentially pragmatic and leave plenty of room for modification and adjustment to individual situations. The essential idea behind "positive neutralism," like that behind Arab nationalism, is independence. "Positive neutralism," Nasser has said, "means independence. In other words I do not yield to one bloc, nor to the influence of any power, and I avoid zones of influence."[2] Nasser's neutralism means action; it is not passive. He has said ". . . our policy is decided in accordance with our interests and in accordance with our conscience. This is the difference between positive and passive neutrality. The latter does not care about what is going on in other parts of the world, but positive neutrality means that our policy is based on our interests."[3] His brand of neutralism does not preclude self-defense: "Our call for neutrality is one thing and our right to self-defense against any aggression is another," he said in an interview in 1958.[4]

Nasser has repeatedly asserted that his policies reflect Egyptian and Arab interests which are independent of the interests and ideologies of the great-power blocs. The criticism most commonly leveled against him in the West, however, is that his neutralism— if it is neutral at all—leans toward the Communist bloc, and in fact, on major international issues he has stood with the Communist bloc more often than with the West. This seems to prejudice his claim to a neutral and nonaligned position.

The five principal objectives of Nasser's foreign policy are: (a)

[2] *Nasser's Speeches*, 1959, p. 275.
[3] Same, p. 419.
[4] *Nasser's Speeches*, 1958, p. 381.

independence and security from external domination for the entire Arab area; (b) arms with which to build military strength; (c) the economic development of Egypt; (d) regional political and economic development and unity; (e) the end of "colonialism" in Asia and Africa and the development of Afro-Asian solidarity in international politics independent of the two great-power blocs.

The realization of these objectives would be acceptable, and probably advantageous to the West. To the Communist bloc they are in the long run unacceptable. Yet Nasser's efforts to achieve them more often than not are carried on in an atmosphere of Sino-Soviet approval and Western disapproval. The circumstances that explain this paradox are significant.

The Objective of Independence

Nasser has repeatedly emphasized his fear that all great powers seek to dominate small nations, and his consequent rejection of communism and capitalism alike. "Our minimum demand of Moscow," he said during a period of strained relations with the Soviet Union, "as indeed of Washington or London is that they understand Arab nationalism, appreciate its dignity and independence and support rather than subvert our stand on positive neutrality."[5] He has often linked Communists, imperialists, and Zionists together as enemies of Arab nationalism. Arab Communists have repeatedly shown their hostility to his conception of Arab independence. He has seen local Communist efforts, with apparent Soviet guidance and support, directed against the integrity of Syria and Iraq. From time to time, as in 1959 and again in 1961, the Soviets have applied pressure when his policies did not suit them.

Nasser has seen plentiful evidence that the Soviet Union has little interest in small states other than to dominate them, but he sticks to the dogma that the Western powers and the Soviet Union are just alike in this respect. However, the Arabs' much greater experience with the Western powers, plus their ingrained suspicion of the West, create a reaction to Western imperialist interference out of proportion to that with which the Arabs respond to the theoretically equal Soviet-Communist threat.

[5] *Nasser's Speeches,* 1959, p. 543.

To the Westerner, it is likely to appear that the issue of Arab independence has been resolved, or nearly so, since the remaining areas of special Western influence are insignificant and are likely soon to gain their freedom. From this point of view, all Nasser's screaming about imperialism appears to be bad manners or chicanery, or both. To the Arab nationalist, however, it does not seem that independence is entirely won. Furthermore, renewed Western intervention by force seems entirely possible. Arab independence and security from great-power interference is an objective with which the West has every reason to agree, but the Soviets usually manage to appear to be supporting the Arabs on this point, although independence is the last thing they want for the Arabs over the long run.

The Objective of Military Strength

The objective of obtaining arms has been important to Nasser for a number of reasons. A strong and loyal army has been both a political necessity and, potentially at least, a support to his policies in the Arab area.

American and British policy has been to provide arms in substantial quantities to Arab states only on the basis of an explicit or implied political alliance, as in the case of Jordan and formerly of Iraq, and also to maintain some kind of balance between Arab and Israeli military power. Convinced as he has been of the reality of the Israeli military threat and of the existence of a considerable body of opinion in the Western governments that his downfall would be in the interest of the West, Nasser found irresistible the Soviet offer to supply him with arms at reasonable prices and in generous quantities in exchange for cotton which he had in good supply, no questions being asked about the ability of his armed forces to absorb them.

Furthermore, the Soviet arms have been made available in such a way as to meet the conditions which he had insisted were necessary for the protection of Arab sovereignty. Arms agreements have been made between the Soviet bloc and Egypt and the U.A.R. without stated political conditions, without the requirement of an alliance, express or implied, without inspection of their disposition and use, generally with abundant spare parts, and with technicians provided only on Egyptian and Syrian request and only for such periods as they were wanted. There have been exceptions to the general pattern: arrogant Soviet officers, technicians who tried to preach communism, periods when spare parts or certain kinds of additional equipment were especially difficult to obtain, and a few occasions when Nasser's anti-Communist policies were brought up when he made requests for more arms.

When asked if the mere fact of dependence upon Soviet arms supplies does not involve a commitment, Nasser has always insisted that he accepted Soviet arms only so long as there was no commitment involved and that he was ready to take the risks involved in breaking off the relationship if necessary. Asked by the Indian journalist Karanjia, at the time of his attacks on Soviet interference in Iraq, if he was not too committed to the Soviets to risk getting into trouble with them, Nasser said, "I can't deal with the question that way. To me the problem is: Am I ready to give up the independence of my country or not?"[6] Meantime, he has insisted that, so long as Soviet conditions do not threaten his independence and while the Israeli threat necessitates maintaining a high level of armament, he has no choice but to accept the Soviet arms.

Nasser has consistently demonstrated his determination to oppose local Communist activity in the Arab world and on occasion has shown that he means what he says about risking the breakup of his relationship with the Soviets if he feels his independence threatened. He knows as well as anyone that the Soviet willingness to supply him with arms is not disinterested. He certainly understands that the Soviets consider that they receive adequate compensation for their arms by the fact that they thereby thwart Western designs in the Arab area and win the Arabs' favor by providing them with the means to defend themselves against a threat that they believe is Western in origin. He also knows that the worse relations are between the Arabs and the West the better the Soviets like it. The question is whether he feels, consciously or unconsciously, that in order to keep the arms channel open it is sometimes useful to provide the Soviets with a *quid pro quo* by attacking the West more vigorously than he otherwise might.

6 Same, p. 542.

The Objective of Economic Development

Nasser is aware that the economic development of Egypt cannot take place successfully without extensive assistance from outside. Fearing dependence upon one of the two protagonists in the cold war he has hoped to benefit from their rivalry and, on balance, he has succeeded. The United States has granted substantial aid and, under Public Law 480, has sold him wheat for Egyptian pounds, half of which are loaned back to him. From the Soviet bloc he has obtained substantial low-interest loans and cotton barter deals which have enabled him to purchase arms, industrial equipment, and some manufactured goods. There has been a rough balance in the over-all quantity of assistance from American and Soviet sources.

The impression given, however, by Nasser himself and by the Egyptian press and radio is usually that the United Arab Republic has considerably more reason for gratitude to the Soviet bloc than to the United States. The reasons for this are extremely complex, but probably boil down, as do so many other matters in Nasser's and the Arab posture, to the basic psychological factors which have often been referred to above. One is the more spectacular and dramatic character of Soviet aid projects. There are also aspects of the general American approach to the provision of foreign aid, irritating to its recipients almost everywhere, which have been particularly aggravating to the sensitive Arab temperament. The complexity of American aid agreements, the great length of time required to complete the administrative procedures before aid which has been promised is actually allocated and delivered, the elaborate machinery for checking and inspecting its use, and the important consideration that American aid has been available only on a year-by-year basis, making long-term projects difficult and risky—all these have adversely affected the Arab evaluation of American assistance, especially in Egypt and Syria. In the field of technical assistance, the American system of sending technicians under the control of the American aid mission for set periods of time has contrasted unfavorably with the Soviet system of making technicians available at the request of and under the authority of the U.A.R. government and of keeping them in the country only so long as the local authorities wanted them.

On numerous occasions some minor irritation has caused an outburst against American aid. Nasser attacked the United States in April and early May of 1960, when U.S. congressmen questioned the continuation of U.S. aid to Egypt while it denied to Israel freedom of transit through the canal. He said: "We tell these people, brethren, and we also tell these Senators, that if Israel and Zionism dominate the U.S. Senate and if the American people bow to and are dominated by Zionism it is because Zionism, through bribery and corruption, exercises domination over the lives and livelihood of many leading Americans." He explained to the senators "who threaten to starve us by ceasing to provide us with wheat" that the American wheat shipments to Egypt were simple commercial transactions supported by loans at 4 per cent interest.[7] He failed to point out that grain purchases under PL 480 are quite different from the normal commercial transaction.

Opening a spinning mill at Damietta built with funds from a Soviet loan, the Egyptian leader said: "In spite of the clouds that have, at times, loomed over our relations, the economic agreement [signed in January 1958] was never affected. At no time did the Soviet Union utter one single word threatening to boycott us economically and on no occasion did the Soviet reproachfully remind us of the economic aid they extended to us or the loans they provided for our industrialization schemes."[8]

It is hard to believe that President Nasser does not understand that the American system permits, and in fact encourages, discussion of every aspect of government activity and that, given the size and outlook of the American Jewish population, discussion of any aid given to him, including a lot of adverse comment, is inevitable. Soviet aid, however, appears to be more graciously and generously given, partly as the result of circumstances and partly owing to careful contrivance.

Nasser's specialists who handle the development program often

[7] Speech at Mansoura, May 7, 1960, *Nasser's Speeches,* 1960 (April-June), pp. 92–93.

[8] Same, p. 98.

appear in private to understand the differences in Soviet and American aid better than the President's public statements would indicate that he does. They understand that low interest rates on Soviet credits are usually canceled out by high prices, and that the quality of Soviet equipment is often much below the Western standard. Bloc technicians, though they may lack some of the irritating qualities of the Americans, often are arrogant and difficult to deal with. The Egyptians, despite their commitment to a planned socialist economy, are eager for the advice of American and other Western economic planners.

In the early years of Nasser's regime the phrase "no strings attached" was in common use. In military assistance agreements, it referred to provisions granting rights of inspection and control to the Western donors, making them, in the eyes of the Egyptians, the senior, controlling partners. In economic aid agreements, it meant the attachment of political conditions such as the Egyptians apparently believed the United States and the World Bank wanted to attach to the High Dam agreement. The continuation of assistance, they believed, would have been contingent upon their satisfying the other parties to the agreement that Egyptian affairs were properly conducted. In the agreement for building the second stage of the Aswan High Dam, the critical issue was not political conditions but rather the choice between two alternatives. If Nasser was really interested in balancing the amount of aid he received from the East and from the West, he might have preferred to obtain aid for the second stage of the project from the West. However, the West offered a combination of separate agreements, some on an annual basis, with several countries and institutions, while the Soviet offered the whole thing in one package. Western leaders also showed a certain lack of enthusiasm for the project, which would certainly have been the subject of debates in Congress and in the American press. Hence, on balance, Nasser's acceptance of the Soviet offer seems to have been logical and practical.

The Objective of Regional Development and Unity

The U.S. government has indicated that it has nothing against Arab unity so long as it is accomplished in accordance with the popular will freely expressed. The Soviet Union has reiterated its support for Arab unity. Nasser probably believes, however, that neither of the two great powers would like to see the Arab states united, and particularly not under his leadership. The U.S. point of view is affected by the belief that unity under Nasser would bring unwelcome changes; the end of the friendly and cooperative regime of King Hussein of Jordan and a transformation in the present role of Lebanon as a kind of entrepôt for Western ideas in the Arab East. There is also the question of the oil concessions granted by Arab rulers with whom the West has established relatively satisfactory relations. Moreover, Nasser has been so often intransigent in his attitude toward the United States that, if he were to gain control of the entire Arab East, there is every reason to expect he would prove even more difficult to deal with. He might even mobilize the resources of the area for a showdown with Israel.

Nasser surely knows that the leaders of the Soviet bloc would be equally opposed to Arab unity under his leadership. It suits their purpose to support him when such support erodes the Western position and encourages anti-Western activity. But having a "bourgeois dictator" like Nasser in a position to consolidate the resources of the Middle East behind an independent and anti-Communist policy would be quite another thing.

Though the Soviets do not look with favor on Arab unity, they support every sort of opposition to the conservative Arab regimes which for the most part object to Nasser's revolutionary nationalism. Nasser, for his part, naturally does not repudiate such support and therefore often appears to be in league with the Soviets on an issue on which both he and they know they cannot agree.

Nasser undoubtedly believes that U.S. activities at the time of the Syrian crisis in 1957 and the U.S. landings in Lebanon in 1958 were designed to prevent his gaining the upper hand in those countries. Also he must regard the frequent mention of the likelihood that Israel would intervene militarily if a pro-Nasser coup were to take place in Jordan as warning that the West will not tolerate steps toward Arab unity under his banner. But he must also recognize that Soviet maneuvers in Syria in the summer of 1957 and 1958 and in Iraq in 1959 had the same objective in view. Thus, on balance, his interest in Arab unity does not put him of the side of either of the great-power groupings.

The Objective of Ending Colonialism Through Afro-Asian Solidarity

On this issue the Soviets have all the advantages and the United States most of the possible disadvantages. Imperialism, as stated by Nasser and many Afro-Asians, links the United States and the West with the evils of the past and the present and puts on them the burden of reform. This means, first, giving up all authority and control and then providing economic assistance "with no strings attached" to the emerging nationalist states. Steps taken by the Western nations to promote independence are often ascribed, not just by Nasser but by a substantial proportion of the Afro-Asian community, to weakness and response to pressure.

On these issues Nasser has had no hesitation in repeatedly voting with the Soviet bloc in the UN. His point is that the Soviets, being on the right side, are voting with him and the other Afro-Asians rather than the other way around. The United States, by contrast, abstained from voting on the resolution put forward at the end of the Fifteenth Session of the General Assembly calling for an end to colonialism.[9] When the American press criticized him on his voting record, Nasser answered in anger:

Positive neutrality means that we are the enemy of our enemies and the friend of our friends. NATO is our enemy in Algeria. NATO is showing us enmity by helping and arming Israel. NATO, the Western states and Western imperialism are showing us enmity and fighting our principles, yet we insist on principles.

What do the Americans say? They say that we are not neutral because we voted 14 times with the Russians and did not vote once with them. We tell them they should understand we do not sell our votes. Our votes are not for sale to them or to the Russians or others. We vote in accordance with our principles.

Take the case of the resolution submitted by the Afro-Asians against imperialism. How could we vote with them so long as they did not vote in support of the resolution which denounced imperialism and recommended the liquidation of imperialism. We vote in accordance with principles. If the Americans see that we do not vote with them,

[9] GA Resolution 1514 (XV).

it is because they vote against the principles of freedom which they announced after the second world war and the Atlantic Charter, which Roosevelt announced, yet on which they later turned their backs.[10]

With respect to the organization of an Afro-Asian entity with a role in international affairs, the Soviets have less advantage than on the issue of colonialism. The Afro-Asian group, so long as it maintains its independence, should become increasingly able to cooperate effectively with the West on international issues as the number of territories dependent on Western powers is reduced. A single issue like South Africa's racial policies can prejudice all Western relations with the Afro-Asian nations, but, even so, trends in the U.S. position since the inauguration of President Kennedy, and in the Western position generally, are likely to render the colonial issue less poisonous.

Nasser certainly does not measure his progress toward his major foreign-policy objectives in terms of the support he has received from the East or from the West, but in terms of the objectives themselves. Nevertheless, he probably takes into account the way in which he has managed to take advantage of the contending forces and his success in protecting his country and the Arab area from great-power ambitions. He has been preoccupied with the impact of power politics on the Arab area since his tour of duty as an instructor at the Egyptian Staff College. He asked R. K. Karanjia, the Indian journalist, on April 17, 1959: "Can anybody today close his eyes to all that is happening in the world outside, not to speak of the events in one's own neighborhood? . . . Today the situation is such that what happens in Berlin affects us. It rather affects us more than what happens in our immediate . . . neighborhood. It is all an issue of the big powers using smaller and less-developed countries as their tools in the game of their cold war. Ours being a very central and strategic region on their chess board we have to be particularly careful. That is a lesson we have learned from our own history.[11]

[10] *Speeches Delivered by President Gamal Abdel Nasser on the Occasion of Victory Day Celebrations at Port Said, Manzalah, Mataria, December 23/24, 1960,* Bulletin issued by the Information Department of the United Arab Republic (Cairo), pp. 34–35.

[11] *Nasser's Speeches,* 1959, p. 538.

NASSER AND THE SOVIET BLOC

On September 28, 1958, President Nasser told Karanjia in an interview, "I can say without reservation that I cannot recall a single incident where they [the Soviets] have sought to exploit our difficulties. Whatever may be their motives in giving us their cooperation and support, they appreciate that we are an independent people with a strong consciousness of our dignity and sovereignty. They have never made any demands on us or tied any conditions to such cooperation as we have received from them."[12] But the following April he told the same journalist that ". . . information in our possession showed that a Communist masterplot [existed] to seize Iraq, establishing a Soviet in this strategic Arab frontier; next to cause a split between Syria and Egypt and break up our union, then to proceed to the ultimate Communist goal of creating a red fertile crescent, that is, a federation formed of Iraq, Syria, Jordan, Lebanon and Kuwait, perhaps to provide the Soviet Union with access not only to the Persian Gulf and the Gulf of Aqaba, but the Indian Ocean as well."[13] He said that the story began with the attempt before the union of Syria and Egypt to turn Syria into a Communist state and continued with the Communist exploitation of the Iraqi revolution. Then, according to Nasser, the Soviets began organizing "an all-Arab Communist underground for purposes of subversion and sabotage against neighboring Arab countries. The foundation for such a front was laid, according to our information, in Moscow at the 21st Congress of the Soviet Communist Party by Arab Communists."[14]

Karanjia then mentioned the heated exchange which had just taken place between Nasser and Premier Khrushchev and asked if it had been "necessary or wise." Nasser's answer was: "The trouble really started when I attacked the Syrian Communists, which was my domestic business. I was shocked when the answer came from Khrushchev in such a manner as to suggest that he had assumed responsibility for the protection of Arab Communists. . . . I wrote to Khrushchev after the Moscow Congress. I cau-

[12] *Nasser's Speeches,* 1958, p. 405.
[13] *Nasser's Speeches,* 1959, p. 536.
[14] Same, p. 537.

tioned him against supporting the Communist party in our country. I reminded him of the fact that the friendly attitude of our people to Russia did not exist because of the Communist party but in spite of them." Finally, said Nasser, events in Iraq convinced him "that Moscow had really emerged as the protector of Communists against Arab nationalism. So I had no alternative but to tell the Russians that we do not want this new type of colonialism. . . . The result was that the enormous goodwill built over three years of friendship was lost in less than three weeks."[15]

In the period between his December 23, 1958, speech in Port Said when he first accused the Syrian Communists of opposing the union with Egypt and attempting to subvert it after it had been formed, and the end of the summer of 1959, Nasser waged a campaign against Arab Communists. Again after the Mosul uprising of March 9, 1959, in Iraq, in which the Arab nationalist and pro-Nasser Shawwaf revolt was defeated, largely with the aid of pro-Communist forces from Baghdad, Nasser attacked communism and the Soviet Union in terms he usually reserves for the Western imperialists.

The theme of the early speeches was that all Communists are agents of a foreign power: "We did not permit the establishment of a Communist party in Egypt because we are sure that the Communist party in Egypt does not act in conformity with its own will or work for the interest of its own country. We are sure that it received inspiration from abroad and worked for the foreigner," he said in one speech.[16] In Damascus on the 20th of March he said communism in the U.A.R. would mean that ". . . a terrorist reactionary dictatorship would be established where dependence would prevail, and under which the country would have no will of its own, and we would follow the line of international communism and receive directives from it."[17] And again, "Communism believes in atheism and believes in dependence."[18]

But in May Nasser told an American journalist that "the friendly relations existing between us and the Soviet Union cannot be shattered by a single crisis. As I have already said, they are worth another test."[19] And on July 9, 1960, Nasser summed up U.A.R. relations with the great powers by saying: "We extended our hand to the United States of America and the Soviet Union as the greatest powers today, and expressed to them our desire for cooperation. It was a matter of gratification for us that the hand we extended to the Soviet Union for cooperation was received with a warm response. . . . At the same time it was a matter of great regret for us that the hand we extended to the United States of America for cooperation did not receive the desired response, on account of the relationship between American policy and that of the imperialist powers from which we suffered."[20]

But this turn of the wheel was not to be the last. After the Congo crisis and a series of colonial issues, plus the Palestine issue, in the United Nations had set the scene for friendly relations between the United Arab Republic and the Soviet Union and strained relations with the United States, Premier Khrushchev and the Soviet press began in the spring of 1961 to needle Nasser.

At a dinner in Moscow for a delegation from the U.A.R. National Assembly headed by Anwar el Sadat, Mr. Khrushchev, referring to Soviet advances in space technology and the prospect of surpassing America's material achievements, raised the question of the Arab nationalist attitude toward communism. "You and we view matters differently," he said. "But this should not stand as a barrier between us. History will stand as judge. We are Communists and you do not belong to this doctrine. Yet history will teach you. It is not us who will teach you. Life itself will teach you. . . . You may think I want to transform you from Arab nationalists into Communists. Naturally, I do not want to do so now, but I feel that some of you present may, in the future, be Communists because life imposes itself on man."[21]

On Arab socialism, the Soviet Premier said, "We operate on socialist bases. You, the Arabs, now understand this, but you do

[19] Same, p. 233.

[20] *Speech of President Gamal Abdel Nasser before the General Congress of the National Union, July 9, 1960,* Bulletin issued by the Information Department of the United Arab Republic (Cairo), p. 10.

[21] "The Sadat-Khrushchev Exchange," *The Egyptian Economic and Political Review* (Cairo), May-June 1961, p. 25.

not understand what socialism which leads to Communism is. . . . You are like a person learning the alphabet. . . . You are learning the 'A.' Socialism is the first letter in the alphabet which organizes human society, while 'B' is the beginning of Communism. If you seek socialism you should not say you are against Communism, since you place yourselves in an embarrassing situation and fall into the trap of imperialism."[22]

Struck by Khrushchev's apparent departure from the oft-proclaimed Soviet acceptance of the Arab nationalists' right to work out their own ideology, opposing communism if they chose, Sadat wrote to the Soviet Premier, affirming the Arab nationalists' intention of working out and living by their own system. The Arabs had rejected capitalism, he wrote, "not because we hate it but because we believe it does not suit the nature, conditions, hopes, needs and requirements of our people. . . . This does not mean that Communism, which proved successful in conditions prevailing in other countries, is suitable for successful application in our country. Our people refuse to be limited to this choice and believe that the ideological scope in the world is bigger than this closed circle. They also believe our people are capable, without becoming isolated from the world's wealth of ideologies, of participating creatively in adding to this wealth."[23]

This exchange was accompanied and followed by a series of items in the Soviet press attacking the U.A.R. for mistreatment of Communists, and U.A.R. journalists for criticizing Soviet communism and casting aspersions on Soviet aid. *Pravda* said that an *Al Ahram* reporter had attacked the Soviet Union for depriving the individual of the right to property and proceeded to attack Arab socialism as "like as two peas to capitalism which is doomed by history—a society in which exploiters rule and people make speeches about democracy, while for their political beliefs progressive people languish in torture chambers."[24] There followed a concerted attack on the Soviet "campaign against the U.A.R." in

[22] Same, p. 26.
[23] Same, pp. 27–28.
[24] Quoted in a postscript to an article by Geoffrey Wheeler entitled "Russia and the Arab World," *The World Today*, July 1961, p. 317. See article and postscript, *passim*, on this subject.

the Cairo and Damascus press and radio in which the Communists were accused of dreaming of world conquest and of being "incensed" at the preparations being made in Cairo for the conference of nonaligned nations which was later held in Belgrade.

In June 1961 "a responsible authority of the United Arab Republic" told Dana Adams Schmidt of *The New York Times* that "we are putting our case . . . before the Asians and Africans at the Neutralists' conference so they can see that power politics are practiced by both sides, East as well as West. They don't differ very much." He went on to say that the Russians "were for us when we were acting against the imperialists," but had grown more and more intolerant of the United Arab Republic's independent policy. "More and more they look at neutralism the way John Foster Dulles did," he said. They say, "the choice is between liberty and imperialism. But we don't see the choice that way. We say there is a third way for all the countries facing the problems of development after they gained independence."[25]

In due course Nasser may again be saying that the Soviets have always been above reproach in their relations with the Arabs. Although he will fight back when he feels that the Soviets are challenging his leadership or Arab independence and probably will again take considerable risks in his relations with them, he always swings back to a friendly position. His willingness to make up with the Soviets may reflect his real dependence upon the Soviet bloc for arms, for a market for a substantial part of Egypt's cotton, and for assistance on the politically important Aswan High Dam project. These factors in his dependence upon the Soviets always pull him back, always limit the risks he will take to jeopardize his relations with them. Furthermore, on colonial issues or other matters which involve a transformation in the international *status quo,* Nasser can usually count on Soviet assistance and on Western opposition. Occasionally the Soviets have twitted Nasser on his impetuousness, cast aspersions on his abilities and the effectiveness of his administration, and questioned the soundness of "Arab socialism." For the most part, however, the Soviets have treated him and his program with a show of respect in marked contrast to the

[25] *The New York Times,* June 7, 1961.

frequently irritating and derogatory statements by public figures in the United States and in the American press.

Nasser is certainly aware of the ruthless determination and the skill with which the Soviet leaders go about the achievement of their objectives. He recognizes also that their long-range objectives in the Middle East and Africa are entirely inconsistent with his own concept of an Afro-Asian community of independent states that will exercise a balancing force in international affairs. But in the short run he believes that he and other neutrals can take advantage of the Soviet Union's interest in dismantling the system by which the Western powers have dominated Africa and Asia. In Nasser's view the liquidation of colonialism and the readjustment of the balance of forces in the United Nations so as to give a greater role to the Afro-Asians are goals which can be achieved only with Soviet help.

Nasser does not seem to be worried about the next stage, when the Soviets can be expected to seek to move more rapidly to extend their control over the Middle East and Africa. Nationalism, he feels confident, is a force which can effectively resist communism in the Arab states and in Africa. He has said, "Communism is a doctrine and doctrines can only be met by doctrines."[26]

Nasser is willing to share ideas and enterprises with the Communists; he finds in their system many things with which he is in agreement. He has been working to establish what he calls a "socialist, cooperative, democratic" society. When he attacked Communist subversion in Syria and Iraq in the spring of 1959, he pointed out that the U.A.R. could not be considered completely alien to the Communist system. The U.A.R. fought communism, not because of its "leftist" characteristics, but because ". . . its inspiration does not spring from its land, but from outside."[27] On another occasion he pointed out that the Afro-Asian countries may have something to learn from the Soviet Union and Communist China. "We pay too much attention," he said, "to the cold war and not enough to the problems and tensions of the newly de-

[26] Interview with Wilton Wynn and Harry Ellis, *Nasser's Speeches,* 1959, p. 587.
[27] *Nasser's Speeches,* 1959, p. 123.

veloping nations." Many countries, those in Africa in particular, are looking at Communist China and wondering if they should not adopt its methods. Egypt, however, he said, "has got beyond that stage of development."[28]

Since the 1955 arms deal, the Soviet Union has made a considerable impression upon the Egyptian people. They know that their army has Soviet arms and believe that the country's security depends on the continuation of Soviet aid. They are aware of the extent of Soviet aid on the High Dam and that Egypt's industrialization, of which they hear a great deal, is being carried out with substantial amounts of machinery and assistance from the Soviet bloc. They know that the Soviet Union and its satellites usually stand with the Arabs and other Afro-Asians on colonial issues, whereas the West is usually on the other side. They see the Soviet Union more and more as the champion of peace, disarmament, the improvement of the organization of the United Nations, and the advocate of negotiation and arbitration in international affairs. Unquestionably, Russian scientific achievements have had an effect on the relative standing of the Soviet Union and the United States in Arab countries.

Granted all this, however, it is significant how little the Soviets have accomplished in the way of injecting communism into the Arab bloodstream. Communism both as an ideology and as an organization has failed to make appreciable headway among the Arabs in recent years. On balance, it has lost rather than gained ground. The Communist effort in Syria and Iraq was more effective in alerting the authorities and the public alike to the alien and authoritarian nature of communism than in winning converts. Soviet assistance programs have made an impression on public opinion, producing a certain sense of gratitude and obligation, but it does not appear that they have resulted in the establishment of institutionalized controls through which the Soviet bloc can manipulate the receiving governments or their people. Economic and arms assistance have created a state of dependence, in the sense that the Arab states have become accustomed to this aid and would be less well off if it were withdrawn. It appears un-

[28] Same, p. 522.

likely, however, that the Soviet Union by threatening to withdraw or withhold assistance could force Nasser, the Syrian government, or General Kassem for that matter, to take actions which they thought violated national independence. In fact, suggestions of pressure would be likely to produce hostile reactions before the physical consequences of withholding aid became apparent.

The resources and effort which the Soviets have expended in making themselves the suppliers of arms to Egypt, Syria, Iraq, and Yemen do not appear to have had any political effect. The Egyptian, Syrian, and Iraqi armed forces have now largely shifted over to Soviet weapons and to the Soviet type of military organization. They depend on the U.S.S.R. for replacements, spare parts, ammunition, and additional arms. Large numbers of their officers and enlisted men have received training in the Soviet bloc. Yet the Arab governments continue to forbid Communist activity within their countries and persistently harass local Communists. In their foreign policies they follow the principle of nonalignment and, on occasion, take positions quite at variance with that of the Soviets. All the evidence indicates that the armed forces, despite Soviet arms and training, support their governments in both internal and external affairs. Stories are current in all three countries about the dissatisfaction of Arab military trainees with life in the Communist countries and with the treatment they received at the hands of their Communist instructors. Current gossip does not circulate rumors of Arab military men who came home Sovietized or communized. The evidence available on these matters is less extensive than one would wish, but what there is appears to show that the Soviets have not bought political support or sympathy with arms and economic assistance. It also shows that their efforts to draw Arab nationalism into such close association with communism that it would lose its identity and independence have succeeded only in stimulating Arab nationalism's particularism.

The Soviets have had their ups and downs in the Arab East since Khrushchev launched his policy of championing Arab nationalism in 1955. Anyone who still harbors the popular assumption that the Communists always establish a fixed policy aimed at set goals and move with glacial slowness and steadiness to its accomplishment need only review Soviet fortunes in the Arab area since 1955.[29]

Khrushchev did offer the Arabs something different from the classical Leninist doctrines of class struggle, dictatorship of the proletariat, and hostility to religion and nationalism. Walter Z. Laqueur has described the new formula:

> The Communism that is striving for power in the Arab world today, though imbued with many Leninist motives, functions as an integral part of the nationalist movement, by no means as an opposition sect. It is not a proletarian party but an authentically nationalist party open to all classes. It has dropped the class struggle and replaced it with the anti-Western propaganda of the cold war. Communism in Asia seldom appears as it frequently did (and occasionally still does) in Europe, as the heir to the ideals of 1789, democracy, liberty, and equality. Its prestige and attractive power are those of a reputedly sovereign means toward the modernization and industrial enrichment of peoples ruefully conscious of their "backwardness."[30]

Nevertheless, the U.S.S.R. made mistakes from the beginning in the implementation of its shrewdly conceived policy and the exploitation of its manifold advantages. In the first place it had exaggerated ideas about the extent to which charity would win the admiration and the allegiance of the Arab people. The Soviet leaders apparently believed after the arms deal with Egypt that Nasser would be beholden to them because they had made him popular throughout the Arab world; what had actually happened was that Nasser had conferred a certain popularity upon them. They also apparently overestimated the extent to which they could exploit Arab nationalism in their own interest.[31]

By late 1960, after failures in Syria and Iraq and disappointment in the development of relations with Egypt, the Soviets were clearly engaged in a difficult rethinking of their policies toward the new nations of Africa and Asia. Part of the problem was apparently a basic disagreement with the Chinese Communists on

[29] See Walter Z. Laqueur, *The Soviet Union and the Middle East* (New York: Praeger, 1959), and Ivar Spector, *The Soviet Union and the Muslim World, 1917–1958* (Seattle: University of Washington Press, 1959) for the development of Soviet policy toward the Middle East.

[30] Laqueur, cited, pp. 343–344.

[31] Cf. Wheeler, cited, p. 312.

policies toward these areas. Whereas the Soviets were reported to be arguing for a policy of cooperation with national revolutions and of seeking to move them gradually along through various stages from preparation for socialism to the final stage of full-fledged communism—a continuation of the Khrushchev policies—the Chinese were said to be urging endeavors to bring violent revolution of the classic Leninist type to the Afro-Asian countries. Differences in the Soviet and the Chinese points of view and objectives were reflected in the "Statement of the Meeting of Representatives of the Communist and Workers' Parties" issued after the November 1960 meeting in Moscow.[32]

The statement generally follows the Soviet line, but the text contains a number of concessions to the Chinese position as well as a tough new look at the national bourgeois governments, presumably agreed upon by the Soviets and the Chinese. "As social contradictions grow, the national bourgeoisie inclines more and more to compromising with domestic reaction and imperialism," it says. "The people, however, begin to see that the best way to abolish age-long backwardness and improve their living standard is that of non-capitalist development. . . . The working class and the broad peasant masses will play the leading part in solving these basic social problems."[33]

This warning that the working class will take over from the national bourgeoisie must have given pause to Nasser and the other national leaders of the undeveloped countries, as did the description of the "independent national democracy" with which the Communists were said to be willing to cooperate. The "national democracy" is a state, like Cuba at that time, which, although not actually Communist, allows Communists freedom of action and is moving in the Communist direction. No Arab state fits the description, although Iraq had come very close in 1959. Communists are urged to fight "anti-democratic and anti-popular" acts, and the U.A.R., Iraq, Jordan, and the Sudan are included in a list of countries in which fighters for the cause of the working class are languishing in torture chambers.[34]

[32] *Documents,* Supplement to *New Times,* no. 50, 1960 (December 1960).
[33] Same, pp. 10–11.
[34] Same, p. 12.

Since the Moscow meeting of Communist parties in November 1960, Communist thinking has gone through still further gyrations. Castro's determined rejection of the "national democracy" label and his insistence on recognition of his country as Marxist-Leninist and of himself—a nationalist revolutionary leader clearly not under the old-fashioned kind of Communist discipline—as the dominant authority in Cuban communism has, doubtless, brought the Communists serious problems as well as satisfying gains and hopes for the future of communism in undeveloped countries.

What all this means for the future of Soviet policy toward the Arabs and for Arab attitudes toward communism remains to be seen. Nasser is obviously not a Castro; the whole record of his career is against his toadying to the Communists and prejudicing the national integrity of his country and of the Arab nationalist revolution, as Castro has done with his country and his revolution. It cannot be said with certainty that some other Arab leader might not follow Castro's course, though it is heartening that even Kassem—who came near to accepting a Castro-like relationship with the Communists—was drawn away from it by the compelling forces of Arab nationalism.

Over the long run the success or failure of the Communists in the Arab East will depend less on what they do than upon the loyalty of Arab nationalism to its basic goal of independence and on the ability of the Arab states to find a stable and satisfactory relationship with the rest of the world.

NASSER AND THE UNITED STATES

Nasser was born and brought up in Egypt at a time when the predominant influences came from the West and reflected the liberal Western tradition. His education in primary, secondary, and military schools was essentially Western. Even revolutionary nationalism and the passion for independence, the ruling themes in his life, came out of the Western tradition. His basic drive is not so much a rejection of the West as a search to find for his people and his country the values which he absorbed from the West.

The bitterness with which Nasser has attacked the West repeatedly since 1955 reflects more than simple fear of the Western powers, more than the conviction that the West is responsible for the problems of the Arabs; it is an emotion charged with the sense of betrayal, the feeling that the West, and particularly the United States, has failed to do for the underprivileged peoples and countries of Afro-Asia what its professed principles and its own traditions obligate it to do. Repeatedly, Nasser has appealed to Americans by pointing out that Washington in his Farewell Address "said exactly the same things that I am saying today."[35] He shares with many Egyptians and other Arabs a conception of America inspired by Wilson's Fourteen Points, the King-Crane Commission, and Franklin Roosevelt's Four Freedoms. It is a concept of a strong, progressive country without colonies or colonial ambitions, remote from the intrigues of European politics, a country to which small nations could look with hope. Like many Arabs he fails to see anything unreasonable in the expectation that America live up to the image created in an earlier and happier day when it had few of the burdens and responsibilities that it carries now.

It has often been claimed that from the Egyptian revolution until 1955 Nasser's policy was based on hope that the United States would provide the resources necessary to pull Egypt out of the morass in which Farouk and the pashas had left it. Jean and Simone Lacouture, veteran French correspondents who were in Egypt at the time, say that there was "an element of ideological understanding" between Nasser and the Americans and the British, "a common determination to block the passage to a violent social revolution by offsetting it with technical reform (the idea being less to bar the road to an imaginary Soviet invasion, than to nip in the bud some Mao of the Nile Valley)." This prospective collaboration broke down, they suggest, not because Nasser thought it unsound but because he could find no support for the idea among the Egyptian public.[36]

Certainly, the expectations of Nasser and his collaborators were raised very high by various indications of American willingness to assist the new regime. Not the least of these was President Eisenhower's letter to President Naguib on July 15, 1954, which gave assurance that "simultaneously" with the conclusion of the Suez

<hr/>

[35] *Nasser's Speeches,* 1958, p. 369.
[36] Jean and Simone Lacouture, *Egypt in Transition* (London: Methuen, 1958), pp. 208–210.

agreement the United States would enter into "firm commitments" with Egypt for economic assistance and for strengthening the Egyptian armed forces. But this pledge is not the only basis for the belief that Nasser looked to the United States for substantial help in the early period of his responsibility as a policy maker. His whole policy was geared to the idea that once the special position of the British in the Sudan and the Canal Zone was liquidated, the revolutionary regime could settle down to dealing with basic problems of economic and social reform, with the assistance of the United States.

Nasser's foreign policy became particularly popular with the Egyptian masses only when he started attacking the West. It is possible, however, to make too much of the contrast between his policies before and after the announcement of the Baghdad Pact. From the outset of his regime, Nasser was perfectly capable of strong anti-Western feeling. In his first public statement to the press after the revolution, at a difficult point in the negotiations with the British over the Canal Base, he declared that if the British did not accept the basic Egyptian position and agree to evacuation, the Egyptians would resume guerrilla warfare and would drive the British out of the zone.[37] On April 13, 1954, in a public speech at land distribution ceremonies at Faroukia, Nasser said that Egypt would oppose efforts to bring Iraq into the Turkish-Pakistani defense pact, which he said was an attempt to "break Arab-Muslim unity in support of Egypt's position in the Canal Zone." He called Point Four a form of "American colonial penetration" and said that the United States would do nothing to displease Great Britain.[38]

Nasser's disillusionment with the United States was inevitable in view of his exaggerated and unrealistic expectations of American assistance in the early period of the Egyptian revolution. But his new attitude developed also as a consequence of his own political education in Pan Arabism, Afro-Asian solidarity, and neutralism. As his ideas on international politics and policy developed under the tutelage of Pan Arabists like Abdel Rahman Azzam, his Afro-Asian ideas at Bandung, and his neutralism under the tute-

[37] *Al Akhbar*, September 27, 1952.
[38] *Middle East Journal*, Winter 1954, p. 74, and Summer 1954, p. 325.

lage of Nehru and Tito, they displaced the rather naïve concept of a relationship with the United States that would replace that with Great Britain but be free of its undesirable aspects. Nevertheless, he and many Egyptians continued to harbor the idea that a special relationship with the United States of great mutual advantage could be worked out if only the United States would cooperate.

American policy makers in 1952–54, it has been argued in the United States, showed too great enthusiasm for the Egyptian revolution, giving the impression in the Middle East that the United States had selected revolutionary Egypt as its chosen instrument. This may have been less of an error than the violent swing in the other direction after the Suez crisis, when through the Eisenhower Doctrine and a series of related actions the United States sought to support the forces of opposition to Nasser in the Arab world. It is not strange that in 1959, when the Indian journalist Karanjia asked Nasser if *rapprochement* were possible between Arab nationalism and the United States, he replied, "The trouble with America is that she has no policy towards us. They want to influence our area like every big power and that creates a contradiction between us."[39] America, in Nasser's view, does not take a positive view on the basic question of Arab nationalism; it simply seeks to exert pressure to influence the Arabs in this way or that in accordance with its own interests and in response to the pressures engendered by the fluctuating international situation.

Over the years Nasser has become more and more plaintive on the subject of American attitudes. He points out repeatedly that "every Israeli point of view meets with great attention from you, and every Arab point of view only meets with neglect."[40] "The New York newspapers," he has said, "are always writing about the rights of Israel but they never mention the rights of the Palestine Arabs to return to their land. . . ."[41] Zionist control of the American press, Zionist influence in the American government, Zionist influence in American intellectual circles, Zionist influence in American business and finance—in Nasser's opinion and in that of

[39] *Nasser's Speeches,* 1959, p. 545.
[40] Same, p. 589.
[41] *Nasser's Speeches,* 1958, p. 374.

most of his advisers, this all-pervasive and all-powerful influence explains the unfavorable attitude of the United States toward the Arab cause.

Nasser and his advisers seem to believe that the United States never does anything about the Arab situation, except when the pressure of events forces it to take action. In their view, it seems logical that they can get action from the United States only by building fires under the American people and government and that they can make us reconsider our position only by heaping abuse on us. The United States can save itself, they believe, only if it heeds the warnings of the neutralist nations. Because of the importance of the Arab and Afro-Asian peoples in international affairs, the United States must eventually take heed of them and grant them their due.

The difference in Nasser's treatment of the Soviet Union and the United States is explained in part by Nasser's belief that, whereas the leaders of the Soviet Union have calculated the international situation precisely and are working with great skill to take advantage of the inevitable trends of the times, the Americans are unaware of those trends or are being misled by special interest groups to take a course contrary to their own national interest and to the interests of the neutral nations. The Russians do not need to be waked up; there is no point in jeopardizing by unnecessary attacks the arms supplies and other assistance he gets from them. The Americans, on the other hand, he believes, are so preoccupied with irrational fears of communism that they cannot understand the most important fact of our time: that a world revolution bringing a third force of Afro-Asian nations into being is changing the whole pattern of world affairs. They are being betrayed by the Zionists and by the European imperialists who are still interested in exploitation of Asia and Africa. The United States must be waked up to the realities of the world situation; its power is needed to balance that of the Soviet bloc, but it should be exerted in favor of the independence of small peoples, not against it.

From the point of view of the West, the important questions about Nasser and his policies are not whether they are pro-Western or Communist. The evidence seems clear that they are neither.

The important questions are whether they represent major historical forces at work in the Arab world, forces which must be seriously dealt with in one way or another; and, if this is so and Western policy takes account of it, whether Nasser and the people to whom he turns for advice and support have the honesty and the capability necessary to bridge the gulf that now separates the West from the majority of the Arabs, as well as much of the rest of the ex-colonial world.

Previous chapters have argued that Nasser's Arab nationalist foreign policies represent valid historical forces. Nasser's has been the strongest and the most dramatic voice speaking for those forces, although it is not the only one. Arab nationalism speaks through many voices. He has captured the mood of the moment and seen the demands of the times.

The authoritarian practices characteristic of Nasser's government, and particularly his management and control of the press and public opinion, are often cited as fundamental weaknesses. But these practices do not differ substantially from those employed in most Arab countries, or in other developing countries in Africa and Asia. They must be related to the stage of political and social development in which the Arabs find themselves, and to the outside interference to which they are subjected. A real question, of course, is whether Nasser and his regime can adapt to changing conditions, whether they have the will and the strength eventually to permit the gradual relaxation of restrictions on public discussion and popular participation in the political process.

One can choose from a wide range of opinion on Nasser the man and on other Arab nationalist leaders and potential leaders throughout the Arab world. In the end any judgment on their honesty, sincerity, and on their dedication to the welfare of their people must be highly subjective. In the opinion of the present writer, Nasser and nationalists of similar stripe throughout the Arab world are honest and trustworthy in their dedication to national goals. What is more important, some of them are marked by a sincerity and commitment to the future of their people that is unusual. Their conduct is less influenced by self-interest than is that of the holders of power in the traditional governments in that part of the world. Their greatest weaknesses, as has been indicated above, are the consequences of the situation out of which they come. Their capacity for growth and development, and for setting aside the suspiciousness, toughness, and lack of restraint which have marked their early years in power, will determine their future and the future of the Arab world.

With all their shortcomings and human weaknesses the Arab nationalists are a real factor in their part of the world today. The United States cannot leave them out of account. It cannot deal with them only to the extent that they meet our standards of respectability. We must deal with them because they are there, because they or men like them will continue to hold political power and determine foreign policy in the Arab world.

XIII

ALTERNATIVES FOR THE UNITED STATES

After the Second World War, America's new strength and responsibility in international affairs imposed upon it new obligations in the Arab area. The natural goal of American policy makers was to preserve the Western position. The security and prosperity of European allies appeared to depend upon special political arrangements with the governments of Arab states providing rights of transit, military base rights, and concessions, particularly for the exploitation of oil resources. American military bases and American oil concessions, many of which were acquired during or after the war, strengthened the community of interest between the United States and other Western powers. In addition, the American concern with strengthening the position of the West in opposition to Soviet-Communist imperialism everywhere was sharpened by the Soviet drive for influence and position in the Middle East. A disturbing factor in the task of policy-making was the association with Israel which brought down on the United States the unmitigated wrath of Arab nationalists and magnified the numerous difficulties that beset the relations of an established, advanced and relatively stable society with a society in the midst of revolution. In brief, the United States, without conscious choice, assumed a position and adopted policies aimed at preserving the *status quo* in the Arab world. Many Americans, deeply disturbed by the ironies in such a policy, sought to bring U.S. behavior toward the Arab East into line with the country's traditional concern for self-determination. The imperatives of organizing the Western alliance, and the hostility and sensitivity of the Arab revolutionaries, however, made adjustments of American policy to the Arab revolution extremely difficult and strengthened the tendency of the majority of Americans, both in the government and among the public, to follow more conservative paths.

The headlong speed with which events in the Arab East unfolded after World War II contributed to the conservatism of American policy makers. However good the intentions of a responsible official and however well aware he may be of the need for considering the long-term implications of some new event, the telegram on the desk has to be answered. When it concerns a crisis which is the tenth or the twentieth in a series, the answer will probably be based on assumptions already formulated and which, although they may have little else but familiarity to recommend them, will be accepted as sound by high officials and by the American press and public.

In the mid-fifties, when crisis became endemic in the Middle East, serious attempts were made to take a fresh look at American policy in this part of the world. Universities increased the attention they paid to the Middle East; government departments set more people to specializing on the Arabs; the oil companies hired research staffs. But the problem had a head start on the newly appointed specialists. Lack of specialized knowledge, preoccupation with the Communist threat, and the confusion which the Arab-Israel issue introduced into so many American minds all tended to delay the formulation of a new policy in accord with American traditions and relevant to the new postwar circumstances.

RULES-OF-THUMB IN THE ABSENCE OF POLICY

In the absence of both consensus and policy in government and among the interested public, responses to Arab problems tended to be based on a set of ideas and practices, a body of common wisdom acceptable to "old hands" and dilettantes alike. The following are examples of a set of easy half-truths, or rules-of-thumb, which had great influence upon American thought and action in the Arab area in the ten years after the Palestine War:

*The Arabs are hopelessly torn by rivalries and conflicts which are
unlikely to be resolved.*

Arab nationalism is inevitably anti-Western and pro-Soviet.

*Nothing can be done to change the American image in the Arab
East; it reflects an ingrained Arab prejudice against the West.*

Force is the only thing which the Arabs can understand.

*The Soviets are moving slowly but certainly to the achievement of
their set goal of communizing the states of the Middle East.*

*The United States must support its friends and see that their friend-
ship is rewarded more generously than the threats and insults of
enemies, whether openly hostile governments or self-styled neutrals.*

One significant thing about almost all these plausible propositions is that they are no more true than their opposites. The Arabs
are united in some ways to a remarkable degree. Despite the anti-
Western theme of Arab nationalism, Arab nationalists continue to
be admirers of many Western characteristics and ways and suspicious of much that the Soviets stand for. The slightest sign of
comprehension of the Arab nationalist point of view exhibited by
an American leader often produces a remarkable change in the
American image in the Arab world. Force, as has been amply
demonstrated by the Israelis, seems to teach the Arabs very little;
it neither makes them respectful nor convinces them that they have
been beaten. The Soviet experience in the Arab world in the past
decade should dispel any idea that the Communist leaders know
exactly where they are going; Nasser has provided them with
greater surprises and greater disillusionments than he has the
United States. And as for the last rule-of-thumb—that friends must
be treated better than enemies—though the opposite cannot be
put forward as an equal truth, it is well to keep in mind that not
everyone who makes friendly noises is necessarily a friend, and
not everyone with a different point of view necessarily an enemy.

Taken as a group, the collection of commonly accepted rules-
of-thumb listed above is more meaningful than the propositions
are separately. Each has its use in a particular situation; they are
all alike in that they are conservative and negative. Together they
say that the Arabs are hopeless people who hate us and who
therefore do not deserve to be understood or to have our position
explained to them. Taken together as the basis for action they lead
to despair, inactivity, and the concession of all the very great ad-

vantages which America and the West enjoy in the Arab area. Acceptance of the idea of the inborn proclivity of the Arabs for communism and the superhuman ability of the Communists to plan well and execute their plans effectively practically gives the game away to the Communists. The only specific policy recommendation included in the popular set of rules-of-thumb accepted by those who do not really want to think about the Arabs is that we should be kind to our friends. Morally and ethically unimpeachable as this sentiment is, it leads to alliances with governments that are either aggressive, unscrupulous, or doomed and to the shoring up of obsolescent groups and institutions.

Clearly enough, a more organized approach is called for. The classic way to go about solving the problem has been to define interests. This has been tried repeatedly.

AMERICAN INTERESTS IN THE ARAB EAST

The steady erosion of Western positions in the Arab East has demonstrated that it is impractical for the United States, or any power, to hold the line, seeking to prevent any diminution of privilege or any modification of territorial arrangements, bases, treaties, agreements, and customs. It is often suggested that there is need for redefining American and Western interests and for establishing minima, thus enabling the West to draw a line beyond which it would not retreat.

It is generally agreed that minimum vital American (and Western) interests are: (a) the independence of the states of the area; (b) freedom of transit through the area and the free movement of oil from Arab fields to Western markets; and (c) denial of the area to Soviet-Communist domination.[1] On first glance, American and Western interests, particularly the emphasis on independence, seem compatible with Arab interests. The only claims made directly for Western advantage, i.e., access to oil and freedom of transit, are also to the Arab advantage. Military bases are not mentioned, nor colonies or protectorates, nor special privilege for Western institutions, nor alliances or pacts.

[1] See the list of fundamental objectives of American policy in the Middle East in an address by Assistant Secretary Rountree, *The Department of State Bulletin,* June 17, 1957, pp. 974–975.

Closer examination reveals how oversimplified and deceptive is the list of three American interests. Consider, first, the independence of the states of the area. Among them is Israel, whose independence, indeed whose very right to exist, is challenged by all the Arab states. Thus, championing the independence of *all* the states of the area brings the United States into conflict with most of them. Further, does U.S. support of the principle of independence mean that we are committed to the perpetuation of the present state system, including the sheikhdoms and protectorates whose foreign policy and defense is in British hands? The American government has more than once indicated that it is not committed to the *status quo,* but that it is willing to accept change only when approved by the majority of the people concerned. In 1958, President Eisenhower told the United Nations General Assembly: "The peoples of the Arab nations of the Near East clearly possess the right of determining and expressing their own destiny. Other nations should not interfere so long as this expression is found in ways compatible with international peace and security."[2] The United States put this principle into practice by recognizing the union of Syria and Egypt in the United Arab Republic in 1958, the revolutionary government of Iraq in the same year, and independent Syria in 1961. But should the United States withdraw its support from governments which no longer command the loyalty of the majority of their people? Or, should the United States accept and recognize a Communist takeover which appeared to have majority support? How is popular support to be measured?

Freedom of transit through the Arab area by general agreement is an interest of the United States, but the Egyptians have closed the Suez Canal to Israeli ships and Israeli goods and the Arab states have stopped traffic with Israel across their borders. Aircraft which land in Israel cannot fly over Arab territory. The United States, although it has opposed in principle this interruption of communications through the area, has accepted it as a fact. When in 1956 the British and French used force to prevent President Nasser's nationalization of the Suez Canal, the United States jeopardized its vital Atlantic alliance by opposing the British and French action.

2 *The Department of State Bulletin,* September 1, 1958, p. 337.

The Suez crisis involved the question of Western access to Arab oil as well as freedom of transit. Western access to Arab oil was also involved when the revolutionary government took power in Iraq. In these cases, Iraqi and Egyptian governments have recognized that their own interests coincide with those of the West, so long as their sovereignty is unchallenged. If, however, Arab states should radically change or cancel the present oil concessions held by Western companies, or nationalize their oil industries, the United States, in view of its interest in continued Western access to Arab oil, will have to decide what changes in the present arrangements it can accept. The generally defined interest itself does not provide the key to practical policy.

Denial of the Arab area to the Communists is an American interest. The vast build-up in the Arab East of Soviet-Communist diplomatic, economic, and cultural activity, and the supply of Soviet arms on a large scale to Arab states, the United States has had to accept. Efforts to oppose these things have often had a boomerang effect. The Arab interest in bolstering their independent position by dealing with the Soviet bloc cannot be denied.

In practical terms, the United States cannot prevent all Soviet activity and influence in the Arab states; our policy can aim, however, at preventing outright Soviet control and domination. The questions that arise will probably not concern intervention and occupation. What happened in Iraq in 1959, when the Communists got a free hand for a time, may give us an idea of the kind of challenge which we may have to face in the future. It is sometimes assumed that a Communist-dominated government can never come to power in any country through a process of self-determination and by the people's free choice. In Arab countries, however, it is seldom feasible to insist on applying the criterion of free elections, with opportunities for campaigning open to all. Iraq might easily have come under Communist control in 1959. At some time in the future the United States may have to decide what to do about an Arab government which claims to be free and independent and based on popular support but which is in fact controlled by Communist agents. It may prove even more difficult to decide what attitude to adopt toward a government which is indeed free, but which for reasons of its own is collaborating with the Soviets and becoming more and more dependent on them. The Cuban case is unlikely to be duplicated exactly in an Arab country, but something very like it could take place.

DESIRABLE SITUATIONS AND VITAL INTERESTS

National interest should not be confused with desirable situations, i.e., situations we should like to see exist or continue, such as the existence of parliaments on the Western model, a free press, Western-run schools, Western clubs, freedom for Western and local business enterprise. These are generally not things that we should be willing to take great risks to preserve; also, by their nature we cannot produce them or maintain them by force or money. Attempts to do so would only divert our national resources from more significant objectives.

Another pitfall in defining national interests is the temptation to include specific positions and rights, like military bases, business or commercial property or concessions, trading or other rights and privileges based on custom or treaties. These quasi-interests are now much less important in the Arab East than before the Second World War. The Suez Base lost its value to the British as a consequence of changes in military weapons and also as a result of political and psychological changes in Egypt. Nasser's seizure of the Suez Canal Company was regarded by the British and the French governments as so great a threat to their interests that they took great risks to defeat him, but much of the world disagreed, not only with this interpretation of their interests, but also with the use of force to defend them.

All over non-Communist Asia, Africa and Latin America, a re-examination of interests, of property and other rights is taking place under the pressures of the anticolonial revolution. In most cases disputes are being settled, for practical rather than moral reasons, in accord with the principle of self-determination. It is significant that countries which have given up their colonial holdings are, for the most part, more prosperous than ever before. Many Britishers who looked on their position in India as a vital interest, and many Netherlanders who felt the same about the East Indies, now recognize that these views are no longer relevant.

In summary, definitions of national interests do not give the policy maker a firm take-off point from which he can move to formulate a sound policy for America. He can identify many situations as desirable, of which none can be labeled "vital" except under certain circumstances and in certain contingencies. Perhaps "national interests" are not always the best basis for policy. Perhaps policy makers should not ask what positions or goals the United States should seek, but rather what approach it should adopt, what kind of over-all relation to the Arab area will prove most desirable.

ALTERNATIVE APPROACHES OPEN TO THE UNITED STATES

American attitudes and objectives are of great importance to the Arab peoples and their governments. What the United States has accomplished, or failed to accomplish, in the past has been the consequence not so much of actions taken as of the American approach, stance, or attitude toward the Arabs. There is more to this than Oriental sensitivity to manners. It reflects the expectation that the United States must have a philosophy of the Arab revolution, an internally consistent conception of what is going on in the Arab world and of what it wants to happen there. Only such a conception can lead to a sound approach in foreign policy.

The United States has the choice of four basic approaches to the Arab states: neutrality, alliance, cooperation with the Arab nationalist revolution, and eclecticism or pragmatism.

The Neutralist Approach

A neutralist or basically disinterested policy for America would mean withdrawing from commitments which might involve the United States in great expense or great risk. It would mean taking no stand, not only on inter-Arab disputes and the Arab-Israeli conflict, but presumably also on Soviet-Arab relations and the growth of Soviet influence. The United States might continue friendly relations with cooperative nations and provide a limited amount of economic assistance, for philanthropic motives and to encourage stability and prosperity. It would not, however, regard the loss of any present position or relationship as a threat to vital interests. It could be argued (1) that American power and influence have proved largely ineffective in the area and that the Communists have advantages which we cannot hope to overcome, and (2) that the American stake in the Western alliance, which is immensely greater than in the Arab world, should not be jeopardized by commitment of political and economic resources in a relatively unimportant and unpromising area. If the Arabs flaunt their neutralism at us, we could return the compliment.

Such a policy, or lack of policy, might seem to offer many temptations, but it leaves out of account a number of things which responsible policy makers cannot ignore. Above all, in the worldwide contest between freedom and communism, American responsibility and the effect of American policy extend everywhere. They are particularly significant in the developing countries. "Neutralism" here, for the strongest power of the free world, can only mean retreat.

Some Arabs would welcome the announcement of an American policy of neutrality, but their approval would be likely to fade if they understood that the policy meant less prospect for economic assistance and withdrawal of the American commitment to confront Soviet power and Soviet pressures with countervailing force.

Alliances with Friendly States

This type of policy would involve the formation of the closest possible alliances with states willing to enter into them. American aid would be concentrated in the allied states to assist them to assume a major or even dominant role in the area. In order to fulfill its commitments the United States would be required to make available substantial military and economic resources.

Aid to friendly states, it could be argued, is easier to justify than to hostile or neutral ones which follow policies in many ways incompatible with our own. Also, the benefits derived from alliances are immediate and tangible, in contrast to the vague and uncertain consequences of supporting a whole variety of countries without regard to their philosophies, institutions, policies or leadership. But the experience of the recent past in the Arab area indicates that a policy based on alliances has no long-term potential. The formation of the northern tier alliance of Turkey, Iran and Pakistan has had some advantages—along with real disadvantages—for the United States; but the attempt to include Arab countries in that alliance has met complete frustration. Offering support to friendly governments seems logical, but it seems doubtful whether the United States could base an effective policy for the Arab area on the kind of relationship it has had with the King of Jordan, the King of Saudi Arabia, or the hereditary rulers of the Persian Gulf sheikhdoms. It is evident, moreover, that none of the Arab states wants alliances of the old type, not even the government of Lebanon or King Hussein. This does not mean that it is unwise to provide the kind of support that now enables Hussein to stay on his throne, but, useful as it is in the present, such assistance is a holding operation, not a policy for the future.

If the Arabs are unwilling to accept alliances, perhaps the United States should base its policy upon an alliance with Israel, presumably a stable and reliably pro-Western nation. But if such an alliance were formalized, and if the United States sought to use its resources to help Israel achieve its goals, it is most unlikely, to put it mildly, that America's position in the Arab area would be enhanced.

Arab leaders today accuse the United States of keying its Middle East policy to supporting Israel—Arab propaganda plays every variation on this theme—but most of them know well that the charge is not true. They must be aware that within the U.S. government there is a great deal of dispute on policy toward Israel and that the governments of Israel and the United States are often in disagreement. A formal American alliance with Israel would be a new departure. It would produce a reaction in Arab states which would bring them much closer to the Soviet bloc. Moreover, it is doubtful whether the Israeli government would give unqualified approval to an American alliance if it were seriously proposed; Israel gains too many advantages from the present situation.

Cooperation with the Arab Revolution

This policy would involve efforts on the part of the United States to identify itself more closely with the dominant forces in the Arab area, taking advantage of the numerous important interests which it has in common with the Arab nationalists—continued independence of the Arab area and freedom from external pressures, economic development, and the development of modern social and political institutions which would provide a base for stability and progress. Where U.S. and Arab interests do not coincide—on the existence of Israel, for example—it would be necessary to agree to disagree, meanwhile seeking to render the conflict less explosive and looking for long-range solutions of an evolutionary nature.

This kind of approach could succeed only if the United States were to demonstrate convincingly that it understands and accepts the policy of nonalignment, and is willing to cooperate with nations which combine such a policy with responsibility for the welfare of their own people and of the international community. The United States would also have to recognize that political and economic development in the Arab area is unlikely to proceed along the lines of Western democracy and the free enterprise system. Business enterprises, particularly the concessionary oil companies, would have to be placed on the foundation of mutual interest, with the expectation that the trend toward greater Arab participation in management and control would steadily continue. The Arab nationalists, it is argued, will dominate the area whatever policy the United States adopts. Within a generation, the outlook of all the men in power will be much like that of the Arab nationalists of today. They will stand for nonalignment with great powers and radical social and economic solutions for the problems of poverty and backwardness. Powerful as the United States is, it does not have the capability of stopping or diverting such a development. Efforts to do so can only turn the Arabs—people as well as leaders—against us and make them more susceptible to Soviet blandishments. Therefore, the case for cooperation with the Arab nationalist revolution rests mainly on the proposition that the United States has more to gain by maintaining good relations, and a basis for friendly influence upon the future leaders, than by trying to keep alive dying institutions.

A serious objection to the proposed policy of cooperation is the fact that Arab nationalist leaders have their own reservations. They are not anxious to be influenced by the United States, much less to be sponsored by it or to become its chosen instruments. Probably for some time they will continue to broadcast their belief in the turpitude of all great powers and in the principle that safety for small states lies in maintaining a position securely between the two great-power groupings. The United States has experienced great difficulty in its efforts to take a stand with respect to nonalignment and neutralism which will evoke a favorable response from the emergent states. So far, it seems that only by accepting all their most extreme positions could the United States satisfy their demands. It is doubtful whether the United States, by making every effort to understand and accommodate itself to Arab nationalist policies of nonalignment in international affairs and in radical reform in domestic affairs, could soon succeed in bringing about many significant changes in the policy or conduct of the Arab nationalists.

Pragmatism

A pragmatic policy would seek to apply all the obvious courses of action, separately or in combination, at appropriate times and places. The United States would maintain friendly relations with Israel, the kings and sheikhs, and the revolutionary governments concurrently, though making special gestures toward one or the other when circumstances made it seem desirable to do so. It would furnish arms to pro-Western Arab states, but none to those who received any from the Soviets. It would, however, give the latter group other types of assistance and would mitigate their anger at not getting arms by limiting or avoiding arms aid to Israel. Israel would be placated by the magnitude of other types of U.S. assistance and by its ability to purchase arms at good prices from other NATO countries. Economic assistance would, on principle, go in greatest abundance to governments whose policies were most compatible with those of the United States, but considerable help would be given to the revolutionary and neutralist governments when the Soviets seemed to be making too much of the opportunities open to them. On appropriate occasions the United States would bestow merited praise on Israel, on the conservative Arab governments, and on the revolutionary states. The United States would announce its acceptance of neutralism in principle, but would not hesitate to disagree with the self-declared neutralist states when their application of neutralist foreign policy was prejudicial to American or Western interests or to the requirements of a just international order.

The pragmatic policy obviously is very like that which the United States has been pursuing. It is the easiest of all policies to apply; also its variable approach seems particularly suited to the amalgam of sub-areas which make up the Middle East.

American pragmatic policy has been accused of weakness, but it is difficult to separate evidences of so-called weaknesses from unpleasant happenings which may have been inevitable in the course of history and which even the wisest policy could not have avoided. Perhaps the real weakness of U.S. policy over the past few years has been its failure to make clear what this country wants and what it stands for in the Arab area. To Arab conservatives it has seemed that the United States was supporting Nasser, and to Nasser that it was supporting the conservatives and Israel, while to the Israelis American policy has often appeared pro-Arab. This is probably the natural consequence of an eclectic policy which will have to be judged not by its consistency but by its achievements.

THE BASIS FOR DECISION

It is not surprising that Americans have found it difficult to choose between neutralism, alliance, or cooperation with Arab nationalism, and that they have found scant satisfaction in eclecticism. None of them promises very much in the way of preserving desirable situations, or creating situations which suit the American ideal—i.e., independent, democratic, free societies willing and able to fend off Communist endeavors and cooperate with the West.

In framing U.S. policy the choices are not between good and evil, or between the familiar and the strange; the future is likely to hold little that is good, judged by older standards, and little that is not new and unfamiliar. Nor is it just a matter of choosing the lesser of alternative evils, but the much more difficult task of deciding, first, what the general pattern of the future is likely to be, and second, given this pattern, what alternative courses offer most hope.

Present drives and present trends in the Arab world, if continued, will certainly see an end of colonial holdovers and of feudal regimes within a generation, however determined their opposition, and regardless of the support they get from the outside. Meanwhile the fulfillment in some form of the dream of Arab unity will persist. Nonalignment and neutralism are most unlikely to be supplanted by alliances linking the Arabs with outside powers, provided the Arabs can choose their international posture. The drive for economic development and improvement of the general welfare will continue to focus interest on foreign aid and means of obtaining it. This drive, if nothing else, will continue to make attractive the policy of bargaining with each of the great-power groupings. Barring some major effort on the part of the Soviet Union or of Communist China to intervene in Arab affairs or to occupy an Arab state, the Arabs will continue to welcome some degree of Soviet and Chinese Communist "presence."

Partly because of rivalries among the Arab states, stimulated by the evolution of new political forms and the emergence of new foci of power, and partly because of the exigencies of economic and social change, the trend for some time is likely to be toward authoritarian governments. Employing socialistic formulas, they will direct and control the use of national resources for economic development. In the early stages, these governments will restrict freedom of expression and private enterprise. Only after the process of self-sustaining growth begins, when some measure of internal stability and security in international relations has been achieved, is there likely to be a loosening of restrictions.

If this is the shape of the future in the Arab world, to what goals should U.S. policy aim? If material interests, including oil, and political institutions in the Arab East have only relative value for the United States, and if the same is true of military bases, what then is our vital interest in this part of the world?

When everything else has been discounted, the interest of the United States in maintaining the Middle East as an area of free and independent nations, in which the Arabs will find their place, stands alone in importance. Within the discernible pattern of the future in the Arab East, either of two alternative courses is possible: (1) a continuation of the fierce devotion to independence and search for self-fulfillment which has characterized the Arab nationalist revolution, and (2) a drift into the circumscribed world of communism from which there is little contact with the rest of the world. The trouble with this formulation, however, is that it implies a clear alternative between freedom and communism. If the experience of the past decade is meaningful, there seems little likelihood that the Arab world is in danger of becoming Communist after the example of Eastern Europe and China. The danger, more likely, is that the Arabs might fall into some variation on communism, like Castro's Cuba before 1962, and, without actually becoming a part of the Communist bloc, cut themselves off from the independent world. What is therefore important to the United States and to the West is that the Arabs not only stay out from under Communist rule, but that they develop independently in the context of their own dream and their own spirit, and that they maintain communication with that part of the world which has not given itself over to the slavery of authoritarian rigidity.

COURSES OF ACTION

The means by which the United States can help to hold the Arab states within the free world are not new. Their effectiveness will depend upon their being informed and stimulated by the recognition that Arab nationalism's drive to independence and to the realization of the potentialities of the area is compatible with basic American interests. Whether courses of action thus motivated can be effectively welded into a rounded, consistent policy will depend upon the style and skill of those who apply them as much as upon the actions themselves. The following formulas involve both attitude and action.

Present the United States as a dynamic country still working out its revolution and sympathetic to the problems and needs of developing countries. The United States must be made to appear progressive and adventuresome in its own life, and in its approach to the rest of the world. The image of the United States must not be that of a nation wedded to the past or convinced that its own methods and institutions are universally applicable. In order to show the face of America more clearly to the undeveloped countries and in order to establish better communication with them, voice must be given to national leaders in all fields including those little heard hitherto, such as labor leaders and advocates of civil rights, of urban development and local government reform. In the United Nations and in the international conferences and congresses which are such an important part of the political life of the world of today, the United States must participate more fully in formulating recommendations for change. It must avoid the role of abstainer on issues of great importance to half of the world.

Encourage fruitful and meaningful cultural and intellectual exchange. In the past, cultural and intellectual exchange has too often been on the colonial pattern, i.e., giving the "natives" an opportunity to learn something about the superior culture of the mother country. Now it is of great importance that American students of Arab affairs and Arab culture be brought into close contact with the universities and other institutions of learning in the Arab countries, and that Arab scholars, technical specialists, and artists be enabled to communicate with their American counterparts. Senior American and Arab scholars should be encouraged to exchange places. American universities which specialize in Arab studies should plan their programs with the current interests and needs of Arab countries in mind. American books of all kinds—literary, scientific, technical—and American scholarly journals should be made available, in their original form and in translation, at prices which Arab students and scholars can afford to pay. Communication between the scholars, scientists, and artists of the United States and the Arab countries can be more effective in their cultural development, and exert more influence on their attitudes and habits of thought, than all the efforts of propaganda specialists.

Contribute to economic development. Economic assistance is of great importance to the Arab states, but its volume is not so important as the way in which it is given, or what appears to be the American purpose in giving it. Conditions are, of course, bound to be implicit in any gift. The United States has limited resources and many demands upon them. Few are so naïve as to believe that aid "without strings" is a rigidly practical concept. Nevertheless, every attempt to withdraw from a commitment or to lecture a recipient state on the propriety of its international conduct has backfired.

On the other hand, treating an aid project as a transaction between equals contributes to its political and psychological success. Few aid projects can be justified solely on economic grounds; most of them are related to political considerations. Aid provided with concern for what is politically important to the receiving nation, as well as what is needed economically, can bring a harvest of benefits to both sides.

Assistance in technical training and in the formulation and implementation of development programs, which are among the most valuable forms of American aid, often will appear to compete with similar activities of the Communist bloc. Clearly it would be unwise for the United States to seek to match everything that the Soviets or the Communist Chinese do for a given Arab country; nevertheless, it is a fact that, if we fail to compete, they may assume a position of dominant influence by default. However, past experience of Arab governments and individuals with Soviet aid and trade programs has generally disabused them of a lot of illusions about the Communists, their methods, and their products. That experience is likely to continue, to the discomfiture of the Soviets. But not if the West has withdrawn from the field.

Deal with the Arab states as sovereign entities, accepting changes within their borders and relationships which they work out for themselves. Accepting the inevitability of change in the political organization of the Arab world, and avoiding favoritism in relations with the several states, will not bring direct benefits to the United States but it will minimize the losses of prestige and influence that follow when a protégé falls by the wayside. Greater efforts are required to maintain good relations with the revolutionary states than with the conservative regimes, but in the long run such efforts are likely to be rewarding, even if today many of the nationalist leaders do not seem to want good relations. Success in dealing with revolutionaries, however, does not necessarily mean that the United States will be riding the wave of the future.

Support Arab unity and regional cooperation. No outside power can establish communication or maintain cooperative relations with the Arab states if it does not recognize the validity of the principle of unity in their political ideology. Decisions on practical means for cooperation, however, must await evidence that the

Arabs themselves have worked out ways of putting principles into practice. Movements toward unity are most likely to touch the material interests of the United States and its allies in connection with the political future of the sheikhdoms and the utilization of oil profits for area development. In these matters, it is of the greatest importance that the Arabs should themselves find a workable, reasonably stable solution.

Efforts to create regional groupings of states for joint action are certain to be a feature of the political landscape in the Middle East, Africa, and Asia in the coming generation. Pan African or Afro-Asian associations will probably not exert as much influence as smaller groupings of states for cooperation in economic development, transportation, and trade. Association or union on that smaller scale will probably become increasingly significant. It is not in the interest of the United States to be the prime mover in any of these developments, but it should be prepared in principle to encourage regional cooperation.

Acknowledge the right of states to follow a policy of nonalignment and neutralism and cooperate with such states in matters of mutual interest. In the present period of transition from dependent to independent status, while most of the new states in Africa and Asia are weak and unstable, it is to be expected that they will continue to harbor suspicions of the great powers. Furthermore, for historical reasons, many of the new states will remain for a long time particularly suspicious of the West and of its standard bearer, the United States. In this situation it probably will be fruitless for some time to argue whether or not the neutrality of the new nations is genuine. The important question is whether they remain independent and jealous of their independence. The deepest interests and concerns of the United States are satisfied so long as the emergent states remain independent; the long-term interests and objectives of the Soviet Union can only be satisfied when that independence gives way to subjection to Communist control. Over the longer run, we may hope that more and more of the new nations will go beyond cherishing their independence, will accept the responsibilities of freedom, and will work with the free-world community for common ends. We should not spoil the chances for such an outcome by an excess of pique over tactical maneuvers which annoy us or which bring Arab nationalists and the Communist powers together from time to time on specific issues.

Convert the struggle against communism in the Arab area into an effort to encourage independence and progress. Important as the contest with communism is to the United States, efforts to engage the enemy directly in the Arab area are likely to do more harm than good. Particularly dangerous is the mistaken identification of nationalist reforms with Communist influence and control. Leninist, proselytizing underground activities are not the principal Communist danger. The Communists, for the most part, are seeking to extend their influence by championing nationalist and socialist reform and by discrediting the West for its squeamishness about such measures. The United States must be prepared to compete with the Soviet Union and the Chinese Communists in the areas that are decisive in the present-day Arab world, namely, political independence and economic progress.

Use circumspectly the potentiality of American military force. The defense of the Arab Middle East, theoretically, is now in the hands of local forces and the United Nations. However, despite the failure of Western efforts to organize regional defense organizations including the Arabs, the failure of the Tripartite Declaration of 1950 to gain acceptance as a defense guarantee, and the rejection of the Eisenhower Doctrine by most of the Arab states, the possibility that external military force might be employed is still an important consideration in domestic and foreign affairs. The stability of Arab-Israel relations and the political situation in some of the smaller and weaker states depend in large part on the present possibility of Western intervention with force.

In public discussions of U.S. policy in the Middle East little attention is paid to the possible use of force; nevertheless it is a contingency which no one is disposed to question. Despite the shrillness of the Arab extremists' denunciations of the United States, it is likely that few of them would be happy to see the United States disarm unilaterally, leaving them at the tender mercy of the Soviet Union. The presence of the Sixth Fleet in the Mediterranean and the air base in Libya are evidence that U.S. military power is available. It is a factor in the calculations of every government and faction. To the extent that there is confidence that it will not be used for aggressive or factional purposes, it is a force for stability.

Maintain a neutral position between the Arabs and Israel. The rule-of-thumb that international problems are not solved but only change their shape does apply to Arab-Israel relations. The United States has made a much more serious effort than the Arabs have given us credit for to give equal treatment to both sides, but we still have a long way to go in this regard. A neutral stance on the part of the United States cannot be expected to bring quick improvement in the situation. The Israelis are unwilling to make any significant sacrifice to get an agreement, and the Arabs are unwilling to consider agreement until the Israelis make some gesture acknowledging the justice of Arab claims. In this kind of controversy in which neither side is completely in the right, the best contribution the United States can make may be to take a scrupulously neutral position.

It is significant that changing American attitudes and policies tend to improve the prospects for good relations with the Arabs, on every issue except that of Israel. American policies on colonial and racial issues, attitudes toward neutralism, and assistance for economic development without political or economic commitment, for example, are opening the way to a new kind of relationship with the countries of Asia and Africa. Is the issue of Israel a fundamental obstacle to the development of such a relationship with the Arabs, one that will assure American influence in the Middle East?

Because the Arab-Israel dispute pervades every aspect of Arab-American relations, it is often asked whether Israel is not the sole cause of Arab-American difficulties. Even if there were a practicable or morally defensible way of eliminating present-day Israel, it does not appear that the implied consequences would follow. For the circumstances that divide the United States and the Arabs are deeply imbedded in the world revolution, of which the Arab revolution is but a part; adjustment on both sides would still be difficult even if Israel did not exist. The manner of Israel's creation and its aggressiveness since becoming a state have acerbated American-Arab relations, but it is not the Palestine question alone which has determined their character.

HOW DIFFERENT THE FUTURE FROM THE PAST?

How different are the courses of action sketched here from those which the United States has been following in the past? Actually, all of them have been pursued at one time or another and with greater or lesser zeal. But the approaches which we have sketched do not include defense agreements and alliances. They also do not include the support of conservative regimes because they are pro-Western, or extending U.S. aid to reward good behavior, or withdrawing it to punish actions which we disapprove.

The principal difference between the old eclectic policy and these new suggested courses of action lies in a different understanding of the basic problem. It is not so much a matter of discovering how to preserve what we have in the Arab countries as of understanding how to participate creatively in the processes of change, while maintaining as the overriding objective of U.S. policy the expansion of the area of freedom in the world.

To understand the Arab situation we must see it from the inside out. And our understanding must be accompanied by a new style of conduct and of diplomacy which will convey unmistakably the interest of the United States in the independence and progress of the peoples of the emerging nations. Under the Kennedy administration much has been done to find this style. In the United Nations, in the statements of the President and some of his principal lieutenants, and in the conduct of the relations of the United States with the new nations, there has been increasing evidence of awareness of the importance of accepting and making the most of the Afro-Asian revolution. There is, however, a long way to go, and much to be learned and accomplished, before the United States and the Arabs can join together with mutual respect and confidence to help each other preserve their independence. Many changes in the Arab outlook will be necessary. On the American side also, new attitudes and new policies are essential if the Arabs are not to go by default across a line beyond which there is little hope for communication or understanding.

BIBLIOGRAPHY

NOTE: Since the author has relied primarily on newspapers, radio broadcasts, and personal interviews in preparing this book, the following list of recent books and articles in Western languages does not represent the whole body of materials used. It may, however, be useful to the reader interested in pursuing the subject further.

Afro-Asian Peoples' Solidarity Conference, Cairo, December 26, 1957–January 1, 1958. Moscow: Foreign Languages Publishing House, 1958. 265 p.

Ahmed, Jamal Mohammed. *The Intellectual Origins of Egyptian Nationalism.* London: Oxford University Press, for the Royal Institute of International Affairs, 1960. 135 p.

Antonius, George. *The Arab Awakening: The Story of the Arab National Movement.* Beirut: Khayat's, 1955. 471 p.

Atiyah, Edward. *An Arab Tells His Story: A Study in Loyalties.* London: John Murray, 1946. 229 p.

El-Barawy, Rashed. *The Military Coup in Egypt: An Analytic Study.* Cairo: Renaissance Bookshop, 1952. 269 p.

Ben Gurion, David. *Rebirth and Destiny of Israel.* New York: Philosophical Library, 1954. 539 p.

Berger, Morroe. *The Arab World Today.* Garden City, N.Y.: Doubleday, 1962. 480 p.

Binder, Leonard. "The Middle East as a Subordinate International System," *World Politics,* April 1958, pp. 408–429.

Boardman, Francis. *Institutions of Higher Learning in the Middle East: A Tabulation and Summary with Some Historical Notes.* Washington: Middle East Institute, 1961. 34 p.

Boutros-Ghali, Boutros. "The Arab League, 1945–1955," *International Conciliation,* May 1954 (i.e., 1955), pp. 387–448.

Bullard, Sir Reader, ed. *The Middle East: A Political and Economic Survey.* London: Oxford University Press, for the Royal Institute of International Affairs, 1958, 3d. ed. 496 p.

Campbell, John C. *Defense of the Middle East: Problems of American Policy.* New York: Harper, for the Council on Foreign Relations, 1960, rev. ed. 400 p.

Caractacus (pseud.). *Revolution in Iraq: An Essay in Comparative Public Opinion.* London: Gollancz, 1959. 207 p.

Colombe, Marcel. *L'Evolution de l'Egypte, 1924–1950;* v. 9: *Islam d'hier et d'aujourd'hui.* Collection dirigée par E. Levi-Provençal. Paris: G. P. Maisonneuve, 1951. 361 p.

Communist and Workers' Parties Moscow meeting, November 1960. "Statement of the Meeting of Representatives of the Communist and Workers' Parties." In *Documents,* Supplement to *New Times,* no. 50, 1960 (December 1960), pp. 1–16.

Dib, G. Moussa. *The Arab Bloc in the United Nations.* Amsterdam: Djambatan, 1956. 127 p.

Egypt and the United Nations: Report of a Study Group Set Up by the Egyptian Society of International Law. National Studies on International Organization. New York: Manhattan, for the Carnegie Endowment for International Peace, 1957. 197 p.

Eytan, Walter. *The First Ten Years: A Diplomatic History of Israel.* New York: Simon and Schuster, 1958. 239 p.

Fisher, Sydney Nettleton, ed. *Social Forces in the Middle East.* Ithaca: Cornell University Press, 1955. 282 p.

Foda, Ezzeldin. *The Projected Arab Court of Justice: A Study in Regional Jurisdiction with Specific Reference to the Muslim Law of Nations.* The Hague: Martinus Nijhoff, 1957. 252 p.

Forum for the Problems of Zionism, Jewry and the State of Israel: Proceedings of the Jerusalem Ideological Conference. Jerusalem Ideological Conference, Forum IV, Spring 1959. Jerusalem: World Zionist Organization, 1959, 398 p.

Gabbay, Rony E. *A Political Study of the Arab-Jewish Conflict: The Arab Refugee Problem (A Case Study).* Geneva: E. Droz, 1959. 611 p.

Gibb, H. A. R. *Modern Trends in Islam.* University of Chicago Press, 1947. 141 p.

Hourani, A. H. *Minorities in the Arab World.* London: Oxford University Press, for the Royal Institute of International Affairs, 1947. 140 p.

——. *Syria and Lebanon: A Political Essay.* London: Oxford University Press, for the Royal Institute of International Affairs, 1954, 3d. ed. 402 p.

——. "The Middle East and the Crisis of 1956." Paper in *Middle Eastern Affairs: Number One.* St. Antony's Papers, no. 4. London: Chatto and Windus, 1958, pp. 9–42.

Hovet, Thomas, Jr. *Bloc Politics in the United Nations.* Cambridge: Harvard University Press, 1960. 197 p.

Hurewitz, J. C. *Diplomacy in the Near and Middle East;* v. 1: *A Documentary Record: 1535–1914;* v. 2: *A Documentary Record: 1914–1956.* Princeton: Van Nostrand, 1956. 291 p., 427 p.

———. "Unity and Disunity in the Middle East," *International Conciliation,* May 1952, pp. 199–260.

Husaini, Ishak Musa. *The Moslem Brethren: The Greatest of Modern Islamic Movements.* Beirut: Khayat's, 1956. 186 p.

Ionides, Michael. *Divide and Lose: The Arab Revolt of 1955–1958.* London: Geoffrey Bles, 1960. 271 p.

Israel Office of Information. *Israel's Struggle for Peace.* New York: Author, 1960. 187 p.

Issawi, Charles. "The Bases of Arab Unity," *International Affairs,* January 1955, pp. 36–47.

———. *Egypt at Mid-Century: An Economic Survey.* London: Oxford University Press, for the Royal Institute of International Affairs, 1954. 289 p.

———. "Negotiation from Strength?" *International Affairs,* January 1959, pp. 1–9.

Kahin, George McT. *The Asian-African Conference, Bandung, Indonesia, April 1955.* Ithaca: Cornell University Press, 1956. 88 p.

Karanjia, R. K. *Arab Dawn.* London: Lawrence and Wishart, 1959. 191 p.

Kirk, George. *Survey of International Affairs, 1939–1946: The Middle East in the War.* London: Oxford University Press, for the Royal Institute of International Affairs, 1953, rev. ed. 511 p.

———. *Survey of International Affairs 1939–1946: The Middle East 1945–1950.* London: Oxford University Press, for the Royal Institute of International Affairs, 1954. 338 p.

Lacouture, Jean and Simone. *Egypt in Transition.* London: Methuen, 1958. 532 p.

Laqueur, Walter Z. *Communism and Nationalism in the Middle East.* London: Routledge and Kegan Paul, 1956. 362 p.

———. *The Soviet Union and the Middle East.* New York: Praeger, 1959. 366 p.

———, ed. *The Middle East in Transition: Studies in Contemporary History.* London: Routledge and Kegan Paul, 1958. 513 p.

Lenczowski, George. *Oil and State in the Middle East.* Ithaca: Cornell University Press, 1960. 379 p.

———. *The Middle East in World Affairs.* Ithaca: Cornell University Press, 1956, 2d. ed. 576 p.

Lerner, Daniel. *The Passing of Traditional Society: Modernizing the Middle East.* Glencoe, Ill.: Free Press, 1958. 466 p.

Marlowe, John. *Arab Nationalism and British Imperialism: A Study in Power Politics.* London: Cresset, 1961. 236 p.

————. *The Seat of Pilate: An Account of the Palestine Mandate.* London: Cresset, 1959. 289 p.

Matthews, Roderic D. and Matta Akrawi. *Education in Arab Countries of the Near East.* Washington: American Council on Education, 1949. 584 p.

Milner, Alfred. *England in Egypt.* London: Edward Arnold, 1899. 448 p.

Nasser, Gamal Abdel. *The Philosophy of the Revolution.* With an introduction by John S. Badeau and biographical sketch by John Gunther. Buffalo: Smith, Keynes and Marshall, 1959. 102 p.

————. *President Gamal Abdel Nasser's Speeches and Press Interviews.* Volumes for 1958, 1959, 1960 (January–March), and 1960 (April–June). Cairo: U.A.R. Information Department, 1961. 442 p., 628 p., 162 p., 169 p.

Nuseibeh, Hazem Zaki. *The Ideas of Arab Nationalism.* Ithaca: Cornell University Press, 1956. 227 p.

Patai, Raphael. "Dynamics of Westernization in the Middle East," *Middle East Journal,* Winter 1955, pp. 1–16.

Peretz, Don. *Israel and the Palestine Arabs.* Washington: Middle East Institute, 1958. 264 p.

Polk, William R., David M. Stamler, and Edmund Asfour. *Backdrop to Tragedy: The Struggle for Palestine.* Boston: Beacon Press, 1957. 399 p.

Qubain, Fahim I. *Crisis in Lebanon.* Washington: Middle East Institute, 1961. 243 p.

————. *Inside the Arab Mind: A Bibliographic Survey of Literature in Arabic on Arab Nationalism and Unity.* With an annotated list of English-language books and articles. Arlington, Va.: Middle East Research Associates, 1960. 100 p.

Royal Institute of International Affairs. *British Interests in the Mediterranean and Middle East: A Report by a Chatham House Study Group.* London: Oxford University Press, 1958. 123 p.

————. *Documents on International Affairs, 1955, 1956, 1957.* Selected, edited, and introduced by Noble Frankland. London: Oxford University Press, 1958, 1959, 1960. 513 p., 768 p., 539 p.

————. *Great Britain and Egypt, 1914–1951.* Information Papers no. 19a: London: Author, 1952. 216 p.

————. *Great Britain and Palestine, 1915–1945.* Information Papers no. 20a. London: Author, 1946, 3d. ed. 177 p.

El Sadat, Anwar. *Revolt on the Nile.* New York: John Day, 1957. 131 p.

Salem, Elie. "Problems of Arab Political Behavior," in Philip Warren Thayer, ed., *Tensions in the Middle East.* Baltimore: Johns Hopkins Press, 1958, pp. 68–80.

Sayegh, Fayez A. *Arab Unity: Hope and Fulfillment.* New York: Devin-Adair, 1958. 272 p.

Shwadran, Benjamin. *The Power Struggle in Iraq.* New York: Council for Middle Eastern Affairs Press, 1960. 99 p.

Smith, Wilfred Cantwell. *Islam in Modern History.* Princeton, N.J.: Princeton University Press, 1957. 317 p.

Spector, Ivar. *The Soviet Union and the Muslim World, 1917–1958.* Seattle: University of Washington Press, 1959. 328 p.

U.S. Department of Commerce. *Foreign Grants and Credits by the United States Government.* A report prepared for the use of the Congress and Government Agencies. June 1960 Quarter, Fiscal Year 1960 Review, no. 63. Washington: Author, 1960.

U.S. Department of State. *United States Policy in the Middle East, September 1956–June 1957: Documents.* Department of State Publication 6505. Near and Middle Eastern Series 25. Washington: GPO, 1957. 425 p.

U.S. Senate. Committee on Foreign Relations. *United States Foreign Policy: Compilation of Studies.* Doc. 24, 87th Cong., 1st sess. Washington: GPO, 1961.

    Study no. 12: "Economic, Social, and Political Change in the Underdeveloped Countries and Its Implications for United States Policy," by the Center for International Studies, Massachusetts Institute of Technology, March 1960, pp. 1165–1268.

    Study no. 13: "Middle East." Staff study, prepared for the use of the Committee on Foreign Relations, United States Senate, June 9, 1960, pp. 1269–1387.

Vaucher, Georges. *Gamal Abdel Nasser et son Equipe; v. 1: Les années d'humiliation et la conquête du pouvoir; v. 2: L'édification de la République Arabe Unie.* Paris: René Julliard, 1959 and 1960. 302 p., 384 p.

Von Grunebaum, G. E. *Islam: Essays in the Nature and Growth of a Cultural Tradition.* London: Routledge and Kegan Paul, 1955. 260 p.

Weizmann, Chaim. *Trial and Error: The Autobiography of Chaim Weizmann.* New York: Harper, 1949. 498 p.

Wheelock, Keith. *Nasser's New Egypt: A Critical Analysis.* New York: Praeger, for the University of Pennsylvania Foreign Policy Research Institute, 1960. 326 p.

Wint, Guy and Peter Calvocoressi. *Middle East Crisis.* Baltimore: Penguin, 1957. 141 p.

Zeine, Zeine N. *Arab-Turkish Relations and the Emergence of Arab Nationalism.* Beirut: Khayat's, 1958. 156 p.

Zuraik, Constantine K. *The Meaning of the Disaster.* Translated from the Arabic by R. Bayly Winder. Beirut: Khayat's, 1956. 74 p.

INDEX

331

FOREIGN AFFAIRS (quarterly), edited by Hamilton Fish Armstrong.
THE UNITED STATES IN WORLD AFFAIRS (annual). Volumes for 1931, 1932 and 1933, by Walter Lippmann and William O. Scroggs; for 1934–1935, 1936, 1937, 1938, 1939 and 1940, by Whitney H. Shepardson and William O. Scroggs; for 1945–1947, 1947–1948 and 1948–1949, by John C. Campbell; for 1949, 1950, 1951, 1952, 1953 and 1954, by Richard P. Stebbins; for 1955, by Hollis W. Barber; for 1956, 1958, 1959, 1960, and 1961 by Richard P. Stebbins.

DOCUMENTS ON AMERICAN FOREIGN RELATIONS (annual). Volume for 1952 edited by Clarence W. Baier and Richard P. Stebbins; for 1953 and 1954, edited by Peter V. Curl; for 1955, 1956, 1957, 1958 and 1959, edited by Paul E. Zinner; for 1960 and 1961 edited by Richard P. Stebbins.

POLITICAL HANDBOOK OF THE WORLD (annual), edited by Walter H. Mallory.

THE SOVIET UNION, 1922–1962: A Foreign Affairs Reader, edited by Philip E. Mosely.

THE POLITICS OF FOREIGN AID: American Experience in Southeast Asia, by John D. Montgomery.

THE ORGANIZATION OF AMERICAN STATES AND THE HEMISPHERE CRISIS, by John C. Dreier.

SPEARHEADS OF DEMOCRACY: Labor in the Developing Countries, by George C. Lodge.

LATIN AMERICA: Diplomacy and Reality, by Adolf A. Berle.

THE UNITED NATIONS: Structure for Peace, by Ernest A. Gross.

THE LONG POLAR WATCH: Canada and the Defense of North America, by Melvin Conant

ARMS AND POLITICS IN LATIN AMERICA (Revised Edition), by Edwin Lieuwen.

THE FUTURE OF UNDERDEVELOPED COUNTRIES: Political Implications of Economic Development (Revised Edition), by Eugene Staley.

SPAIN AND DEFENSE OF THE WEST: Ally and Liability, by Arthur P. Whitaker.

SOCIAL CHANGE IN LATIN AMERICA TODAY: Its Implications for United States Policy, by Richard N. Adams, John P. Gillin, Allan R. Holmberg, Oscar Lewis, Richard W. Patch, and Charles W. Wagley.

FOREIGN POLICY: THE NEXT PHASE: The 1960s (Revised Edition), by Thomas K. Finletter.

DEFENSE OF THE MIDDLE EAST: Problems of American Policy (Revised Edition), by John C. Campbell.

COMMUNIST CHINA AND ASIA: Challenge to American Policy, by A. Doak Barnett.

FRANCE, TROUBLED ALLY: De Gaulle's Heritage and Prospects, by Edgar S. Furniss, Jr.

THE SCHUMAN PLAN: A Study in Economic Cooperation, 1950–1959, by William Diebold, Jr.

SOVIET ECONOMIC AID: The New Aid and Trade Policy in Underdeveloped Countries, by Joseph S. Berliner.

RAW MATERIALS: A Study of American Policy, by Percy W. Bidwell.

NATO AND THE FUTURE OF EUROPE, by Ben T. Moore.

AFRICAN ECONOMIC DEVELOPMENT, by William A. Hance.

INDIA AND AMERICA: A Study of Their Relations, by Phillips Talbot and S. L. Poplai.

JAPAN BETWEEN EAST AND WEST, by Hugh Borton, Jerome B. Cohen, William J. Jorden, Donald Keene, Paul F. Langer and C. Martin Wilbur.

NUCLEAR WEAPONS AND FOREIGN POLICY, by Henry A. Kissinger.

MOSCOW-PEKING AXIS: Strengths and Strains, by Howard L. Boorman, Alexander Eckstein, Philip E. Mosely and Benjamin Schwartz.

CLIMATE AND ECONOMIC DEVELOPMENT IN THE TROPICS, by Douglas H. K. Lee.

WHAT THE TARIFF MEANS TO AMERICAN INDUSTRIES, by Percy W. Bidwell.

UNITED STATES SHIPPING POLICY, by Wytze Gorter.

RUSSIA AND AMERICA: Dangers and Prospects, by Henry L. Roberts.

STERLING: Its Meaning in World Finance, by Judd Polk.

FOREIGN AFFAIRS BIBLIOGRAPHY, 1942–1952, by Henry L. Roberts.

AMERICAN AGENCIES INTERESTED IN INTERNATIONAL AFFAIRS, compiled by Ruth Savord and Donald Wasson.

JAPANESE AND AMERICANS: A Century of Cultural Relations, by Robert S. Schwantes.